HUNTED

CLASS | NEW
2 | STUDIES
0 | IN
0 | RELIGION

EDITED BY Kathryn Lofton AND
John Lardas Modern

HUNTED

Predation and Pentecostalism
in Guatemala

KEVIN LEWIS O'NEILL

The University of Chicago Press
Chicago and London

The University of Chicago Press, Chicago 60637
The University of Chicago Press, Ltd., London
© 2019 by The University of Chicago
Published 2019
Printed in the United States of America

28 27 26 25 24 23 22 21 20 19   1 2 3 4 5

ISBN-13: 978-0-226-62451-8 (cloth)
ISBN-13: 978-0-226-62465-5 (paper)
ISBN-13: 978-0-226-62479-2 (e-book)
DOI: https://doi.org/10.7208/chicago/9780226624792.001.0001

Library of Congress Cataloging-in-Publication Data

Names: O'Neill, Kevin Lewis, 1977– author.
Title: Hunted : predation and Pentecostalism in Guatemala / Kevin Lewis O'Neill.
Other titles: Class 200, new studies in religion.
Description: Chicago ; London : The University of Chicago Press, 2019. |
   Series: Class 200, new studies in religion | Includes bibliographical references and index.
Identifiers: LCCN 2018061412 | ISBN 9780226624518 (cloth : alk. paper) |
   ISBN 9780226624655 (pbk. : alk. paper) | ISBN 9780226624792 (e-book)
Subjects: LCSH: Church work with drug addicts—Guatemala—Guatemala. |
   Drug addicts—Rehabilitation—Guatemala—Guatemala. | Involuntary treatment—Guatemala—Guatemala. | Evangelistic work—Guatemala—Guatemala. | Pentecostalism—Social aspects—Guatemala—Guatemala.
Classification: LCC BV 4460.3.O54 2019 | DDC 277.281/1083—dc23
LC record available at https://lccn.loc.gov/2018061412

For Ignatius

_____

CONTENTS

NOTE

HUNTED IS AN ETHNOGRAPHY OF PENTECOSTAL drug rehabilitation centers in Guatemala City and their practice of bringing (oftentimes dragging) users to Christ. The faithful call it hunting. Focused on the chase, this book is a provocation to interpret the world from the perspective of predation. It invites readers to appreciate how forms of sociality can be understood as a series of calculated targets and attempted escapes. This means sitting with some rather uncomfortable content, with those who hunt and those who have been hunted. The turbulence of this dynamic ultimately transformed this book into an experiment in form. Itself organized around the logic of captivity, *Hunted* proposes predation as a root experience of the contemporary.

As will become clear, the fieldwork for this book, which began in the winter of 2006 and did not end until the spring of 2018, grew increasingly fraught both for my interlocutors and for me. Slowly, what I perceived to be reciprocal economies morphed into uneven lines of pursuit that offered very few avenues of escape. At some point, it all caught up with me, and I found myself trapped by my own commitments. And so you, reader, will judge me. You might also judge the people described inside this book. Just know that I also judged them and especially myself until it became clear to me (as it may to you) that predation upends any stable notion of right and wrong. *Hunted* has nothing to do with the good.

PREFACE

ALEJANDRO HANDED ME A LETTER ON June 2, 2016. He did it quietly, when no one else was looking. We sat shoulder to shoulder inside one of Guatemala City's Pentecostal drug rehabilitation centers, listening with fifty-five other captives (*internos*) to sermons about sin and salvation. The center was a grey stump of a building, a simple two-story house that held drug users (often against their will) for months, sometimes for years.[1] Alejandro was one of these users. A proud man in his midthirties, with tired eyes and strong arms, Alejandro often waxed philosophical, but this time he didn't. After pressing the piece of paper into the palm of my hand, he leaned in to say: "Get me the fuck out of here."

The letter read:

Help Me National Police!

My name is Miguel Alejandro Gonzalez, born January 15, 1982. I am of sound mind and body. I know clearly that I do not want and do not need to be in this ministry and in this rehabilitation center.

On April 28, 2016, the pastor tracked me down, found me, and then brought me back to his house against my will. He forcefully detained me with the help of two men from the house by throwing me in the back of a truck.

I told them that I did not want to go to the house. I do not want to be held captive. Every day that passes I tell them that I do not want to be inside the house, but the pastor tells me that he is going to kick my ass.

The punishments here are severe. Here are some examples:
- *They withhold food from me*
- *They yell at me in a loud voice*
- *They make me clean the house*
- *They keep me in a very hot room all day long*

- *I sleep on the floor*
- *They tie me up with ropes for hours*

Please, I do not want to be here. I am here against my will. My family did not put me here, and they do not know where I am. They did not sign a contract, and they are not paying for me to be here.

Please send help so that I can get out of this house.

Thank you,

Miguel Alejandro Gonzalez

Alejandro had been hunted. At the outer edges of today's war on drugs, where the state is weak and churches are strong, Christian vigilante groups scour the streets of Guatemala City with singular intent: to pull drug users out of sin by dragging them into rehab. Often in the middle of the night, when the capital city is an absolute ghost town, three or four recovering users drive with their pastor to the house of an active user. At the request of a wife, a mother, or a sister, each at wits' end, this hunting party (*grupo de cacería*) hovers over the man while he sleeps. They say a short prayer, and then it gets physical. One man takes the legs. Another two grab the arms. A fourth (if there is a fourth) controls the neck. Sometimes they choke him out. All the while the user, suddenly and unexpectedly crucified to his bed, struggles in vain.

"They just grabbed me right off the streets and threw me in here," Alejandro later explained. "They've done it a few times before. I was here six months, and then they let me go. I was out fifteen days, and then they came and got me again. I did another two, maybe three months, and then I got out again." Alejandro looked exhausted. "And now I'm back."

These hunts can be harrowing. I once saw four men from the center corner a young man inside his parents' house. Too strong for his own good, he fought his huntsmen for what seemed like an hour, wrestling with each of them one by one. As I paced nervously off to the side, wondering why the four didn't just rush him all at once, it occurred to me that they were tiring him out. When the young man eventually flagged, the four hog-tied him with such force that I suddenly found myself speaking up. The ropes are too tight, I pleaded. You crossed a line, I stammered, but as I stepped into the fray, I felt a hand holding me back. "Don't be stupid," someone said. That voice was Alejandro's.

Alejandro's letter did not just open a window into the horror of human vulnerability and the experience of being prey; it was also a stark reminder that Alejandro had hunted, and he had hunted for years.[2]

"How many?" Alejandro mused, taking a moment to count. "Three hundred." He quickly checked himself: "No. I've been on more than 300 hunts." Alejandro's best guess signaled his years spent inside these centers as well as his ability to hunt down drug users. "I had to pick up some guy a few nights ago," he told me not too long after handing me his letter. "See the guy over there? In the green shorts?" Alejandro pointed to a young man named Santiago. "I had to grab him from his bed," Alejandro explained, "because his mom paid [the pastor for] us to do it." Alejandro shook his head. "And it's not the first time," he said. "It's actually the second time I've hunted him this year." He then paused just long enough to get the story straight, adding, "And the worst thing is that I end up having to tie people up. We have a jacket with ropes, like a fucking straitjacket, and when someone doesn't do what the pastor tells him to do, I have to tie him up."

Alejandro cringed. "I'm tired of hunting," he said, "because when I leave here, the people I've tied up come looking for me." He seemed to grow indignant. "But they don't understand that I have to hunt. It's what I have to do to eat better, to sleep a little longer, so I can get a shower here." Alejandro then connected the dots for me: "Hunting is why the pastor keeps me here. The pastor hunts me because I hunt for him."

This is a book about humans hunting humans. It is an ethnography of Pentecostals who track down drug users, as if they were animals, to remind them, in classic Christian fashion, that they are human—that, in the words of so many missionaries before them, it is not enough to be human: one must also act human. After years of fieldwork alongside Alejandro but also many others, I came to understand this hunting as a kind of predatory pastoralism. This is the Christian impulse to seek out, tie up, and drag back those sheep that have wandered from the fold. It is a disruptive insight for at least three reasons. The first is that it upends the more standard philosophical position that pastoralism and predation have opposed genealogies—that persuasion is different from coercion. I now regard pastoralism and predation as not really at odds with each other but rather as interdependent modes of governance.[3] "It's about saving a life," Alejandro insisted. "That's why we beat these guys, tie them up, and drag them here like pigs."[4]

The second realization is that every hunt presupposes a theory of its prey, a clear sense of who can be hunted and why. Whereas manhunts tend to presume an ontological distinction between the hunter and the hunted, predatory pastoralism announces that everyone is a sinner in the eyes of the Lord. This means that salvation is the only way to escape—and that what must be evaded is not the chase or the center but oneself.

The third insight is that predation upsets an increasingly bundled set of images about pastoralism.[5] Across the humanities and the social sciences, from a range of theoretical and methodological commitments, scholars deliver steadfast portraits of state withdrawal, their key terms telling all: dispossession and disposability; expulsion and exposure; precarity and social abandonment. While each advances an analytically distinct proposition, each also contributes to a single, powerful image of the failed shepherd, of people left to die.[6]

Hunted tells a different story. Its subplot is not that the masses have been left behind. Instead, a more constructive reading, a more challenging line of inquiry, is that they have been given a head start. "I climbed out of that window," Alejandro said, "before they put the bars up." On the second floor of his pastor's center, Alejandro gestured towards the light. "I slid out that window, hung from the sill, and then dropped to the sidewalk." Alejandro walked me closer to the windows. "I was high a few hours later," he then said, "but I made sure I got a gun. I knew that they would come for me. I knew that the pastor would hunt me down." And the pastor did. The details of this hunt repeat themselves across Guatemala City with such consistency that one begins to wonder whether the failed shepherd is really such a failure after all. The shepherd seems quite capable of catching and releasing his prey. That is the point. The political demand nipping at the heels of Alejandro as he escaped from the pastor's center was not to make live or let die but rather to hunt or be hunted.[7]

The manhunt has multiple histories, but in Guatemala, predatory pastoralism begins with the war on drugs.[8] "I am convinced," President Richard Nixon announced in 1971, "that the only way to fight this menace [of drug abuse] is by attacking it on many fronts." And attack he did—with the fumigation of Mexican hemp fields and a crackdown on Mexican marijuana smugglers. But this show of military might did little more than kill enough cannabis to pique America's interest in cocaine. As demand soared, cocaine corridors connected Medellín to Miami and Cali to Northern Mexico, all by way of the Caribbean. The United States responded with hugely militarized antidrug policies, but these increasingly expensive, progressively effective maritime blockades only prompted traffickers to shift their transport operations from sea to land, eventually making Central America a principal transit route. Soon planes, boats, and submarines ferried cocaine along the Pacific coast to northern Guatemala. There, beyond the reach of US interdiction efforts, traffickers prepped their product for its eventual trip north. And they have continued to do so at a growing clip. In 2004, some 10 percent of the cocaine produced in the Andes and bound for the United States passed through Guatemala. A decade later at least 80 percent of this product touched Guatemalan soil.[9]

The movement of all this material came with considerable logistics. Equipment, labor, infrastructure—traffickers need all of this, but pay for none of it in cash. Instead, they pay with cocaine, which itself never held much value in Guatemala. There have never been enough Guatemalans who can afford the drug. To monetize this material, to convert cocaine into cash, laboratories began mixing the drug with baking soda to make crack cocaine. Sold throughout Guatemala City, crack cocaine has proven to be a far more affordable and far more addictive version of powder cocaine. Smoked through a pipe one rock at a time, crack is as intense and fleeting as it is cheap. In the United States, the rise of crack cocaine met growing urban violence and decidedly racist antidrug policies in ways that tripled the country's prison population. Yet in Guatemala City, with a homicide rate often twenty times the US average, crack cocaine was not criminalized so much as Pentecostalized.[10]

The Pentecostalization of drugs and drug use in Guatemala hinges on an extreme lack of social services. As a part of economic restructuring—which has included the privatization of state enterprises, the liberalization of trade, and the relaxation of government regulation—less than one percent of Guatemala's total health budget addresses issues of mental health. Hospitals also flatly deny medical service to patients seeking support for substance abuse while the Roman Catholic Church has proven absolutely impassive. The Church runs one detoxification center in Guatemala City for alcoholics. Expensive even by middle-class standards, the center only has six beds. Pentecostal drug rehabilitation centers, when taken in the aggregate, have over 6,000 beds. This radical disparity in cots has long mirrored equally disproportionate rates of conversion. Once overwhelmingly Roman Catholic, Guatemala is now at least half Pentecostal and Charismatic Christian.[11]

More important than numbers are the visceral truths that Pentecostal Christianity promises its people. They include that salvation is real; hell is eternal; and Jesus loves you. These principles have set the conditions for something called theological therapy (*teoterapia*). This is a mashup of

Pentecostal theology, twelve-step programming, and self-help psychology. Its most basic assumption is that captivity will give way to conversion. It rarely does, but this has done nothing to slow the growth of these centers for a simple reason: they provide a practical solution to a concrete problem. Drug use is up, state resources are down, and only Jesus saves. The net result is a shadow carceral system infused with Pentecostal imperatives about who can be hunted and why. It is a theological construction that carries considerable consequences. By 2016, more Guatemalans found themselves literally tied up in Pentecostal drug rehabilitation centers than locked up in maximum-security prisons.[12]

Populating these centers presents pastors with a fundamental challenge. Users often do not want to enter rehab, and so they must be brought to rehab. They must be hunted. There is near consensus on this last point: the police condone hunting; families pay for the service; and centers profit from the practice, both financially and spiritually. Much of this has to do with the immediate social context—with an extreme lack of social services, for example—but there is also great theological precedent to the hunting of wayward souls.

Consider the crosier. The shepherd's crook, that abiding symbol of pastoral power, bends at the top, fashioned in such a way as to fit tightly around the neck of an animal. To read this rod is to appreciate pastoralism's physicality. A combination of pulling and prodding, dragging and drawing, puts into context that iconic image of Christ as shepherd, the one with the sheep on his shoulders, and how Christ, to get that sheep on his shoulders, must have grabbed the beast by its legs and controlled its neck. Not unlike a user suddenly and unexpectedly crucified to his bed, the sheep must have struggled in vain. It is an unsettling image that Pedro, Alejandro's pastor, invoked with a lilt of inspiration: "I do not kidnap men. I rescue them."

Pedro's logic is open to interpretation, but in the end, it is interpretation to which he opened himself—not simply by allowing me to shadow his work for years but also by lining his center with theologies of predation. Across the top of a wall, just outside his office, there hung the image of an eagle. It could have been classic Christian iconography. The Bible often evokes the image of a soaring eagle, its flight symbolizing the resurrection or ascension of Christ, and yet here, in this rehab, for this pastor, the eagle on this wall was not ascending. It was diving, with talons drawn. This bird of prey was hunting. "God the Father," Pedro once mused while we spoke in his office, "has a fish in one hand and a whip in the other." Pairing salvation and slavery, the fish and the whip, this pastor took as intuitive the overlooked observation that pastoralism is predatory.

Yet hunting as pastoral mandate too often fades from sight. Scholarship about pastoralism tends to pivot between two archetypes. The first is the good shepherd, who governs with "constant kindness"—through what Michel Foucault has called the "art of conducting, directing, leading, guiding, taking in hand, and manipulating men." Its counterpart is the bad shepherd, who "disperses the flock, lets it die of thirst, [and] shears it solely for profit's sake." This strict dichotomy between the good shepherd and the bad shepherd reflects a strict analytic division between research programs on humanitarian intervention and zones of social abandonment. The former aligns with "the management of life in the name of the well-being of the population." The latter invokes what Giorgio Agamben takes to be the progressive animalization of man and what Foucault laments as the bestialization of biopolitics. What is ethnographically obvious, however, is that at the very limits of the pastorate, where the state is absent and the souls are unmanageable, the shepherd does not simply either administer or abandon his sheep but also makes them his quarry.[13]

·

Pedro was very proud of his work, and he was eager to share it. In his mid-fifties, with fading tattoos down his arms, Pedro often preached about saving souls, but too often, he felt, society misunderstood his labor of love. A local news team once filed a story on his center, assigning a camera crew to one of his hunts. The mission was routine enough. A father had called Pedro to bring his son to the center for drug rehabilitation, but the story that aired stopped just short of giving Pedro his full due. Bookended by buttoned-up newscasters behind a station desk, the two-minute report showed Pedro and his men barging into a family's house, tackling a young man, and then restraining him with a pair of handcuffs that Pedro had lifted from the National Police years earlier. The climax came when Pedro pulled a knife from the young man's hand. Holding the weapon up to the camera, Pedro announced with no small amount of pride: "This is the kind of work that we do!"

The problem was that a private security guard witnessed the events from afar, mistook the intervention for a kidnapping, and immediately called the National Police, who arrived with guns drawn to throw Pedro and his men up against a wall. All the while, the cameras kept recording. The police quickly realized their mistake, apologized to Pedro and his men, and then thanked them for their service. They even accompanied Pedro and his new captive back to the center, but the apology and police escort never made the final cut. Even though the news story proved sympathetic to Pedro, advancing in no uncertain terms an unqualified appreciation for this kind of predation, the image of the police frisking the pastor lingered with him for years. It ultimately made him very wary of journalists, with their rushed timelines, but rather warm to me, an anthropologist, whose commitment to understanding his predatory pastoralism extended over years. Pedro also appreciated the nuance that ethnography made possible, valuing our conversations about such broad theological themes as freedom, justice, and love as well as sin, grace, and the will. Pedro saw my fieldwork and this book as one way to get the story right.

I too wanted to get it right, but these centers, especially Pedro's, often proved so extreme that descriptions of them never seemed to translate well to a general academic audience. Anthropologists always seemed concerned that my conclusions were far too normative while scholars of public health often pressed me to make more of an abolitionist argument. Historians of religion never seemed entirely convinced that these centers were actually Christian, and human rights activists wanted a list of abuses. Nothing I ever described seemed quite right.

To the activists, I would concede that a book could be written that details the human rights violations committed inside these centers. The houses tended to be far too small to hold as many men as they did; there was no way for anyone to appeal their captivity, and dozens died every year while inside.[14] In fact, the violence that occurred across this industry could support a formal truth commission, with personal testimonies and historical analysis not only evidencing that human rights abuses occurred but also that the Guatemalan government left its people to fend for themselves amid terribly uncertain times. But such a book, I came to realize, would flatten the moral and political ambiguities of predatory pastoralism. It would also obscure my own ambivalence. If these houses were such problems, then why did the police apologize to Pedro, thank him for his service, and then escort him back to his center—without ever stopping to question why the pastor had a pair of their handcuffs in the first place?[15]

For more than a decade, I attempted to answer this question by walking with those who hunted as well as those who had been hunted—if only because they tended to be the same people. It was an intimate project that admittedly made my efforts at observation look a lot like participation, with fieldwork proving to be a kind of pursuit in its own right, a style of hunting, with its own targets and objectives. Committed to the promise of ethnography, to the idea that extended participation can yield otherwise illusive observations, my fieldwork traced very particular webs of predation to make certain persons (Alejandro, Santiago, and Pedro, but also hundreds of other individuals) objects of inquiry and, thus, people to track and capture through reflection and analysis. In methodological terms, however uncomfortable the conclusion may be, this research led me to understand ethnography too as a mode of predation. My notes and photographs, archives and spreadsheets, demonstrate an almost compulsive attention to an underemphasized anthropological obsession with acquisition.

Bronislaw Malinowski is best known for describing fieldwork as a way of enduring alterity. "Imagine yourself," he famously writes in *Argonauts of the Western Pacific* (1922), "suddenly set down surrounded by all your gear, alone on a tropical beach close to a native village, while the launch or dinghy which has brought you sails away out of sight." Less cited but possibly more relevant to explaining the workings of ethnographic research is a metaphor he crafts only a few pages later: "The ethnographer has not only to spread his nets in the right place, and wait for what will fall into them. He must be an active huntsman, and drive his quarry into them and follow it up to its most inaccessible lairs."[16] For over a decade, I tracked and captured knowledge about predatory pastoralism, spreading my nets across Guatemala City and waiting for what fell into them.[17]

The material that I gathered tended to fold along three lines of inquiry, with this book's narrative arc ultimately focusing on Pedro's center as well as the plights of Alejandro and one of the young men he had hunted: Santiago.[18] The first line of inquiry always felt like a loud rush. Much of my fieldwork took place in the streets, with users, dealers, and cops as well as the family and friends who witnessed the consequences of drug use. Organized by pastors, such as Pedro, these hunting parties collected users from the streets and their homes. More often than not the hunters were themselves in rehab, also under lock and key, but they were bigger, stronger, and sometimes smarter than the average captive. Hunting was a privilege, and the rewards were immediate: status, adventure, and a bit of sunlight. "I'd be lying if I said that I didn't enjoy the hunt," Alejandro once told me. But hunting also opened the hunter to the possibility of being hunted. "People are after me," Alejandro worried. "Every time I leave the center, I know that people are looking for me. I hunted them, and so now they want to beat me." It is, in fact, amid a series of home invasions and back alley chases that my fieldwork drilled down into the frantic realities of predatory pastoralism.

The second line of inquiry always seemed like little more than a whisper. It came from inside these centers, alongside these captives. Unlike the hunt's frantic pace, the rhythm inside these centers was slow. There were often no twelve-step programs or group sessions. None of the captives had case workers or even files. Progress was unevenly measured, with captives hardly ever better or worse—only free or not. "A lot of people say it's a process," reasoned one pastor, "but it's not a process. Rehabilitation is a miracle." Like a switch that flips on and off, there was often nothing in between, and so I waited alongside these captives for a miracle to happen amid brutal patches of boredom.

Along the way, Pedro allowed me to enter and exit his center as my schedule saw fit. This provided me with a gross amount of privilege, but somehow (and to my surprise) my mobility never seemed to stir these captives so much as my apparent lack of vice. As Pedro's population changed from month to month, with users caught and released, I found myself answering a familiar set of questions not just about fieldwork but about my soul. Did I drink? Not often, I would answer. Did I use drugs? They never interested me much, I would say. To have a conversation with a captive, to listen to him speak about his inability to control himself, proved uncomfortable for both of us when it became clear that we did not have the same appetites. "You don't have any vices?" I remember one man asking me in complete disbelief. "None?"

The third line of inquiry proved to be nothing more than a series of handshakes with police officers, judges, lawyers, human rights activists, and public health officials. Every meeting began with an earnest effort on my part to understand the relative regulation of these centers, but they always ended with a firm sense that reform was not possible. When I began fieldwork on these centers in 2006, Guatemala boasted one of the highest homicide rates in the world and one of the lowest conviction rates. By the end of this project in 2018, after extraordinary efforts at judicial reform, conviction rates had risen (incrementally) as homicide rates fell (modestly), but Guatemala City remained one of the most dangerous cities in the world, with three (rather than two) percent of murders resulting in a conviction.[19]

Throughout those years, in the face of extreme urban violence, consensus held among government and church officials that these centers had become an accepted solution to a dynamic problem. In some effort to nuance this belief, I began to work with a photographer to tell a story that, like ethnography, evades any easy or singular interpretation. This led to a series of photography exhibits in Guatemala City, in addition to staged debates among public health officials, human rights activists, and members of the Christian community. To jumpstart a public conversation about compulsory drug rehabilitation centers, I also engaged the British Broadcasting Company and the United Nations Committee Against Torture. Perhaps predictably, the images I curated and the life stories I advanced provoked a wide range of responses, with even the most challenging of photographs leading to unanticipated optimism about the promise of Christian renewal. "This is the work of God," Pedro insisted while appreciating the photograph of a young man held behind a set of makeshift bars. "This is the absolute work of God."[20]

Understanding Pedro's perspective meant becoming subject to and at times ensnared by predatory pastoralism. This was the situation when Alejandro handed me his letter on June 2, 2016. His note directly interpellated me as an active participant rather than as a passive observer. The letter caught me with its very form. I could have treated it as an artifact that provided yet another perspective on predation, but the letter itself demanded not an interpretation but rather a response.[21] How would I respond? This book, one such reply, details the webs of predation that pastoralism spins, pinpointing those moments when apparent lines of flight become absolute dead ends. Alejandro had indeed been hunted by the pastor, physically tied up but also tethered to a set of social relationships that would not let him go. Yet Alejandro's plea also set me in motion, scrambling to figure out how to honor his request without endangering lives.

Alejandro addressed his letter to the National Police in the hopes of triggering a raid, but my deep familiarity with these centers had taught me that these police actions almost always end poorly, with the newly liberated either picked up moments later by other pastors or found dead in the streets in a matter of weeks. And so I approached the police as well as lawyers and public health officials, while also working with Alejandro and his pastor to find him a way out of the center, the drugs, and the hunting. No easy solution ever emerged. "You want to get Alejandro out of here?" Pedro eventually asked me. "Then buy me a pair of Nikes. Or better yet, just give me $100 [USD]." As money changed hands, with lives forever altered, the fact remains that hunting is itself a genre with a narrative arc that even I could never really escape.[22] The Hunt. Captivity. Escape. Return. This fieldwork tied me up, which is why this book starts on the run, so to speak, with Santiago, the young man whose mother paid to have him hunted (by Alejandro no less), and it ends with Alejandro, who never really found his way out.

THE HUNT

I will send for many hunters, and they will hunt them down on every mountain and hill and from the crevices of the rocks.

—JEREMIAH 16:16

ONE

_____

The central market is expansive. It stretches six city blocks, with sheets of corrugated metal covering almost every square inch. Each sheet was puzzled into position by someone wanting to extend the market by just a few more feet. A labyrinth of stalls piled high with everything from bags of tooth-paste to boxes of broccoli, the market echoes with different reggaeton tracks as hawkers compete for customers. So unplanned is the place that it once burned to the ground because there was no clear way for the fire engines to enter the area. Volunteers ran in and out of the flames with buckets of water.[1]

How did they know where to go? Because it is the shadows that really set the scene. An almost complete lack of natural light meets an uneven as-sortment of low wattage bulbs, each hanging from a cord. With aisles that sometimes pinch so tightly that you have to turn sideways just to pass, the market can conjure a sense of vertigo. I, for one, did not know which way was up, let alone out, which is why I tried my best to keep up with Santiago as we paced the market. It wasn't easy.

"They've hunted me before," Santiago said. He looked weathered, with a beard that seemed unintentional.

A man carrying a bucket of tomatoes suddenly pushed past us as a pastor preached into a bullhorn. The machine made him sound distant, from another world. "He paid the ultimate price," the pastor said, "to save us from our sins. Christ rescued mankind and all he asks from us is that we obey him, that we bathe ourselves in baptismal waters to know the true glory of God."

Santiago wasn't listening. He was visibly uneasy, with what seemed like paranoia setting in. Some of this had to do with the crack cocaine. Vapor-ized with a lighter and then absorbed through the lungs, the drug hits the bloodstream almost immediately, flooding the brain with dopamine. This jolt causes crack cocaine's characteristic high. It constricts blood vessels, dilates pupils, and increases the user's body temperature, heart rate, and blood pressure. But this euphoria only lasts about five minutes, even less if the crack is of poor quality (and the crack sold at the market is almost always of poor quality). This sudden spike and equally abrasive drop can foster a sense of anxiety, of near despair—but so too can the hunt.[2]

In a series of sharp lefts and hard rights, Santiago dodged vendors in an attempt to bury himself even further in the market. "The deeper I go," he reasoned, "the harder it is for him to find me."

Him? I wondered.

At first I thought that Santiago had a plan, that he knew where he was going. Maybe he was looking for a friend who might hide him somewhere. A needle in a haystack, I thought. No one would ever find him here, but it eventually became clear to me that Santiago's only strategy was to keep moving, to compulsively wend his way through the market.

He did this for hours, and I followed the movement of Santiago's feet in the hopes that they might give me some advanced warning as to which way he would turn, but he often pivoted so quickly and with such purpose that I struggled to keep pace. Either incapable or unwilling to stand still, we ended up discussing his history with hunting in short bursts.

"I wasn't working," he said, "I wasn't doing anything. I was just smoking, and so she had me hunted." Santiago tripped past someone selling pirated DVDs.

She? I asked.

"My mom," he said.

Santiago had not worked in weeks. In his early twenties, with sturdy hands and a quiet demeanor, Santiago's natural strength availed him to the city's construction sites, where multinational corporations built condominium complexes, office towers, and shopping centers. More than one hundred high rises had gone up over the course of a decade, presenting Guatemala City with a new skyline while at the same time providing Santiago with a steady stream of income. He shoveled dirt and cleared debris for cash-in-hand, throwing grey chunks of concrete into dumpsters for upwards of twelve hours a day.[3]

"He's an excellent worker," his mother later told me as we spoke in her living room. Maria owned a two-bedroom house in a rather poor part of Guatemala City. It was a cinderblock structure with an aluminum roof, but it also had fresh tiles on the floor. Her two eldest children had paid for the flooring. They lived in the United States and wired money to Maria in small denominations. One hundred dollars here, two hundred dollars there. It added up in ways that elevated Maria and her family toward some sense of middle-class respectability, but then there was Santiago, her youngest.

"He scares me when he smokes," Maria said. She then whispered, as if the neighbors might hear, "Oh, Lord, no one can hold him down."

Over the years, a number of substances had made Santiago rather hard to pin down: marijuana, solvents, paint thinner, the occasional pharmaceutical, and, to a growing extent, crack cocaine. He also drank, but that no longer held his attention. Instead, crack bounced Santiago between increasingly shorter bouts of work and progressively longer stretches of drug use, which made Maria concerned not just for her son's safety but also for his soul. "The way of the Lord," she said, "is the only way to truly liberate someone from sin."

So will you have him hunted? I asked.

Maria's Bible answered for her. She turned to Romans 5:3–5 and began to read aloud in a slow, steady voice: "We also glory in our sufferings because we know that suffering produces perseverance; perseverance, character; and character, hope." She traced the words with her finger while striding from one end of her living room to the other. Soft-spoken and gray-haired, Maria always seemed inspired when she had a Bible in her hands. "And hope does not put us to shame," she read, "because God's love has been poured out into our hearts through the Holy Spirit, who has been given to us." Maria then fell silent, eventually answering my question. "Yes," she said, she would have Santiago hunted.

Back in the market, under the sheet metal, Santiago speculated that "she's going to call the pastor." He paused just long enough to talk, to square himself to me, adding, "Maybe she's already called him . . . I bet she's already called him." Santiago then ticked off the reasons why he thought the hunt was already underway: "This is what happened last time," he said. "I stopped going to work. I couldn't handle the crack. I stopped going home to sleep. I was gone for days."[4]

So why are we at the market? I asked. The crowds seemed absolutely antithetical to an escape. Wouldn't Santiago want to distance himself from people rather than run right at them?

Santiago explained to me what scholars have long known—that the crowd can be a resource. The crowd can turn a blind eye to abduction, but it can also turn the tables. Or, as Santiago said, "If you scream and make a scene, then sometimes people help you out. Sometimes people will step in long enough for you to slip away." Upon a second look, the market did present a confounding web of alleyways that Santiago could use to his advantage. "All I need is a head start," he said, "and I can disappear."[5]

But wouldn't it be easier to just go back to work? I asked.

By work I meant the construction sites, with their steady pay, rather than the errands that Santiago had been running for vendors inside the market. He would haul bags of onions and boxes of dried fish from the trucks to the stalls for spare change, eventually earning enough to smoke for an hour or two, and when his high faded, he would hoist yet another box onto his back. Not having been out from under the market for nearly a week, avoiding the light of day for far too long, Santiago found himself trapped by his own desires, seemingly bound hand and foot.[6]

"I can't get myself back to work," Santiago admitted, "not on my own, and if I did, I'd just smoke the money." He was being honest. Steady work had always been a problem for him—largely because a two-hour crack session can cost upwards of $50 USD, and these crack sessions rarely ever lasted two hours. They tended to extend across a day, even two, and so Santiago ended up spending all of his money to keep the sessions rolling. Then he would steal. This meant taking cash straight from his family's pockets but also stealing hard-earned appliances from under their noses. He even sold the family's microwave for pennies on the dollar and pilfered light bulbs straight from their sockets. "He sold my table saw," his brother huffed, "and that [machine] was how I made money."

Santiago's family was not alone. Prior to 2006, when there were only dozens rather than hundreds of Pentecostal drug rehabilitation centers in Guatemala City, hunting parties would track down and capture those who drank too much. This was a different kind of hunt, with a different set of techniques. Alcohol slows down the user, even puts him to sleep, which can make hunting look a lot like fishing. "If he drinks," a hunter once explained to me, "we let him drink. And then we'd give him more to drink. Until he couldn't talk. Until he couldn't walk. Then we'd take him." With just a bit of bait, the hunter would reel in user after user. The work was easy. It was also inspired. "If you're in the streets," Alejandro said, "you'll end up dead."

But then nets turned into hooks as crack cocaine flooded the city. Unlike alcohol, crack cocaine does not slow down the user but instead speeds him up. It speeds everything up, which is why Santiago looked over his shoulder. He scanned the horizon, reading every vendor for signs of a chase. Though he occasionally mistook a pedestrian for a predator, Santiago knew who was looking for him.

Alejandro had hunted Santiago before. Ten years older than Santiago, with a stronger, wider frame, Alejandro was an imposing figure. "I don't feel anything anymore," Alejandro told me. We sat inside Pedro's center, among the general population, while Alejandro kept watch over the captives. "You know that feeling," Alejandro asked me, "when you're about to get into a fight, like when your hands start shaking? I don't feel that anymore." With a round face and strong arms, a nose that broke stage left, Alejandro walked smoothly when he wanted to be seen, but he could also hide in plain sight when he needed to disappear. Accustomed to wearing secondhand T-shirts with the sleeves cut off, Alejandro had a tattoo on his left shoulder. It looked like the earliest version of Mickey Mouse, the one with the spindly legs and a button nose. The tattoo was the kind of commitment that some people might regret, but Alejandro never seemed to care. "That's the least of my worries," he once told me.[7]

Inside the center, well before Santiago's panicked tour of the central market, Alejandro described the market as one of his hunting grounds. "We pick up guys there all the time," he said. "It's not easy. The lighting is terrible, and there are thousands of people. And stuff's everywhere. I've twisted my ankle there while chasing down a guy."

How do you find someone in the market? I asked.

"The family calls us," he said. "They let us know where he is, and what he's doing.'" Alejandro then echoed Santiago's strategy about the crowds. It seemed to be common knowledge. "But you need to watch out for the crowds," Alejandro said. "They'll back a guy up if you just try to hook him in the market. You need to wait a bit, watch the situation."

By this time, Alejandro had relaxed against a wall and was taking his time to answer my questions. He seemed to enjoy these moments of reflection, the chance to really consider his techniques.

"I'm waiting for the guy to separate from the group," Alejandro said, "to go buy some more drugs or just take a walk. You need to wait until he's alone, on his own."

And then?

"And then you walk up to him," Alejandro said, "and grab his thumb." Alejandro took my hand and turned my palm upwards. My arm locked as I suddenly found myself standing on the tips of my toes. "I then tell him that 'you either walk out of here with me quietly, or I'll break your arm and drag you to the car.'" He paused. "It's actually pretty wild," Alejandro said, "to know that you're being hunted. You don't know where to go. You don't know what to do. You just start to panic because it could be anyone. Different guys hunt for different centers and they're all from the streets. So you don't know who is going to grab you." Alejandro knew both sides of this exchange.

"When I'm hunting," he said, "I use it to my advantage. I hang back, watch the situation, and let the guy get comfortable. Because maybe he doesn't see me waiting for him. Maybe he doesn't know I'm the guy hunting him." Alejandro then flipped perspectives. "But when I'm being hunted," he said, "it scares me. Because I'm usually pretty fucked up [by the time I'm being hunted] and I don't know who is watching me. I mean, it's like you got God calling out your name."[8]

TWO

_____

Pedro often called out Alejandro's name.[9] A man of faith, with long hair and a bulging stomach, Pedro was well past middle age. In the past, a quarter of a century earlier, Pedro had spent a year inside of a Pentecostal drug rehabilitation center for drinking and drugs and living on the streets. "How is it that I managed to escape from drug addiction?" Pedro once wondered aloud as we stood inside the center. "How is that I managed to escape from smoking marijuana, from injecting cocaine, from having gone mad, from ending up a prisoner, from getting to the point where I had to sleep in the streets?" Pedro paused. "I experienced God's mercy," he said. "Christ rescued me. He brought me to a place where I met . . . where I met myself, where I met God." Pedro would later start his own enterprise out of a two-story house. We talked on the first floor of his center, inside his front office, while a wall opposite of us announced in bold blue font: "The man who falls and then gets back up is greater than the man who has never fallen."

"We give the family peace," Pedro said, "because they prefer to have their father or brother or son locked up here so that he doesn't get himself killed." Pedro rested his elbows on his knees, leaning forward until he was balancing on the edge of his chair. He looked uncomfortable, with his soccer jersey starting to bunch around his belly. "There are people here against their will," he said, "and they want to get out, but why do they want out?" Pedro answered the question for me: "Because they want to do drugs." At the time, fifty-five captives lived above Pedro's front office. Santiago would make it fifty-six.

The house was never meant for any of this. While Pedro lived with his family on the first floor, using the space largely as it was intended, with family meals eaten around a kitchen table, the second floor strained to keep up with the demands of captivity. Roughly 1,200 square feet, the second floor had a total of three bedrooms. Two of them had been converted into dormitories, with each holding a cluster of bunks stacked three beds high. Pedro called the third bedroom the morgue (*la morgue*). This is where new arrivals recuperated from withdrawals. Offering nothing more than a king-sized mattress splayed out on the floor and a few buckets, the morgue held three to five captives at any given time.

Then there was the family room, with its southern facing windows. It was not large, maybe 400 square feet, but it served a number of different purposes. It was where the captives ate their meals, listened to sermons, and slept on the floor. Every night, as many as thirty men zigzagged across the room, piecing themselves together so that they fit just right. The second floor's toilets, both of them, still functioned as such, but they strained from overuse.

The bars were also conspicuous. Pedro secured every possible avenue of escape. He capped the door at the top of the stairs with a metal gate, and he plugged the morgue with a heavy door. Both had padlocks. Pedro also lined those southern facing windows with bars and then topped them with corrugated metal.

A door connected the former family room to a balcony. I often imagined the kind of plans that the architect must have had for this space. The house was obviously built with upward mobility in mind. The architectural intention, it would seem, was to have the balcony just off the family room—so that the patriarch and maybe even his wife could have a drink while the children played with toys or even roughhoused until the man of the house told them to cut it out. I could even imagine a real estate agent touring a young couple through the house, quickly admitting that the space was obviously much too large for them "for now" but that they would one day grow into it. The agent might have even tried to sell the very same scene that came to my mind whenever I looked onto the balcony: the kids, the cocktails, the stern but loving plea to just be quiet. But none of that made sense anymore, given that Pedro had fortified the balcony's door with padlocks, lined the edges of the veranda with razor wire, and posted two guard dogs there.

I asked Pedro about human rights.

"Talking about human rights," Pedro waxed, "makes me sad." He leaned back in his chair, resting his forearms atop his stomach. His front office lent him a kind of executive aesthetic, with its filing cabinets and calendar, but everything within eyesight was secondhand, down to the desk blotter. He had even fished his office chair out of a landfill.

Why do human rights make you sad? I asked.

"Because people want human rights for the thief or the addict or the trafficker or the murderer, but what about the rights of the mother who right now is calm and relaxed because she knows that her son is in good hands?" Pedro looked tired. He had been up well past midnight on a hunt that dragged him across the city, into alleyways, and eventually to the very edge of a canyon. "And what about a father who is too old to physically dominate his son," he asked, "but he knows that today his son is here? He knows that his son is not going to turn up dead." Pedro looked me in the eyes, adding: "This is not about the individual. This is about the family and society."[10]

Is this why you run this center? I asked with a kind of naiveté. I always prodded the pastor with the most basic of questions, which sometimes he appreciated and other times he didn't. I had apparently caught him at a bad time.

Pedro scoffed, answering, "I do all of this because I love my neighbor, and I love helping the needy." He pointed at a locked door, one of four that held fifty-five users against their will, adding, "And I will not turn my back on these victims. They are dying because of drugs."

Pedro was right. Drugs are deadly serious in Guatemala City, not necessarily because of overdoses but because users tend to make increasingly poor decisions as they overextend themselves with their substance of choice. They steal from their neighbors, go into debt with their dealers, and pick fights with gang members. They even pass out in the streets. All of this can add up to a death that very few people mourn. "Try to get the police to give a shit about someone on crack," Pedro once challenged me. "You should see the look of relief on their faces when they toss one of those guys into a bag."

Pedro's center kept users alive. Pedro often preached about the power of conversion, about the thrill of standing on one's own two feet, but he also was patently aware that his mission was to hunt down those sheep that had wandered from the herd.

Pedro had inherited this mandate from the center that once held him. Opened in 1981 and shut down thirty years later, that house was Central America's first Pentecostal drug rehabilitation center. The founding pastor was a former soldier and a convicted criminal, but he was also a changed man. In his early years, he went by the nickname Bad Luck (*Malasuerte*) and served multiple prison sentences. On July 5, 1970, following an uneventful military career, he was sentenced to twenty-four months of prison for theft. On June 11, 1971, while still in prison, he was sentenced to another forty-eight months for disorderly conduct, and on August 8, 1977, he was sentenced to prison for three and a half years for drug trafficking. But, as people would say metaphorically, "Malasuerte died in Pavón."[11]

Malasuerte, otherwise known as Jorge Ruiz, found Christ in Guatemala's largest prison: Pavón. This sprawling prison farm once represented the very cutting edge of liberal reform in Latin America but then fell into disrepair, with prisoners eventually taking full control of the institution. For decades, guards never entered Pavón. Instead, they walked the perimeter.

In Pavón, Jorge learned about prison, and these were lessons that he would articulate through the classic Christian idiom of warfare. "One wonders if it is worth it," Jorge writes, "I mean to engage in a direct war against evil, when in most cases one becomes a victim of the very system that one fights." In search of higher ground, amid his own conversion to Christianity, Jorge took aim at drugs.

Reflecting on humanity's inherent weaknesses and its predilection toward sin, Jorge narrated his life as folding along a bright divide. He sinned before his conversion in prison, but after salvation, he thrived as a Christian through his rehabilitation center. His redemption, he insisted, came by the grace of God. The prison itself did nothing to better him. It only made him more of a criminal. He sought a context in which people could change, where the individual could come to terms with sin. And so, within an ever-changing capital city, one tested not just by unemployment and gross socio-economic inequalities but also a genocidal civil war, Jorge met the woman who would become his benefactor.

María Elena was an eccentric Pentecostal whose wealthy husband had been murdered by leftist rebels during the country's civil war. The heir to her husband's estate, María Elena found herself taken by Jorge's swagger. A photograph of Jorge from the mid-1980s has him leaning against an American roadster with tight blue jeans, a white T-shirt, and a gold chain. A comically oversized cellular phone hangs from his hip.

"He was so charismatic." She blushed. We spoke in one of her homes as she petted a white lap dog. Another sat at my feet. "We used to discuss the Bible, the power and the authority of God. He treated me like his mother, and I treated him like my son. And oh how he would protect me." María Elena told a story of a man who loitered by one of her many stores. He bothered the customers, she said, but the police were unwilling to do anything about it. So she told Jorge about the man, and he was gone the next day. "Jorge just grabbed him, put him in his van, and took the man back to his center." She smiled. She then admitted to missing him terribly. Jorge died in a car accident in 1991, and so Jorge's wife ran the center for a decade until his daughter took over for another ten years. "I miss him so much," María Elena said.

Jorge spent much of his time hunting sinners. He would wait for the sun to set, for the city to turn quiet, and then he would wake a pair of his most trusted captives. They would cast about the city, searching for lost souls passed out in the streets or huddled in doorways. There are also stories of Jorge and his men stalking specific users. They would park their truck and then follow on foot the tracks of someone on the lam not simply from society but, more importantly, from God. There was an obvious thrill to this kind of pursuit, which mixed the adrenal pleasures of domination with an evangelical sense of purpose.[12] It was this sense of adventure that attracted people to Jorge.[13]

María Elena was one such admirer, eventually lending one of her homes to Jorge at no cost. Located in the very center of the city, just steps away from the national cathedral, the house's floorplan boasted fourteen rooms, four bathrooms, two expansive terraces, and an industrial-sized kitchen. Jorge used every square inch of it. At the height of its run, roughly twenty years before the police would raid the house for harboring members of organized crime, the center held as many as 250 captives.

"We sleep on the floor like spoons," a man once told me with tears in his eyes. We were speaking inside Jorge's center—in 2011, just months before the raid. Jorge's daughter managed the enterprise, largely by handing over all pastoral duties to a cohort of former captives. Her lack of interest in the everyday running of the center had created innumerable opportunities for abuse. The very same captive explained how he had to scrub the floors on his hands and knees, naked. "As punishment," he told me.

During that same visit, another captive whispered to me, "No one is going to tell you the truth." We sat in the front office while Jorge's daughter entered and exited, going about her business.

"It has been a real opportunity to be here," the captive suddenly back-pedaled when she reentered the office, "a real blessing."

Jorge's daughter left again, and the captive mouthed a few words that I couldn't understand. I squinted until he spoke up. "Out of control," he whispered. "This place is out of fucking control." He kept his eyes trained on the door. "She has two friends," he said. "They always come here at night. All drunk and shit, with two Rottweilers and machetes. Just to fuck with us. Just to have the dogs growl in our faces."

"Then leave," I told him. "Call your family."

"They put me here," he said. "My family has no idea what they've done to me." He leaned toward me to keep his whisper at a minimum. "The only thing I can say about this place is that at least I know where I'm gonna get hit from. Out there I'll get killed. In here, I'm not gonna get more than a beat down."

Jorge's daughter entered once more. "That's about everything," he said. Full stop.

Given the uneven quality of care that Jorge's center provided, expansion might have seemed improbable, but the radical absence of government programs allowed the center to become a recognizable social resource, with transfer sheets lining its archives. State institutions (courts, prisons, mental hospitals) brought men of all ages to the center—even young boys. A civil servant from the Secretary of Social Services signed over a fourteen-year-old drug user on October 16, 2001: "The minor says that it has been a year since he has seen his parents. He says that he has no brothers or sisters." Another transfer sheet describes a ten-year-old boy as "very disobedient. Cries at anything. And poorly behaved." The center took them all.[14]

Jorge's pastoral efforts eventually set the conditions for a much larger kind of expansion, with a dozen or so captives leaving Jorge's center to start their own outfits. Pedro was one of them. By the late 1990s, Pedro had saved up enough money to open his own rehab. These second-generation centers often proved to be far more improvisational than Jorge's, if only because pastors such as Pedro never enjoyed the support of a benefactor like María Elena. Instead he and other former captives scoured the city for abandoned buildings and low-rent opportunities, spending all of their money on the basics: bars, padlocks, and razor wire. Many of them didn't even have furniture, but Pedro knew that all he needed was two dozen or so captives not only to recoup his initial investment but also to keep his center afloat. These entrepreneurial efforts eventually formed a web of some two hundred Pentecostal drug rehabilitation centers in Guatemala City. "They all had their start with Jorge," Pedro once mused. "Even the new centers have a connection to Jorge." Only months earlier, one of Pedro's first captives opened a center in one of Guatemala City's outer suburbs. Having been hunted by Pedro, who had been hunted by Jorge, this third-generation pastor now hunted at the margins of the capital.[15]

THREE

Back in the market, still beyond the reach of natural light, Santiago found himself at a decision point. Midday had become late afternoon, with the sun beginning to set and vendors starting to close up shop. Uninterested in spending yet another night in the market, Santiago considered returning home to have a meal. He also wanted to talk to his family. "It's better than smoking all night," he reasoned. I agreed.

We took a series of public buses back to Santiago's home, with no small amount of trepidation. As the bus sputtered and choked its way across the capital city, Santiago insisted that we hover near the back of the bus in case a huntsman entered through the front door. "We can slip out," Santiago reasoned, but then he caught himself, knowing full well that the pastor's men often rush the front door of buses in the hopes of pushing their prey out the back door. "They then tie you up right there on the side of the road." Santiago winced.

I felt compelled to calm his nerves, to reason with Santiago that no one could possibly know which bus he was on and that he should probably just rest for a moment, but Santiago was beside himself, afraid of the inevitable, and yet growing ever closer to his family's home, where he would most certainly come into contact with the pastor's men.

Did Santiago want to be caught?

I once had a conversation with one of Pedro's captives. The young man had been hunted by Pedro's men and described his capture in crisp detail. There was an alleyway and a chase; he ran as fast as he could, but then he tripped over something. Tumbling to the ground, the men quickly picked him up and tossed him into the pastor's car. "But I'm not here [inside the center] against my will," he then told me. Reading a look of confusion on my face, he added: "I let them catch me." The young man didn't seem to be making excuses—for running, falling, or even being caught—but rather he wanted to communicate a delicate point about submitting to the hunt. "Once they had a hold of me," he explained, "I knew it was over, and so I let them take me."

Was this bus ride home a moment of Santiago "letting" Pedro take him?

As we hopped off the bus and walked the last two blocks to Santiago's home, past some of the very places where he bought his drugs, Santiago seemed more confident in his decision to return home—to have a conversation with his family about a fresh start. "I'll talk to them," was the last thing Santiago said to me before he walked through the front door.

Maria received her son with a sigh of relief. "When he passes out in his bed," she told me, "then I know where he is, and I know that he's safe." But an ulterior motive also piqued Maria's interest in her prodigal son. As Santiago collapsed onto his bed, his shoes still fastened to his feet, Maria fished a business card from her Bible. It was for Pedro's center. Maria had called the number before, and so she knew full well what she was about to do. "I hate having him hunted," she told me, "I hate to see them grab him." But Maria dialed the number anyway, and as she did, I caught a glimpse of the card. It read: "Drugs in your family? There's a solution. Call anytime. Open

24 hours a day." Next to the text sat a sketch of Christ as shepherd, with a staff in his hand and a lamb slung across his shoulders.

Maria had first come across Pedro's card years earlier. A neighbor's son had struggled with drugs, resisting his family's help at every turn. Fed up, the family paid the pastor to hunt him. Four men tied him up in the middle of the night and brought him to Pedro's center. Before driving away with their catch, one of the huntsmen left a dozen cards with the family. Maria's neighbor then passed her one of those cards, which she tucked into her Bible—just in case. When I asked her why she had kept the card, Maria simply said: "Santiago makes me cry. He's always made me cry."

Pedro's center was not the only outfit handing out cards. The expanding network of centers produced a thicket of paper that circulated throughout the city, each making promises in language that had been lifted from the corporate worlds of hospitality management and customer service. The first was usually that the center is "at your service 24 hours a day." Many of them went even further, insisting that they provide "a friendly, agreeable environment" for drug rehabilitation. "Do not give up!" other cards encouraged. "We are here to help!" The vast majority of these cards were results oriented. "If there's a problem of drugs in your family, then there is a solution." A different card squeezed the following information into a single frame, with exclamation points punctuating nearly every phrase: "Open 24 hours a day! Visiting hours Saturday to Saturday 10:00am to 5:00pm. Ring the doorbell! Or call now! It would be a pleasure to serve you!"

They often included multiple phone numbers and the occasional email address. One notorious center handed out cards that announced its mission in suspiciously oblique ways: "Helping those with problems with drugs, alcohol, and etcetera." The "etcetera" signaled just how undefined a center's mission can be. Serving as a kind of moral catchall, centers often did not target addiction so much as sin and, thus, did not hunt users but rather sinners.

Variations of stock images also appeared on the cards, usually featuring a silhouette of a businessman running from one corner of the card to another, briefcase in hand while his tie trailed behind him. Another set repositioned the businessman so that he held his hands above his head to show the chains of addiction.[16] Yet another depicted him trapped inside a bottle. "Call now!"

Other pastors, such as Pedro, adorned their cards with images of Jesus Christ, depicting their savior in a range of settings—as a shepherd with a sheep atop his shoulders; as a prophet extending his hand towards the heavens; or as a beneficent father figure walking children through open fields. One card placed a user at the foot of Christ's cross in the midst of full supplication.

Pedro's son, Roberto, had designed his father's business card using an online template. In his midtwenties, with his two young children almost always by his side, Roberto's entrepreneurial spirit had helped make the center successful. In addition to the sheer force of the hunt, these business cards proved vital to Pedro's pastoralism. They enabled Pedro to communicate legitimacy, authority, and piety, the sense that there was a plan of some kind, a modicum of expertise at play. These cards transformed desperate families into willing clients.

The strategy seemed relatively straightforward. Roberto made his father's center look credible by modeling a level of corporate formality. Albeit designed on a secondhand computer and printed at a local internet café, with paper purchased at the central market, these cards provided Pedro's center with a sense of gravitas. Every detail seemed to be meticulously considered, down to the weight of the card, its cut, and its glossy finish.[17]

"We had to throw away a hundred of these cards," Roberto once told me, "because we didn't cut them right."

So what? I wondered aloud, but my flippancy missed how these centers prioritized aesthetics over information, and so Roberto defended his decision.

"Who's going to take us seriously with an imperfect card? Who's going to trust us with their son? Or their father?"

Roberto knew all too well that the size and shape of each card was essential to the center's performance as a believable entity. Their card needed to be on the same level as any other business card produced by a government agency or international organization. He did it to increase awareness of the center, to be sure, but he also wanted to create an air of lawfulness. Roberto needed to feel legitimate so Maria could feel like a client. To leave a dozen business cards with a family after dragging their son into a vehicle was a modest effort at networking and also an effective way to transform a kidnapping into a business transaction—to convert a manhunt into a fee-for-service arrangement.[18]

To spread these cards across a tabletop, to take them in all at once, demonstrated the ways both empathy and abduction formed overlapping webs of predation. It also charted the affective dimensions of being chased as well as living in captivity—while also addressing the paradoxes of escape as not a singular event but a constant effort. For while Pedro had most clearly hunted Santiago, Maria too was prey to the pastor, as a customer. These cards also demonstrated that the pastor's enterprise was not entirely hegemonic. Roberto deployed market strategies to position himself within the industry; he actively sought out customers by presenting them with a solution to a problem that he himself tried to frame. Yet Maria was no fool. She was never duped; in fact, she may very well have been the most informed consumer in the capital city.[19]

"Did you know that they shot Santiago?" Maria once asked me.

Who? I asked.

"Some kids in the neighborhood. He was buying drugs, and they shot him in the stomach." Santiago later showed me a thick scar that snaked up his abdomen. He also insisted that I touch a nub of bone that never properly healed. It was a piece of rib that protruded whenever he lost too much weight.

"The doctors had to open me up," Santiago said, "to make sure that my organs were okay. That everything was good."

Distracted by a wave of memories, Maria eventually added, "He almost died." Without Pedro's center, with its standing offer to hunt loved ones at all hours of the night, even to the very edge of canyons, Santiago would have walked the streets. "But in the center," Maria insisted, "Santiago is safe. No one can shoot him there."

The fundamental obstacle was that Santiago had absolutely no interest in entering a drug rehabilitation center. Also adding to the problem was a lack of muscle. No one in Santiago's family had the strength needed to bring him to the center. Pedro's house was also an hour away from the family's home, and so with no steady access to a car, there was simply no conceivable way for the family to get Santiago to the center without having him hunted. After haggling with Pedro over Santiago's monthly fees, even downgrading Santiago's stay from a bed to a floor mat, the family eventually agreed to stretch their budget and pay a lump sum to transport Santiago from the streets to the center.

Alejandro did the honors.

FOUR

The bat hung in Pedro's front office, right above his desk. Weathered and metallic, made for children's T-ball games, the stick was strong enough to break grown men.

"I hit them," Pedro admitted. "I get down to their level and sometimes I take a swing."

Santiago had told me the same. "The pastor beats people," he said as we circled the market. "He'll beat people with his fist and then with his bat." Pedro would also poke them in the gut, pushing a captive onto his heels with each prod until his back was up against a wall.[20]

Pedro dominated both body and soul, his hunts demonstrating day in and day out that caring for the sheepfold demands as much muscle as it does heart. "Above all," he insisted, "I put salvation in the hands of God, as he's the only one who is able to rescue us." But staging an audience before God took some effort on Pedro's part.

Pedro's central task, as he understood it, was to get users to sober up just long enough for them to hear the word of God, and so he fielded a hunting party to grab their attention. "I make mistakes," Pedro admitted, "so I can't tell the guys here that I'll be able to help them. But it's not about me helping them. It's God who helps them, in the same way that God helped me."[21]

Pedro never hunted by himself. Part of this had to do with his age. Since starting his center he had grown sluggish, gained weight, and picked up a slight limp. He always denied the limp ("I walk just fine") just as he dismissed his diabetes ("It's not a problem"), but both strapped his mood to a rollercoaster of emotions.

Pedro usually hunted with four men, whom he pulled from the second floor. "The first thing you have to realize," Pedro explained, "is that hunting is a privilege. How many guys do I have here? Close to sixty or something? Not all of them can hunt. Not even a handful of them can hunt."

Why? I wondered.

"Because they'd run away!" he said. We spoke in his front office as he stretched out in his chair behind a desk. "They'd take one step outside the center and then just disappear, and I don't want to make more work for myself."

There are stories of a hunting party losing men. A group of four suddenly becoming a group of three. It is a remarkable moment of reversal. For when the hunter makes a break for it, he suddenly becomes the hunted, and he rarely gets far. Once the remaining three complete their immediate task, those same huntsmen then set out to find the escapee. "We drag that guy back to the center," Pedro huffed, "and beat the shit out of him." He then said, "Because only a few of these guys can be trusted, and it takes months to gain that kind of trust, to know if someone is really sincere."[22]

By sincere, Pedro meant transcendently trustworthy. He was talking about whether a captive could be brought to the very brink of freedom, shown a clear pathway for escape, and then trusted to return to his own captivity—with the pastor's newest catch, no less. "Do I know the man's heart? Can I trust his soul?" These are the questions that Pedro asked himself about each of his huntsmen, and only the most sincere, only the most transparent of these men, ever hunted on his behalf.

Sincerity inside this center was always a performance; it was far more a matter of doing than being. Within the Christian tradition, going as far back as the sixteenth century, the rhetoric of sincerity has tried to reconcile the paradox of the forced confession with an authentic affect, and in the end it has generated a field of expectation that routinely attempts to connect inner states to external representations.[23] The important amendment here is that these centers have made sincerity a technique of governance.

Sincerity structured so much of life inside Pedro's center that captives self-consciously tried to make their inner self outwardly legible to the pastor. These signs of sincerity included clean clothes, an upright posture, and a positive attitude. "But I really know that someone has changed," Pedro once told me, "when I can wake him up in the middle of the night and tell him to hunt." All of this made the practice of hunting the most prized privilege inside the center—not simply because the hunt pleased Pedro so much (and it did) but also because hunting was the purest means by which to perform Christian sincerity.

This led to one of hunting's most confounding paradoxes: "The pastor knows that you're ready to leave the center," Santiago once explained to me with a bit of a shrug, "when you no longer want to leave the center."[24]

Tomás no longer wanted to leave the center. In his midthirties and originally born in Nicaragua, Tomás moved to Guatemala City when he was a young boy, but then his parents abandoned him. Tomás lived on the streets of Guatemala City from the age of ten. He never joined a gang, though he also never finished school, instead relying on petty theft and drug dealing to get him from one day to the next. By the time he was twenty, Tomás had become dependent on a constellation of substances, with rubbing alcohol and solvents topping the list. He also smoked crack cocaine when he could afford it, but those opportunities were few and far between. With no family to fall back on, Tomás often had nowhere to go until he found himself hunted by Jorge's center.

"I was just walking the streets one night, looking for a place to stay," Tomás remembered, "when this truck pulled up. Three guys got out and wrestled me into the truck. I ended up back at the center." Tomás spent a year inside of Jorge's center, completing a home renovation project to pay for his captivity, and then he began to hunt.

Tomás proved to be an excellent huntsman—not so much at tracking, for he was often far too slow to keep up with the group, but he was deft at capture. His muscular back and chest proved invaluable. So too did his swagger. He felt unnervingly comfortable approaching his prey, talking to the user calmly, and then giving the person an ultimatum. Either the person could come to the center or he would be brought to the center. Tomás was also willing to take a hit, with a captive once breaking his nose in a way that permanently deviated his septum.

Given his abilities, Jorge kept Tomás for an additional twelve months. Afterwards, upon his release, Tomás found himself on the streets again. Far from sober, after only two weeks of freedom, Pedro picked him up. "Someone told me that a guy from Jorge's center was back on the streets," Pedro remembered, "and so I went looking for him. I knew that he could hunt, and so I wanted to have him."

Tomás's memory of the event paralleled his first abduction all too well: "I was in the streets. It was night. This truck pulled up and a bunch of guys got out. They dragged me into their truck and took me to the center." Tomás started to hunt for Pedro almost immediately.[25]

Emilio was one of the four men who hunted Tomás, and then the two eventually hunted alongside each other. Solidly middle class, Emilio used to steal from his father's pharmacy, working his way through an assortment of over-the-counter pain killers before trafficking drugs. The police caught him in the late 1990s moving bricks of marijuana across the capital, but his father raced to his side, calling in a favor with a judge. Instead of sending Emilio to prison, the judge allowed the family to commit Emilio to Jorge's center. This kind of offloading became increasingly common as government officials found that families often preferred Pentecostal drug rehabilitation centers to state prisons.[26]

Spindly and at times hauntingly quiet, Emilio's work ethic eventually earned him the opportunity to hunt for Jorge's center, his calm demeanor providing a nice counterbalance to a cohort of reactive personalities. Hunting also made Emilio's time inside the center more comfortable. "Huntsmen get better food," Emilio said. "They get more privileges, more freedom. You get to leave the center [for the hunt] and sometimes get to sleep late." After two years at Jorge's center, Emilio bounced between the streets and other centers until Pedro hunted him.

Bautista was the youngest huntsman by years. Exceedingly scrawny, with a tattoo of a marijuana leaf behind his left ear, he never knew Jorge's center. "Everyone talks about it like it was hell," Bautista said, "as if I care about any of that." Having been hunted for his crack cocaine use, Bautista quickly rose through the ranks of Pedro's center, becoming the pastor's right-hand man after only a year.

"His family called me," Pedro explained. "They said that Bautista couldn't stop smoking. So we grabbed him and brought him here." Pedro painted a quick picture of the kidnapping. "He's skinny," Pedro said, "so it wasn't too hard."

When did Bautista start hunting for the center? I asked.

"After only a few months," Pedro answered. "I could tell that he's smart. I liked him, and I could trust him with everything."

By everything, Pedro meant the keys, the front door, and even the bat from time to time. Bautista shuttled newly acquired users past the front office and up the stairs to the general population. He also answered the phone. This tended to place Bautista in the front office, lounging on a couch, watching television with his feet propped up on a chair. It sometimes looked like Bautista owned the place.

You ever get jealous? I asked Tomás.

"The favorites fall fast," he said with a shrug.

None of this seemed to bother Bautista, probably because he had not yet experienced a fall from grace, and so his responsibilities expanded to the point of becoming Pedro's surrogate. "It's better if I speak to the families," Pedro reasoned, "but Bautista can handle everything else."

The final member of Pedro's quartet was Alejandro, who had been in and out of Pedro's center for years. I had actually met Alejandro five years before he handed me his letter for the National Police. He was inside a different center, on the other side of town, and trying to find his way back to Pedro. Alejandro never had any real family in Guatemala. He arrived in Chicago in the late 1980s and quickly became a ward of the state. He shuffled from one foster family to another until getting married at fifteen. He worked union jobs for years while making deliveries for members of organized crime. Then Alejandro got arrested, serving five years with the Illinois Department of Corrections across a number of institutions until the United States Immigration and Customs Enforcement deported him to Guatemala. "They put me on a plane," he said. "I didn't really know Spanish. I didn't have any family. I didn't know what I was going to do."

Ever since he was thirteen years old, Alejandro struggled with substance abuse, mostly alcoholism, but he increasingly came to use whatever drug was within arm's reach. "I drank a lot in the States, and I did some co-caine. I got out of control too many times and that wasn't fair to my wife." They separated after a few years.

Once deported, Alejandro struggled to find work in Guatemala City. With only an inattentive aunt in the capital, Alejandro took to the streets, trying to make money by moving drugs. "I thought to myself, 'I don't know how to sell but I know how to move stuff from one dealer to the next.'"

Cocaine's commodity chain in Central America proved completely foreign to Alejandro in ways that prompted him to smoke more than he sold. "I mean, how fucked up is it that I come to Guatemala and end up smoking crack? I never smoked in the States. Never. But here I end up los-ing days to that shit." Alejandro lived on the streets, often spending weeks inside the market moving produce from trucks to stalls. Pedro eventually picked him up while casting about for new captives.

"These days, we usually wait for families to call," Pedro explained, but years earlier he actively sought out the deported. "They have more money than other people here in Guatemala," Pedro explained. "The deported have family in the States that can pay for their captivity." Money orders from West-ern Union lined Pedro's archives, with distant family members often paying above market rates for captivity. None of this was true for Alejandro. No one ever paid for his captivity. Yet before Pedro could wash his hands of him, Alejandro proved to be a leader. He began to run the general popula-tion, discipline the men, and manage a whole range of activities, including the kitchen. Alejandro had a knack for making himself useful.

Pedro's huntsmen were all rather senior except for Bautista. Each had years of experience, which eventually allowed Pedro to pack as many as sixty captives into his second floor. The sight was often difficult to see, with cap-tives literally pressed against each other, but Pedro never seemed concerned. "The important point," he insisted, "is that this is about love rather than hate; this is about rehabilitation rather than retaliation. We want users to live rather than die. This is about forgiveness and not retribution."[27] I remember think-ing to myself how sincere Pedro sounded when he said those words to me.

FIVE

Not everyone thought that Pedro sounded sincere. Even though these cen-ters provided a necessary service to the city, as the government flatly refused to provide any kind of care for drug users, the most cynical of citizens un-derstood Pedro's mission as nothing more than a business. They would call Pedro the equivalent of a shyster and a charlatan, and a whole range of people dismissed these centers as fee-for-service providers that took advan-tage of vulnerable families. In a series of interviews that I completed over the course of many years, government officials called pastors such as Pedro "vultures." Public health workers shrugged them off as parasitic while hu-man rights lawyers saw them as nothing more than agents of greed. Even the pastors of established churches would raise their eyebrows, often won-dering whether any of these centers did more good than harm.

Much of this suspicion had to do with the business model that most of these centers maintained—which they relied on not necessarily for profit but survival. It was a hardscrabble kind of strategy that admittedly made Pedro look like he was running a bit of a hustle, but none of it seemed out of step with the city itself. As I would remind those working in government, public health, and human rights, only a third of Guatemalans at any given moment work in the formal economy.[28] Everyone else is just trying to cob-ble together a bit of stability.

Cultivating compassion for Pedro's business model was admittedly hard for me—not necessarily because I was suspicious of Pedro but because money is not an easy topic to discuss, whether in Guatemala or elsewhere. And given that the price of captivity and the promise of salvation are slip-pery topics at best, it took years of fieldwork inside of Pedro's center to mus-ter up enough courage to ask him a relatively simple set of questions. I re-member first broaching the subject of money inside his front office, with Pedro sitting high in his office chair and me slumping forward on a stool. The conversation felt uneven from the get go.

What do you pay your huntsmen? I asked.

Pedro just stared at me.

Over time, Pedro had become completely forthcoming about most ev-ery aspect of the industry, from his own history of addiction to the hunting of drug users, but the money was always a mystery. I had seen cash change hands and had often heard him haggle with families, but telling me the spe-cifics of these exchanges always seemed out of bounds for Pedro. Never did my fieldwork feel more like a cat and mouse game than when we discussed finances.

"What do you mean?" he eventually asked. I repeated the question, asking as clearly as I could how much money he gave each of his huntsmen in exchange for his labor. I had always been amazed by how much labor

Pedro was able to squeeze out of his men. They not only tracked and captured drug users, often in the most extreme circumstances, but also kept the second floor from erupting into a riot. They were often obedient to Pedro and yet strict with the captives, respectful of the house but unbending with the men. They could be cruel at times, but they always performed in a way that allowed Pedro to float above the messy details of running his center. Yet my sense was that Pedro did not pay them. So I asked again.

What do you pay your huntsmen?

Pedro again stared back at me. The question seemed impolite, even crass. It also seemed to call into question Pedro's own sincerity—his motives and aspirations. He knew better than anyone that a misinterpretation of his intentions, a small adjustment to his objectives, could transform him from a shepherd to a mercenary.

This is one reason why Pedro did not answer my question. Instead he avoided eye contact while feigning dumb in ways that not only confirmed that he did not pay his huntsmen at all but also that I had not yet learned the right language to ask him the right questions.

What I did know was that Pedro had bootstrapped his center from the very beginning. This meant paying out of pocket for renovations and repairs, food and medicine, as well as the unwavering march of utility bills. With these demands, many pastors found it difficult to stay in business, and it was common to see centers open and close within a matter of months. So I tried a different tack.

Can you make a living doing this? I asked.

"It's like this," he said, weighing his words carefully. "They say that every job has its wage." We spoke in his office as he straightened himself up in his chair. "I do other things, right? I have some small jobs on the side. So I make a bit of money from that." He then squirmed toward a more satisfying answer: "But I don't need money, because this isn't about getting rich." Trying to strike just the right balance, he added, "The Bible says something like, 'Look at the birds in the field. They don't sow or harvest, and yet their father feeds them.'" He then posed a question: "If that's what God does for the smallest of creatures, then why wouldn't he do it for me? I am a child of God." He finally leaned back, adding, "So to be here, with a bit of bread, is more than enough." Pedro looked satisfied.

But how much does each person pay to be here? I pressed. I wanted to understand his business model, but I again felt that my questions were missing the mark. I could also feel my forehead beginning to perspire as I burned the social capital that I had worked so hard to earn with Pedro.

All the trust and affection that he bestowed on me came from years of my observing and then obeying a million little rules—about what I could know and what I could not; about where I could go and where I could not; about whom I could interview and whom I could not. And it had paid off, with me gaining access not only to the hunts, the center, and the families but also to long stretches of conversation with Pedro that always proved intimate and, at times, inspiring. My question about money seemed to risk all of this.

Pedro asked me to repeat the question. Again he acted as if he did not understand, almost as if giving me one last chance to sidestep the conversation—to back out before we ever really got into it. But I pressed on. These centers obviously functioned through a moral economy of exchange, but their captivity also had a political economy.

How much does each captive pay to be inside the center? I asked.

Pedro just shook his head. The question was impossible to answer—not because there was no number to name but rather, he explained, because the question opened onto a rambunctious theological debate. "No one pays to be here," Pedro said. "This is not about money, and I do not charge for this house." He was very clear about this last point. "I do not charge families for this house," he said. He then doubled down on the impossibility of paying for redemption: "I do the work of God here, and you don't pay for the work of God. You do not pay for salvation. You can't put a price on redemption." Pedro's voice began to rise: "I don't let anyone pay for this place. No one is paying for this place. I wouldn't even let someone pay to be here." Pedro was visibly upset.

Then how do you pay your bills? I asked.

"Offerings," he answered. "People make offerings."

Offerings are not payments? I wanted clarification.

His answer seemed simple enough. "No," he said, "offerings are not payments. They are not the same thing at all."[29]

Payment for Pedro was money for work done, goods received, and debt incurred. Pedro paid for renovations and repairs. He paid for food and utility bills. An offering was something different. Families did not pay Pedro to save their loved ones. Instead they offered Pedro gifts of money at the very same time that he saved their loved ones from sin. These two gifts—offering and salvation—ran parallel to each other. They never overlapped, at least for Pedro. It was a distinction that allowed Christian compassion never to be confused for economic compensation.

"I do this out of love," Pedro insisted. "I do this to save people."

All the while families offered gifts of money. This was a delicate dance, especially given the fact that redemption has always been an economic metaphor for salvation. Redemption, theologically speaking, straps the sinner with a debt that only the grace of God can repay.[30] And so while business cards demonstrate how these centers align with the logic of capitalism, Pedro's insistence on offerings as opposed to payments bent the entire operation back onto more redemptive terrain.

"I am telling you," Pedro insisted, "nobody pays me." And to argue otherwise, the logic extends, was to confuse taking care of someone with simply taking them.[31]

So how do you make money? I asked.

"I do not make money," Pedro answered.

Then what do the families offer?

Pedro seemed more comfortable with this question and so he laid out some of the numbers, but not before schooling me on the centers themselves. As he would explain, his bottom line began with an affordable space. Most of the city's centers started out as factories, garages, store fronts, apartment complexes, single family houses, and military barracks—until something failed, be it a family, a neighborhood, a business, or the state. All of these structures sat empty until pastors renovated them into rehabilitation centers. The process was apparently not hard.

"It doesn't take much to turn one of these places into a rehab," Pedro explained while touring me through his own center. "You add a few doors. You secure the windows. Maybe you change some of the rooms." He noted a few other items that would complete the transformation, such as a desk for the front office and some cots for the general population. "A new sign is always important," he added, "but the first step is finding cheap space." Pastors have done this for decades by searching Guatemala City for abandoned buildings and low-rent opportunities. These pastors have steadily shadowed the disaggregation of the capital from an urban formation with a recognizable city center to a sprawling region studded with pockets of blight. "You can't just tie a bunch of guys up," Pedro once said. "You need to put them somewhere."

Once somewhere, the families of captives made their offerings. The average family, he said, offered him Q800 ($100 USD) per month, with the hunt requiring an extra Q400 ($50 USD), but the families of some users offered as little as Q200 ($25 USD) per month to have their loved one sleep on the floor. Others offered as much as Q1,600 ($200 USD) per month for a private bed in one of the dormitories. The family of a mentally ill captive could offer anywhere between Q1,600 ($200 USD) and Q2,400 ($300 USD) per month for long term care. The center tended to hold at any given time about a half dozen captives with schizophrenia, bipolar disorder, or severe depression. The money quickly added up. Holding an average of fifty captives at a time, with each family offering an average of Q800 ($100 USD) per month, Pedro's center generated around Q40,000 ($5,000 USD) in offerings every month.[32] Padding his margins, Pedro also completed anywhere from ten to thirty hunts a month for both his own center and for smaller operations, moonlighting for pastors who had not yet formed a sincere enough hunting party. Together, all of these hunts pulled in as much as Q12,000 ($1,500 USD) a month.

This is considerable money in Guatemala City. Pedro's living expenses were always pretty low. Pedro paid Q3,200 ($400 USD) per month in rent for the center, around Q3,200 ($400 USD) per month in food for the captives, and less than Q1,600 ($200 USD) per month in utilities for the building. Local churches often lightened those numbers with donations of bread and vegetables, and Pedro routinely received hundreds of pounds of charitable provisions from the United States Agency for International Development. Boxes of vitamin-fortified lentils sat on the roof, brought there by subcontractors who saw Pedro's center as a charitable organization.

There were also dozens of other tactics that redirected resources toward Pedro. Once, while holding an electrician captive, Pedro had the man splice a mainline so that the center could pirate electricity from the city, cutting the electricity bill in half. And this was only the start. Given that Pedro often held mechanics, barbers, and carpenters, he never paid for car repairs, haircuts, or home repairs. He also never paid for any of the labor that sustained his center. Everything from the cleaning to the cooking, even down to the hunting, involved conscripted labor; each of these assignments offered captives an opportunity to perform their sincerity to Pedro.

All of this seemed to make Pedro financially comfortable, especially given the fact that he and his family lived onsite. While this made him available at all hours of the day and night, it also allowed him to sidestep the cost of maintaining a private residence. And so while the average Guatemalan earns around $2,750 USD a year, Pedro cleared about $5,000 USD per month after expenses, propelling him and his family well into Guatemala's middle class. "Oh," Pedro added, "the center is registered as a church property. So I don't pay taxes."[33]

SIX

There would be nights when Maria would lock Santiago out of the house and make him sleep in the streets. "I'd also lock him inside his room," she told me, "and I'd keep him here in the house. But then he'd just get mad and fight his way out." Along the way, he would tear his room apart, breaking furniture and throwing objects. So Maria began a conversation with Pedro about her options, which revolved around the saving powers of Jesus Christ.

As both Santiago and his mother grew older—he in his twenties and she in her sixties—the future prospects for long-term care seemed to diminish, and Pedro's center emerged as the only viable solution for Santiago's survival. "I've fasted," Maria said. "I've fasted for twelve hours and then for twenty-four hours. But nothing works. Nothing at all."

We spoke just outside Maria's home. She leaned against a door as she thought out loud. "He needs help," she said. "I've spoken so often with him about his vices." She was careful to use the word vice as opposed to sickness. "We've prayed together about his vices," she said, "and I've told Santiago that he needs to make the decision to change." Maria began to calculate the cost of it all. She did not have the money to put him in a center more than once. "And so I want to put him inside the center for a long time," she told me. "I want to make the decision to put him there for a really long time."

How long? I asked.

"A year," she said, "maybe more." She flinched at hearing herself say those numbers out loud: "I want him with me. I want him with me right now, but he just doesn't make the decision to change. He always says that he'll come to church with me tomorrow or the next day, but he never does." And the risks were real. "I hurt so much for Santiago," she said, "and at night, I dream for my son and I pray for him." Out of sheer heartache and pure love, but also through streaks of anger, Maria eventually called Pedro. "Santiago also needs to be punished," Maria once told me.

Maria revisited the center before she called Pedro to hunt her son the second time, wanting to see the house one more time before making her decision. Fighting traffic on a Saturday afternoon, transferring from public bus to public bus, Maria eventually arrived at Pedro's front door. She rang the doorbell and Alejandro welcomed her into Pedro's front office.

Entering the center was no small task. Opening the front door meant finding the right key, unlocking the padlock, and then carefully positioning

one's body to allow a visitor to enter the center while guarding against the
off chance that someone might make a break for the door. This process took
time—to find the key, which was not always where it should be, but also
to prepare the room for a momentary breach in security. Each metal door,
outfitted with a padlock, demanded the same kind of discipline for entry.
There was the front door, which Maria entered, and then there was the door
at the top of the stairs, which Tomás and Bautista kept watch over. Alejandro was also tasked with managing the door to the morgue.[34]

Walking into the center was nothing short of an event. It was a common occurrence for Bautista to scream for Alejandro and then have Tomás
open the door at the top of the stairs just enough that Alejandro could reach
the front door. To the unfamiliar, this production might have seemed ludi-
crous, but such measures were absolutely necessary for Pedro to maintain
a sense of control. Never did any single person have all the keys to each of
the doors.

To further boost security, Pedro eventually added another locked door
between his front office and the hallway that led to the stairs. This meant
that a few months into Santiago's eventual captivity, four different doors,
four different padlocks, and four different keys separated those inside the
morgue from the streets.

Aren't four doors a little extreme? I asked Pedro.

He stared past me, refusing to engage with what seemed like a naive
question. I pressed on: Isn't it at least dangerous? A fire could spread faster
than any effort to unlock those four doors would take. Even at their best,
the guys took twenty minutes to get me from the morgue to the streets. Pedro also passed on answering that question, saving it for a future conversation. Instead, he wanted to focus on Maria.

With Christian murals hanging along the wall and Roberto's children
toddling about the office, Maria asked some standard questions—about the
quality of the food, where Santiago would sleep, and how many men the
pastor held upstairs. Pedro answered each question with a confidence that
came from years of experience.

"The food is fine," Pedro said. "And Santiago will sleep on the floor, unless a bed opens up. Are you interested in Santiago having a bed?" Maria
avoided the question, not wanting to negotiate over anything at that time.
"And I hold as many men as God wants me to hold," Pedro added. "No
more. No less." She then asked Pedro for a tour of the facilities.[35]

Pedro first showed Maria the front office. "Here is the phone." He gestured. "And this is one of our diplomas." The certificate, written in English,

came from a training workshop hosted by the United States Embassy. These
are two-day events held inside one of Guatemala City's international ho-
tels. North American experts on mental health and addiction guide pastors through a series of PowerPoint presentations, instructing them on the
rights of the patient (not captive) as well as evidence-based approaches to
rehabilitation (rather than theological therapy). These are quick events. "I
like the lunches," Pedro once mentioned, "but the lectures are terrible. They
don't know what we go through. They don't have any experience working
here in Guatemala City. They don't even know the people we help." Christ
is also conspicuously absent from the conversation. "And Jesus. Faith. They
don't talk about any of it," Pedro said.

The real payout comes at the end of the two-day session, when each
participant receives a certificate for completing the course. The piece of paper is easily mistaken for a diploma, especially when pastors frame them
for their front offices, allowing the English to obscure the scope of its significance.[36] "I haven't learned a single thing from those events," Pedro once
told me, "but the families appreciate the paper." Pedro hung several of these
certificates in his front office as if he were a doctor or a lawyer with his de-
grees on display.

Maria took it all in for a second time. "Here is a photograph of a young
man before he entered the center," Pedro said as he pointed to an image that
he had taped to one of his walls. "And here is an image of him after he left
the center." Roberto had edited the two images together, dividing them with
a split screen and pasting "Before" at the bottom of one image and "After"
at the bottom of another. The transformation on display was dramatic, with
a shower, shave, and a fresh shirt signaling a new beginning for a man who
had come straight from the streets. Pedro then led Maria to a small side
room. Here she could visit with Santiago any time she liked. "Every day is
a visiting day," Pedro insisted. "You want to visit Santiago? Then come visit
Santiago." The visits could only happen in that room, he said, ensuring that
Pedro could eavesdrop on conversations from the comfort of his desk.

Pedro then led Maria up a small flight of stairs to a barred door. Locked
from the outside with a key, the door separated the first floor from the second floor. "I can't take you inside the general population," he told Maria. "I
don't let people inside, but you can take a look." Maria leaned toward the
door, pressing her forehead against a pair of bars. She then looked from
side to side.

Directly in front of Maria was a gray wall and to her right was the
morgue, but she was not at the right angle to see inside the room. To her left,

Maria could see, even if only out of the corner of her eye, the former family room. It was midmorning and the men had gathered inside the main room to listen to a sermon from a visiting pastor. It was a delicate scene, if not a reassuring one, suggesting a comfortable level of care and Christianity's central role in the center. At one point, as we stood at the top of the stairs, with Maria's face pressed against the door, we could hear the pastor read from his Bible, allowing Psalm 27:4–6 to echo across the second floor.

"One thing I ask from the Lord," he read, "is that I may dwell in the house of the Lord all the days of my life, to gaze on the beauty of the Lord and to seek him in his temple." He read with some force, pushing his words at the captives. "For in the day of trouble, he will keep me safe in his dwelling; he will hide me in the shelter of his sacred tent and set me high upon a rock." All Maria could see from her perch was the pastor behind a thin pulpit. "Then my head will be exalted above the enemies who surround me; at his sacred tent I will sacrifice with shouts of joy; I will sing and make music to the Lord."

What Maria could not see was Tomás watching over the captives, making sure that the man at the podium delivered an acceptable sermon and that everyone listened intently. Maria also could not appreciate the intimate dynamics of nearly sixty captives living in such a small space—for weeks, months, and sometimes years.[37] There were often fistfights between captives over what seemed like the scarcest of resources: a piece of bread, a sliver of soap, or even a week-old newspaper. Maria could also never have anticipated how hungry these men got, especially when the center's already bland menu lost its taste because of extreme bouts of depression. Some captives even experimented with starvation, refusing meals in the hopes that that their family and friends might visit them and see what the center had done to their bodies. Captives would lose ten and then twenty pounds, the most extreme of them holding their pants up with makeshift belts.

From where she stood, Maria could also not see the stretches of inactivity that these men endured. There were sermons and meals, and these men also cleaned rooms and engaged in a series of chores; but there was also often nothing to do for hours on end. "It's the boredom that's the most difficult part of all of this," Tomás once admitted to me. Finally, Maria could not have anticipated how easy it could be to not see any of this. Many people would visit their loved ones weekly, even daily, at first, but then slowly pulled back until those in captivity became an afterthought.

Instead of seeing any of this, Maria listened to a pastor preach about the Lord sheltering sinners inside his sacred tent. With such an amenable vision of the center in full view and with no other options in sight, Maria ended her tour with a bit of optimism. "Just call me," Pedro told her as they walked to the front door. "Call me if you ever need me, and listen, if possible, call me when he's asleep. It's easier that way."

SEVEN

So much had changed over the years. For a stretch of time, Santiago drank too much, and this was a problem, but it was a different kind of problem than drugs. Santiago could stay drunk for less than $1 USD a day in Guatemala City. In many ways, that was a simpler time for Maria and her family. Rubbing alcohol (*quimica*) is incredibly cheap. It is also unbelievably accessible. Most corner stores sell it for a few cents, which explains why little plastic bottles often litter the sidewalks of the capital city, pooling next to men too drunk to pick themselves up off the ground.[38] But Santiago no longer wanted to get drunk. He wanted to get high, and he wanted to stay high.

"It can get bad," Alejandro admitted. "A mother had us pick up her son the other day. The problem was that he was high when we showed up, and so he took off running once he saw us. We chased him, but then he climbed up a three-story building." Alejandro paused to let me imagine the scene. "He made it all the way up to the roof. And along the way he picked up a pipe." The problem was suddenly obvious even to me, but Alejandro spelled it out: "He had the high ground and there was only one ladder leading up to the roof. So it was impossible to get up there without getting hit on the head."

So what did you do? I asked.

"We waited him out," Alejandro said, "and then we distracted him while two guys scaled the other side of the building. They took him from behind." Alejandro then paused, shaking his head. "But that hunt took five hours."[39]

Santiago did not make it to any roofs. Instead, moments after Santiago returned home from the central market Maria called the center to say that Santiago was asleep in his bed. Pedro's four huntsmen arrived by car within the hour. They spoke to Maria just outside of her home, insisting that she leave for a few minutes.

"Bautista told me that it can get really bad," Maria said.

"It does get physical," Bautista later explained to me, "and then mothers sometimes want to call off the hunt. They want to stop it, and then I don't know what to do. Because the pastor wants us to bring the guy in, but then the mother all of a sudden doesn't want us to hunt her son." Bautista closed off that option by pushing Maria out the door.

With Maria across the street inside a neighbor's kitchen, Bautista and Alejandro quietly searched the house for weapons. The home was quiet and completely dark, and so they tiptoed around the space looking for anything that could be used against them just in case Santiago wrestled free, but they found very little. There were a few knives in the kitchen, but this seemed like an improbable place for a struggle. There were also a couple of plastic chairs that he could throw at the men, but this was a minor concern. There were no stones, bars, or bats as well as no guns or needles. The room was clear. Bautista seemed satisfied.

The four men then moved into position, slowly creeping into Santiago's bedroom. It was well past sunset, and the room did not have windows. Hauntingly dark, without any light, Bautista cast a soft glow across the room with his cellphone. This allowed Alejandro to find his way to the left side of Santiago's bed and Emilio to the right side. Tomás then took his position at the foot of the bed while Bautista managed the doors. All the while Santiago slept on his side, his chest expanding and contracting at a calm, meditative pace. He had absolutely no idea what stood above him. Emilio asked the group to bow their heads as he whispered a quick prayer. He prayed for their safety, for Santiago's redemption, and for peace to return to this household.

Bautista then nodded and the men pounced. "You have to move quickly," Tomás later explained to me, "with as much force as possible. This is not a conversation. You need to dominate the person immediately, so that he knows who is in charge."

Emilio grabbed Santiago's left arm, pinning his shoulder to the bed. Alejandro did the same to Santiago's right arm while also pressing on Santiago's chest. Tomás controlled his legs, wrapping his arms around Santiago's knees in such a way as to press Santiago's shins into his chest. They then picked him up and carried Santiago through the front door while Bautista kept a step ahead of everyone, arriving at the car just in time to open the door.

In a matter of seconds, Santiago had gone from his bed to the car, finding himself wedged between Alejandro and Tomás as Bautista started the engine. Emilio rode shotgun.

From start to finish, Santiago's hunt took less than five minutes. Santiago was sober and so his capture was without incident. He did not struggle when they carried him to the car. "I knew it would happen," he later told me, "and once I knew it was happening, I just let them take me." But this was not always the case. The drive to the center is often a matter of chemistry. The hunted can be belligerent, erratic, and violent. They can also punch and kick the entire car ride or arch their backs like defiant children.

"We just hold their arms at their side," Emilio explained.

Do you ever hit back? I asked.

"Of course," Tomás said. "We punch, but only in the stomach. We don't want him bleeding for the pastor."

The abducted can also be nauseous, paranoid, and desperate. It is not uncommon for Alejandro to arrive at the center with vomit on his pants. When adrenaline mixes with alcohol and crack cocaine, the abducted are sometimes completely overcome.

"I hate it when they beg," Alejandro once complained. "They beg us to set them free. They promise to never get high again, and I just tell them to shut the fuck up."

The huntsmen also play with their catch, telling them fantastic stories that often leave these poor, vulnerable men frantic for answers. "Sometimes we tell them that we're taking them to a bridge." Emilio chuckled. "A lot of these guys don't know who we are or why we're there, and so we tell them that they owe someone money and that we're going to throw them off a bridge."

Bautista found this particularly funny, adding another layer to the gag. "I'll even convince them that we've got the wrong guy. I'll call them some other guy's name and tell them that they owe us money. They spend the whole time trying to convince us that we have the wrong guy." Bautista, chortling at this point, delivered his punchline: "And then they end up at the center."

Over the years, I often tried to account for such cruelty, sometimes wedging it into some broader theological statement about pastoralism, but no easy answer ever really emerged. When I pressed the point that such antics were anything but Christian, Emilio, and Alejandro as well as Tomás and Bautista would double down on a rather rough and tumble take on their faith. What mattered to them and to Pedro were the ends and not the means—that these users would land inside the center rather than die in the streets. And by committing themselves to sustaining life, to making sure that the sinner lived to see another day, these men forgave themselves for enjoying what could only be described as the thrill of the hunt.

None of it seemed to contradict their Christianity. Instead, the raucous ways in which they hunted these lost souls allowed Pedro's huntsmen to imagine themselves not just on the margins of society but also at the vanguard of Christ's Great Commission—as not just fishers of men but, more interestingly, as bounty hunters for Christ. It was a freewheeling kind of faith that answered to nothing but Pedro's singular question: Did you get your man?

Given that these new captives would soon have to perform their own sincerity to Pedro through such classic Christian techniques as proper hygiene, upright posture, and a positive attitude, the latitude that these four huntsmen enjoyed always foregrounded the Christian realism that so often structured the center's commitment to predatory pastoralism. Their mission remained as simple as it was salvific: drag wayward souls back to the fold.

In this instance, the four huntsmen had captured their man, and so Santiago stared straight ahead, letting the city race past him as Bautista drove the car. I later asked Santiago what he was thinking. "Nothing, really," he said. "I guess I was thinking about the last time I was locked up in the center, and how long I'd have to be inside this time." He paused for a bit, adding, "I was also thinking about how much I had fucked up."

The only real hiccup came when Alejandro and his men transferred Santiago from the car to the center. There is a short stretch between the curb and the center's front door, a seemingly inconsequential patch of concrete along an otherwise quiet residential street. But it is almost always a hurdle. The hunted can lull his hunters into a sense of calm with an uneventful car ride and then access a final jolt of energy, of sheer desperation, when he finds himself out of the car but not yet inside the center. This is when Santiago made a run for it, pushing past Tomás and Alejandro. "I just wanted to escape," he later told me. "I just couldn't accept the idea that I would be inside the center for months." But Santiago did not get very far. The four men took chase, caught him a half a block later, and pulled him into the center. They even smiled as Santiago struggled, enjoying the inevitability of it all.

Santiago never really had a chance.[40]

CAPTIVITY

If you do not listen, I will weep in secret because of your pride; my eyes will weep bitterly, overflowing with tears, because the Lord's flock will be taken captive.

—JEREMIAH 13:17

EIGHT

Alejandro mixed the drink with sacramental precision. Standing behind Pedro's desk, inside his front office, Alejandro held a plastic mug filled with hot water and rubbing alcohol. As steam rose from the cup, painting the room with a medicinal smell, Tomás and Bautista stood on either side of Alejandro like a pair of wayward altar boys. They kept close watch over Santiago's every move, as if he might make another break for freedom, but Emilio had already locked the center's front door, the key now safely stowed in his pocket.

"The hot water makes the alcohol hit the guy harder," Alejandro told me.

Why do you want that? I asked.

"To keep him alive," he said.

Worried about the immediate symptoms of detoxification, the cocktail was a makeshift effort to manage the dangers of withdrawal, as well as to induce users into a state of calm as they slowly weaned off their drugs of choice. And so Santiago gagged his way through the drink while Alejandro hounded him to finish it even faster.

I mentioned to Alejandro that Santiago was not drunk, that he was in fact completely sober, but Alejandro wouldn't take me at my word. "You don't know that," he said with some wisdom. No one ever really knew the full details of any of these men, he explained. During a conversation later in the week, Pedro admitted that he had missed the signs of withdrawal, which can include disorientation, confusion, and hallucination, far too many times.

"We've lost ten guys this year," Pedro told me.

So what do you do with the bodies? I stammered, knowing full well that some centers ditch them in the streets, especially if the pastor had not been in contact with the families.

"We call the police," Pedro said, "and they collect the body."

But then what do you do with all the men? I followed up, wondering how a police officer could enter the center without asking questions. Even one mention of coercion from a captive could hypothetically initiate an investigation, inviting the officer to ask each one of the men whether they were inside the center of their own free will. To Maria's horror, Santiago would have been the first to step forward, and the scene would have undoubtedly cut Pedro's population in half, if not more, within a matter of minutes.

"We put them in the [former family] room," he said. "I tell them to shut up and then I lock the door." Pedro looked a little defensive. "We aren't doing anything illegal here," he reminded me. "We just don't want the guys talking to the police."

Or passing them a note, I thought to myself.

Alejandro continued to shout at Santiago to finish the drink. "Even if they aren't drunk," Alejandro later told me, "the alcohol calms them down. It takes the edge off. We even slide sedatives into the drink sometimes, if the guy is really wild."

But Santiago wasn't wild. By the time Santiago stood inside Pedro's front office, he seemed to be thoroughly wiped, appearing almost resigned to the situation. You could see it in his shoulders. In the market, he would bow his chest, as if reassuring himself that he knew what he was doing, but now he slumped forward, completely bereft of the confidence that I had witnessed earlier that day. Now well into the night, amid the calmer space of Pedro's front office, we all watched Santiago while hints of the hunt lingered, radiating off of everyone's bodies. Santiago was the most visibly worn out, with beads of sweat forming on his forehead. His shirt was also wet, in parts translucent.

The fluorescent lighting invited an almost surgical gaze. My attention immediately landed on the patches of lint that clung to Santiago's beard. I also noticed for the first time that the tips of his fingers had been burnt from smoking out of metal pipes and that his teeth had yellowed. A rash of bug bites studded one of his forearms. All of these details had escaped me in the market, its shadows softening the severity of Santiago's state. Under a new light, in a new space, Santiago looked like a completely different person.

It was this crushed vision of Santiago that Bautista captured with a photograph.[1] "We take a picture when they enter the center," Pedro later explained, "and we take a picture when they leave." The photo would prove vital in determining when Pedro would release Santiago from his center. "It's so that I can show the family how much the guy has changed," Pedro explained. He later added that he wanted to capture a visceral sense of life before the center so that he could stage a redemptive vision of life after. Part of Pedro's process included producing a classic Christian division between a life before Christ and a life after Christ. If there is no before, Pedro reasoned, then there can be no after. The taking of men was dependent on the taking of photos.[2]

Unbeknownst to me, Bautista had also made a smartphone recording of Santiago's capture. It was not a perfect production by any means. There was not enough light, and the phone's fixed-focus lens simply could not keep up with Bautista's jittery camera work. What eventually appeared on screen proved to be nothing more than a mix of shadows and muffled sounds, most of which came from Bautista's own finger tripping over the device's embedded mic. The video would have been completely incomprehensible to the unfamiliar viewer, and yet, for me, it was nothing short of haunting. I was immediately struck by how differently events unfolded in the video versus how they replayed in my mind. Fully aware of the intricacies of memory, with its tricks and discrepancies, it was nonetheless odd, even perversely intimate, to reexperience the abduction from the foot of Santiago's bed, to hear that muttered prayer one more time, and then to see Santiago set upon. At the time of his taking, Santiago seemed to have gone so peacefully, with more of a shrug than a struggle, but the video showed him resisting far more than I remembered. At one point he arches his back in sheer horror.

What do you see in this video? I later asked Pedro. We spoke in his office, days after the hunt. Both of us huddled over his smartphone in some effort to make out the video. It wasn't easy but Pedro seemed confident in his interpretation.

"I see someone who needs to change," he answered.

After the drink, Pedro ordered Alejandro to move Santiago from the front office to the morgue.[3] This meant pushing Santiago down a short hallway and then up a set of stairs. Along the way, a half dozen of Pedro's lap dogs howled at Santiago. One bared his teeth. The barking and nipping put me on edge as Santiago walked past a message that Pedro had written on one of the house's interior walls. Painted in big black letters, for newly acquired men to read as they lumbered towards the morgue, the letter taunts:

> Dear friend,
>
> Value the roof over your head. Value the food. Value your family. You alone choose between the bitterness of alcohol and drugs and the love of your mother, wife, and children. Keep consuming, my stupid little friend, and I'll keep waiting for you here.
>
> The Pastor

Alejandro knew the morgue well. The room was the color of mildew, yet it smelled like disinfectant. With no windows and only a king-size mattress flopped on the floor, a couple of buckets sat in the corner while a stool lingered near the door. The stool was for one of Pedro's huntsmen—so he could manage the morgue—and the bucket was for those who couldn't make it to the bathroom in time.

"I once woke up in the morgue," Alejandro remembered. "I asked this guy next to me if he'd stop me if I tried to escape." The man told Alejandro that he would not. "And so I got up and started acting crazy." Alejandro apparently banged against the morgue's metal door, screaming for help. Pedro unlocked it to see what was going on, which allowed Alejandro to push past him, grab a chair, and start hitting the locked door at the top of the stairs. "You either let me out of here," Alejandro screamed, "or I want drinks." Pedro had someone fetch three glasses of rubbing alcohol. "But they must have had pills in them," Alejandro guessed, "because I started to get all quiet. I was all wired on cocaine, but I started to calm down." Alejandro did the math: "I had an eight ball of cocaine before I got picked up. I smoked ten rocks the night before, but they just kept giving me pills and drinks." Alejandro eventually settled into his cell.

Santiago proved to be far more submissive. He had been defiant when they dragged him across those last few meters of freedom, but then he capitulated, quietly obeying every order. Perhaps the most invasive was to strip naked in front of the other captives before entering the morgue. This strip search was standard practice.[4]

On the second floor of the center, just outside of the morgue, Santiago stood naked as he waited for instruction—to be told to bend over and then to squat down; then, at the bottom of the squat, to pull his scrotum to one side and to cough. All of this was to search for contraband and concealed weapons, but also to enact an intimate kind of dominance over the captive, to communicate to him that he had no right to privacy, that his body was no longer his own.[5]

The strip search often took only a moment, but if the captive resisted, the process could drag on across an entire afternoon. Santiago did not put up a fight. He stumbled into a fresh set of clothes that Bautista handed to him. Green shorts and a secondhand sweatshirt—this would be his uniform for his foreseeable future.

This intake process was more or less the same at the 200 or so centers around Guatemala City. Pastors would capture and then search captives, though sometimes they would just drag them straight to the morgue so that they could cool off or sober up. The only part of the process that Pedro left out was a ritual that had become legendary years earlier in Jorge's original center.

In the 1980s, a man named Frener was living in Maryland, learning English and building a life for himself. He was undocumented and spent years working small jobs until one day he slipped into a kind of depression, started using drugs, and spiraled out of control.[6]

In a terrible state, Frener walked to a gas station, doused himself with gasoline, and then swallowed a lit match. His body erupted into flames, from his mouth outward. He survived, but only after a long stretch in a public hospital to treat the third-degree burns. His body was crippled and his hands bent inward, their tips melted off in the fire.

When telling me the story years later, Frener explained how he had been medevaced to a hospital in Maryland. "I flew in a helicopter," he said, reflecting some pride that someone, somewhere, took an interest in him.

Once he was stable, the United States deported Frener back to Guatemala, and he convalesced in a hospital. On March 3, 1989, his family sent him to Jorge's center, where he would stay for over twenty years. The stated reason, as scribbled on his intake form, was the use of drugs and bad conduct (*mala conducta*). Frener was in the center when police raided and closed it in 2011, but even after that, after every captive had scrambled to escape, Frener found himself unable to leave. He wandered the house, not knowing where else to go.

"I just feel locked up sometimes," Frener mentioned to me as we toured the empty center, which the police had raided only a few days earlier. "I can't really get through the door." He walked through the main hall, where his fellow captives once lived. "The penalty for leaving is kind of bad," Frener explained. "They keep you locked up in the morgue, or we need to be against the walls." With the voice of a child, he confessed that "they mostly be mean with us." After twenty-three years of captivity, Frener felt positively trapped even when the front door hung open.

For years, Frener played a special role at Jorge's center. During the strip search, after a new captive had been told to bend over and squat down, Frener would slyly join the circle. After being prompted by another captive, Frener would approach the new man, stand close to him, and announce: "Welcome to hell!"

The joke was that Frener, because of his burned body, was thought to resemble Freddy Krueger, the evil protagonist from *A Nightmare on Elm Street*. "Frener Krueger," they called him.

The alcoholic drink, the photograph, the strip search, and even Frener's nearly forgotten routine, all confirmed that while the hunt is a game, captivity is a ritual, with Pedro's acquisition of Santiago opening a window into a deeply patterned process.[7] And so, exhausted and a little drunk, Santiago entered the morgue and collapsed into a deep sleep.

NINE

Maria arrived at Pedro's front door the next morning having again worked her way through city traffic with a combination of public buses. The trip took over an hour, but she nevertheless looked rested. Following the hunt, while Alejandro and his men drove Santiago to the center, Maria took a few minutes to straighten up her home. Tomás and Baustista had dragged dirt into the house and knocked over a few chairs on their way out. She also found patches of mud on her tiles. But none of this took long to clean. With a quiet house and Santiago off the streets, she had gone to bed with a weight lifted from her shoulders. Her son was safe inside a center. There was even a slight skip in her step as she walked through Pedro's front door. Maria would later mention to me that she had never slept more soundly. No longer in the streets or at the market and well beyond the reach of those kids who had once shot him, Santiago was now under lock and key.

Maria took a seat on a rickety stool while Pedro sat commandingly in his office chair, a desk dividing the space between them. The optics of the front office made clear who was in charge. Pedro's chair literally lifted him ever so slightly above Maria as the stool forced her to slump forward. Upstairs, Santiago sat in the morgue.

Maria looked nervously around the office as Pedro pulled an intake form from his desk drawer and slid it through a typewriter. With his reading glasses slipping to the tip of his nose and his posture accentuated, Pedro hunted and pecked his way through a series of questions that he posed to Maria, carefully establishing a modicum of a paper trail. I sat in the back on a stool.[8]

"What is Santiago's complete name?" Pedro asked Maria. He punched out the answer with two fingers.[9]

S-a-n-t-i-a-g-o . . .

"What is his date of birth?" Pedro took his time, documenting every detail with a snap of a key.

D-e-c-e-m-b-e-r-0-9-1-9-9-0

"What is his level of education?"

P-r-i-m-a-r-y

"What is his permanent address?"

Z-o-n-e-2-1

"What are the phone numbers we should call, if we need to contact the family?"

5-5-7-6-3-3-4-1-and-5-5-8-8-3-2-1-0

Pedro then arrived at the most important question of all: "Who will be the person to decide when Santiago can leave?" There can only be one person, Pedro explained. Convincing or comforting more than one guardian was both taxing and confusing. Instead, he preferred a single point of reference, which was perfectly fine for Maria. She alone would make the decision to set her son free. Pedro typed out that answer.

M-a-r-i-a

Months after Santiago's hunt, during a bit of downtime, I asked Pedro why he used a typewriter. Over the years, I had often seen him struggle to collect basic information, and the machine always seemed to jam or the ribbon would break. And sometimes, when Pedro would strike two keys at roughly the same time, they would tangle and he would have to separate them in ways that inked his fingers and, in turn, the forms. Wouldn't it be easier to use a pen or maybe a computer?

"I like how the typewriter sounds," Pedro admitted. "You can't hear a pen and you can't hear a computer." Pedro apparently wanted his clients to experience the formalization of their loved one's captivity. The sound of every keystroke gave authority to a contractual relationship that was otherwise dubious at best. More than creating a set of coherent files, Pedro cared about cultivating an atmosphere. The process of completing the intake form was less about collecting information than delivering a sensation. The main message was that a son or brother or husband was now under Pedro's jurisdiction.[10]

The intake forms were also part of the process. Pedro had lifted much of his legalese from Jorge's forms. One of Jorge's original forms read: "The center offers security to the detainee, delivered by professional and specialized staff members trained to recuperate the fallen from such problems as alcoholism, drug addiction, delinquency, homosexuality, and other problems."[11]

Jorge's intake forms also stated that detainees are only allowed to have a toothbrush, toothpaste, underwear, a change of clothes, soap, toilet paper, and a BIBLE. Bible was written in all caps. "There will be no phone calls," the form flatly stated. If the detainee tried to escape, the center was "not responsible for this: neither for what happens during an escape nor for what happens after the escape." If the detainee turned violent and destroyed furniture inside of the center, "the family is responsible for replacing these broken objects." The very bottom of the intake form cited Isaiah 40:10: "The Sovereign Lord comes with power, and he rules with a mighty arm."

And then there was the contract that the captive signed. Above the space for the signature read: "For my own rehabilitation and my own good I promise to comply with the regulations of this house, and also to comply with its disciplinary rules." The form continued, "As I have stated when seeking rehabilitation, I have no outstanding warrants for my arrest with either the civil or military authorities. And I also authorize the authorities of this house to keep my belongings in case I ever escape." If the captive could or would not sign the form, he provided a thumbprint against his will.[12]

The filling out of the form, with all of its overextended language, was part of a broader performance. From the stool upon which Maria sat to the office chair in which Pedro perched, the imbalance between them was embodied in their postures and compounded as Pedro pecked at his typewriter. But Pedro's performance was also an obvious conceit, for the relationship was not as asymmetrical as Pedro would have liked. Without Maria's consent, without her business, then Pedro had nothing. This ritual of signing bound Maria to Pedro, confirming his authority over her son through an act of submission.[13]

Maria nervously tapped her heel as she balanced atop the stool, remarking, "He's a beautiful person until he gets money in his pocket." She then got deadly serious: "And he's going to die in the streets without this center." Her dark prophecy hung in the air as she began signing the papers that Pedro placed in front of her. Written in the first person, the following are only some of the conditions to which Maria agreed on behalf of Santiago:

> I hereby voluntarily enter this ministry to submit myself to treatment for alcohol detoxification and/or drug rehabilitation, located at the address stated clearly at the top of this form. I give formal consent to my total, complete, and voluntary submission for the restoration of my complete person during what will be my internment. I commit myself to strict observation and follow the given rules for the reestablishment of my health. I will be transferred to another ministry within this network if I do not comply.
>
> a.   I understand that the treatment will last seven months, which the institution understands as an appropriate length of time for my restoration and recuperation.
>
> b.   At the moment of entering this center, I have given a nonreimbursable donation of the following amount: _____.
>
> c.   To cover any additional medical, psychiatric, or psychological care, I have provided a nonreimbursable sum of money of the following amount: _____.

d. Whatever debt that I incur through the destruction of furniture and equipment will be paid by me or whoever is responsible for me.

e. I promise not to ingest toxic substances, drugs, and/or alcohol during my time of treatment for detoxification with this ministry because it can be hazardous to my health and contrary to the interests and the objectives of my restoration.

f. I accept to see visitors on Thursdays and Sundays but only after the first fifteen days of my treatment and only by family members, such as a father, mother, wife, brothers, and children.

g. I accept that I may be subjected to the following laboratory tests: 1—drugs, 2—HIV/AIDS, which would immediately cancel my stay at the center.

h. The decision to enter the center is mine. I enter because of alcohol and/or drugs, my own loss of control, and the danger to which I have put my family and society.

i. So that there is no confusion about my decision to enter this center, I have asked a family member to accompany me to serve as a witness. He or she signs this paper along with me and shares in the responsibilities detailed by this contract.

j. I accept this contract completely, and by the power and authority of this institution I have read, accepted, ratified, and signed (or give a thumb print from my right hand because I cannot sign) this document, confirming with a witness that has accompanied me and has been previously identified.

With pen in hand, Maria signed her name at the bottom after negotiating some conditions. Both she and Pedro agreed that Santiago would stay inside the center for seven months; Maria would also offer the center Q600 [$75 USD] per month; the offering would cover three very basic meals a day but not a bed. Santiago would sleep on the floor. Maria handed over another Q600 for possible medical expenses and added another Q400 [$50 USD] to cover the hunt. "That was nearly all the money that I have." Maria winced as we walked out of the center.

As we spoke on our way to the bus stop, Maria marched more confidently than I had ever seen in the past. I asked her if she understood the form that she just signed. "To tell you the truth—" she blushed "—I didn't really read it." The details, she said, seemed like an afterthought. Santiago was already inside the center and she had already given Pedro her money. Most importantly, Santiago was off the streets.

What else could you ask for? I asked.

"A miracle," Maria answered with some certainty. "I want him to change."

TEN

Alejandro once complained that "there's just so much time inside the center. What do we do with all of this time?" The answer was to wait.[14] Over the years, I found that waiting could look a lot like sleeping, with a captive's head propped against a concrete wall, arms folded across his chest. Santiago often wore a hooded sweatshirt that he was able to pull over his head, straining the strings to close the hood almost entirely over his face. Only Santiago's nose stuck out. Others sat on the floor, hugging their legs in such a way as to create a tent when they stretched their T-shirts over their knees, allowing them to duck under their collars for a bit of privacy. As the second hand pushed the minute hand and the hours added up, these captives created their own spaces and simply waited for the day to end.

"But then you go to bed," Santiago said, "on the floor, next to these same guys." And so waiting for the next moment ultimately became a meditation on waiting itself. The question that emerged for all captives at one time or another was not how to wait, but, rather, what they were waiting for. Nothing about life inside the center ever proceeded according to concrete markers. There was no talk of steps and stages or even progress and growth; the dominant experience of captivity was just waiting.

"Waiting keeps these guys off the streets," Pedro told me, knowing full well that the therapy he offered did not lead in any particular direction. "It's better that Santiago is upstairs just waiting around rather than running the streets." He added, "You can get yourself killed out there." This is no exaggeration. The principle argument for holding these men captive was to keep them alive. At the very least, even during the most excruciatingly repetitive days, while listening to yet another testimony, these captives were nonetheless passing the time rather than waiting to die. "Because out in the streets," Pedro insisted, "you're going to get shot. At least here you're not waiting for that." A few weeks later, having thought about my question more, Pedro approached me again. "They're waiting for a better perspective on life," he added. "They're waiting for a chance to make a good decision. They're waiting for a chance to know better." Waiting apparently had therapeutic value in itself.

The captives were also waiting for their families to heal. "The families need a break," Pedro also told me. We spoke just outside the center, a few days after Santiago's capture. "They come here with their son or brother or husband, and they are tired. They've had their money stolen. Their sleep stolen. Their pride broken. Their loved one has been scandalous, and so they come here for a break." The language of warehousing suddenly became literal—families stashed a loved one inside this center not so they could be saved, but rather so they would be stored.

"I'll come back later for him," a mother once told me. We had just driven away from the center after delivering her son to the pastor. She was angry at her son and somewhat pleased that Pedro's men had roughed him up; she was also relieved that she could go home to sleep. "I don't have to worry about him at night running around getting high," she said. "I don't have to keep counting my money and hiding my stuff." With the city streaking past us out the window of a taxi, the woman said, "He can just wait there. He can just wait there. Until I'm ready to get him out, he's just going to have to wait." She then turned to me. "And he might have to wait there for a very long time."

Most of Pedro's captives found themselves waiting for a very long time, which is why Pedro committed them to a daily schedule that he had also borrowed from Jorge's center. The schedule was, in many ways, inspired by the very penitentiary system that once held Jorge.[15]

5:00	Bathroom
5:30 to 6:00	Hygiene and house cleaning
6:00	First worship service

During these two hours, detainees dedicate themselves to prayer, praise, and testimony as well as prayers for the pastor and singing in chorus. Prayers led by the pastor. Meditation on the Word of God is followed by songs and then a closing prayer.

8:00	Breakfast
9:00	Cleaning

The following hour is dedicated to playing ping-pong and chess and reading the Bible, until the next worship service begins.

10:00 to 12:00   Second worship service

12:00 to 14:00   Lunch

14:00   General cleaning

15:00   Third worship service

The detainees practice "fencing" between worship services. This is a game to see
     who can find the appropriate Bible verse first.

16:30   Visits

Visits by family and friends until 19:30. During this part of the day, detainees
     spend time maintaining and repairing the vehicles used to evangelize, assist,
     visit, and collect people from the streets.

19:30   Dinner

20:00   Evening prayers

The schedule could look busy, at least on paper, but there was never
much to do.

The vast majority of the captives didn't have responsibilities. They were
either straight from the streets, such as Santiago, or unfit to work. The latter
routinely spoke out during sermons, constantly barking their frustrations
at having been locked up by their family. Their anger was understandable.
My own daylong shifts inside the center often left me breathless, sometimes
forcing me to fumble my way out for fresh air. Stretches of fieldwork left
me with a mix of horror and admiration that individuals could sustain that
style of captivity for so many months without revolting. But frustration,
as understandable as it was, also kept a captive from working through the
system and, thus, working their way out of the house. Pedro never released
captives for good behavior, but they could perform a kind of Christian piety for Pedro that suggested a certain degree of salvation. This is why the
rebellious never really got anywhere. "They don't let me do shit here," one
captive told me, "because of my attitude." He thought about it for a moment
and then fell back into the same trap that Pedro had set for him months ago.
"Well, fuck 'em." He shrugged, and Pedro obliged, quashing any chance for
this young man to ever prove himself inside the center.

Cleaning the floors was one way for captives to prove themselves. It
was also a way to keep them occupied, as they essentially walked in circles
while mopping. The process went something like this: Those charged with

washing the floor would get everybody's attention at the top of the appointed hour. The most senior among them would then actively shepherd everyone against a wall, huddling the men together to expose as much of the floor as possible. The newest of the captives would then collect and discard any debris. Scraps of paper. Used tissues. A broken pencil or two. The others would mop the floors and later dry them by snapping towels just above the tiles to create a trace amount of wind. When the captives were done, they would allow the rest of the men back across the room.

Cleaning the floors took up an hour and a half of every day, with the rest of the day largely spent waiting. Alejandro, for one, would wait to use the bathroom. He would wait for his morning tortillas. He would wait for worship services to end. He would then wait for lunch and for dinner, and even for the end of the day so he could fall asleep. "And once you start thinking about all of this waiting," Alejandro admitted, "it can drive you crazy. Like, you can't do anything but wait. It can start fucking with your mind."

The mind-numbing nature of it all was palpable. Users often entered the center, sobered up, and dove into the sessions before the repetition became obvious. Each day would bleed into the next, losing any distinct quality from one to the other. Fridays could be Wednesdays, and Tuesdays would feel no different than Thursdays. "The only day that saves us is Sunday," Tomás explained. "There are no sessions on Sunday, and so that breaks the rhythm a bit." Tomás sat on the floor, slowly kicking a bottle cap with his foot. "So Saturdays can feel a little different because it's the day before Sunday, and Monday is a little better because it's the day after Sunday."

What do you do on Sundays? I asked.

"Oh, we don't do anything," he said. "There are just no sermons. So we just sit around all day instead of having to do the sessions."

In the same room? I asked.

"Yes, in the same room," he said with a bit of impatience. "There isn't any other room here."

On Sundays, the captives chose where to sit, when to sleep, and how to pass the time. No one forced them to sit up, keep their eyes open, and/ or listen to each other. They could turn away, which was exactly what Santiago did on his first Sunday. He sat himself in a corner, with his hood over his head.

"People deal with this in different ways," Tomás said. "Some guys come here ready to fight. Others start working right away for the community, helping with stuff around the center, and others just get really quiet. They're here, but they're not really here."

Like a ghost? I offered.

"Like a ghost," Tomás echoed.

The breaking point would come when captivity felt utterly without end. There were few ways to gauge the passage of time, except the walls. The walls marked the change of seasons.

On the second floor, inside of the center, the walls changed colors. They were once green, and then they were blue and then white and then blue again. I knew this because the captives scratched at the walls. There was nothing desperate about it. They just quietly picked at the paint with their fingernails, gently scratching the surface so as to carefully (if not compulsively) separate one layer of paint from another.

"You have to go slowly," Alejandro explained. "You have to take your time or the paint just falls off the wall." You could tell from the sound of his voice that this frustrated him when it happened.

In the former family room, where most of the captives ate, slept, and prayed, men would lie on their sides for hours and slowly peel their way from one layer of paint to the next. Sometimes I would see them doing this during sermons or as they drifted in and out of sleep. These were not expansive projects. No one ever tackled more than a small patch at a time, usually something the size of a postage stamp, and most of these men placed their work near the bottom of a wall. These were discreet efforts that could easily be overlooked. I'm not even sure Pedro ever noticed them, but picking at paint occupied a good deal of the men's time.

Repaintings took place on a regular basis, and they happened through the bartering of goods and services, with a family exchanging the captivity of a loved one for a fresh coat of paint. This was also how Pedro had his car serviced, appliances updated, and center fumigated. Pedro once landed a commercial refrigerator for a hunt and a few months of captivity.

I once asked Alejandro about the significance of picking at the paint, of literally scratching at the walls. I could see that the colors allowed him to move from one era to another, to link the present to his expansive history of captivity. Each layer of paint seemed to harbor a different set of memories for Alejandro, with each era somehow color-coded in his mind. "When the room was blue, that's when things were pretty bad. There were lots of fights between the guys. No one was really in control. Green was a lot calmer."

The scratching always struck me as an effort to repurpose the room into a resource for rehabilitation, with the paint itself providing these men with the means to work with their hands as they thought through their lives. I pressed Alejandro on the therapeutic possibilities that literally scratching at the walls provided. The question immediately felt naïve. Does it help? I asked.

"Guys are just trying to kill time," Alejandro said. When these captives scratched at the walls, they did so out of boredom, for the simple delight of peeling one layer of paint from another. "There's not much else to it," he added.

More defiant men would make their mark in deliberate ways. With a paper clip or pen cap, they would scratch their name into a wall, usually with the dates of their captivity. They would write the month, day, and year of their arrival, and then they would make an open-ended dash. Many would commit to completing the record on the day of their release, but no one ever did. The thrill of release always overshadowed the little promises that these men made to themselves during the quieter moments of their captivity, and so their names hung on these walls with open ended dashes, suggesting that confinement may never actually have an end date. It might just go on forever.

ELEVEN

Sermons always seemed to go on forever, with visiting pastors sometimes showing up multiple times a day. Pedro preached on occasion, but he typically outsourced most of the sermons to a cohort of preachers who spent their days travelling to different centers across the city. One day, I walked up to the second floor and encountered a man I happened to know well. He was older, or maybe just weathered by life, with a gaunt face and a brown suit. His tie was tight around his neck. I had first heard him preach at Jorge's center several years earlier. At that time, Jorge's center was just beginning to slow down, and held fifty rather than its usual 250 captives. Frener was still one of them, as was a young man hiding from the police. He had tattoos across his fists and face and would always ask me if the police had come to the front office for him.

"Are they here?" he would ask me.

No, I always answered, assuring him that he was well beyond reach of the law.

When I first heard the visiting pastor speak, I was struck not so much by his moral ambition but rather by his commitment to engage these centers. He himself had been taken captive years ago for drinking too much.

His daughter had apparently paid a pastor to hunt him, and now he seemed committed to staying out of places like Pedro's, which oddly meant visiting them almost every day. The sight of someone like Santiago seemed to scare this visiting pastor straight in ways that made this man of God need the center as much as the center needed him.[16]

Back inside Pedro's center, the visiting pastor greeted me with a business card that peddled his Pentecostal skills as a spiritual director, theological therapist, and motivational speaker. There was also a phone number and an email address. Before he began preaching, however, he insisted that I make a digital recording of his sermon so that he could hand out copies to whoever would listen. I happily obliged as he settled behind a makeshift lectern.

The pastor would deliver the very same sermon that he had given at Jorge's center years earlier. With its well-rutted peaks and valleys, the pastor preached on a single virtue for over an hour: a positive attitude. It was a message that shifted the scale of the hunt from the streets to the soul, with the sinner suddenly invited to hunt himself—to track down his own appetites and put them in a cage.

"So let's talk about having a positive attitude," the pastor said to all fifty-six men. Some sat on chairs but most had found space on the floor. The lucky few leaned against a wall in ways that allowed them to pick at the paint. They surreptitiously scratched, studied, and then scratched some more. Santiago was in the very back of the room with his hood over his head. He seemed to be sulking. I sat attentively on a stool.

"If you think you can do something, you can do something," the pastor said, "and when people change their attitude, they change their life." He effused positivity, his energy almost assaulting this seemingly anesthetized audience. The contrast in affect could not have been more dramatic. "Jesus Christ came," he said with verve, "to set the captives free, to give freedom to the prisoners and to the oppressed. And the biggest discovery of this generation is that human beings can change their lives by changing their minds." He shot a quick glance at my digital recorder, to make sure that it was working—and so tipped me off to his real interest. Preaching at a clip that far outpaced the energy of the room, the pastor obviously had his ambitions on accessing an imagined audience through the recording.

"In other words," he said, "all people can change, but what do you need to have?" The question hung in the air until he answered it: "You need to have a positive attitude. We all have problems in life, and God has the solution for us. Jesus is the way. He is the truth. He is life, and no one comes to the Father except through the Son."

"Thomas Edison," he then proposed, "was the one who invented the light bulb. And how often did he fail? He failed nine hundred times. But he also succeeded. He just kept trying over and over again." The pastor's point seemed to be about persistence. "You have to persist over and over again. Because you don't have to stay here." Santiago flinched at this last point, shaking his head side to side. "You can get up," the pastor reasoned. "You must get up! God wants to bless you. He wants you to prosper. He wants the best for whatever you touch. Whatever you do in life—be blessed."

He then instructed the men to turn toward each other. "I want you to tell something to the person next you," he said. "Tell him: 'Jesus has something special for you.'" The men turned to their side and repeated the phrase. "Then say: 'He wants to change your life.'" The men did this. "Then add: 'God has miracles for you. God will do extraordinary things in your life.'" The group echoed the words back to the pastor in sync. "Now say: 'God will change your attitude.'"[17] They all did—even Santiago joined in this time.

"We can change," the pastor explained, "but it all depends on us. You have to have the desire. If you have the desire to change, then you will change. You need to say to yourself, I'm going to do it." He stood firmly in front of the men, acting out success through his bodily comportment. "Success lies in your habits and customs. People who have bad habits fail. People who have good habits succeed. A winner is not born super gifted or with high intelligence. A winner's advantage is his attitude, not his fitness. Attitude is the standard for success. It is crucial because it determines the way you act."

Alejandro stood over the men to ensure that everyone participated.

"But do not pity yourself," the pastor insisted. "We instead need compassion. Because compassion is one of the most remarkable emotions that we have as human beings. Self-pity is possibly the worst. Self-pity is an emotional disease. It's a terrible thing to have. But compassion is what we need to have for ourselves and our neighbor."

The sermon halfway through, the pastor asked captives when they were going to improve their attitudes. Without pause, he answered his own question with zeal: "Today! Today is the day when the weak will become strong! Today is the day that the fool will become smart!" He tapped his Bible while surveying the room for a pair of eyes to engage. He settled on Tomás. "God gave us special gifts," he announced. "God gave us talents. And God has special things for each of us. But everything depends on us. We need to have the desire to do these things." He took a step back. "Look," he said, "your attitude is very important. I am constantly amazed by how many people have a poor attitude but still want others to be optimistic. If you have a poor attitude and tell your family, 'Well, that's just how it goes,' then what?" No one offered an answer.[18]

"And I'll tell you something," the pastor continued. "Your family is my family. It doesn't matter if you tell me that your dad is involved in drugs or that that your mom is doing drugs. Those things do not matter. God wants something special for you." His voice began to peak: "You can leave this house. You can do it, but it all depends on your desire to do so. Is your desire weak? Or is your desire strong? You have to want to change your life."[19]

Santiago seemed to bristle at the message; he started to squirm.

"And keeping a good attitude is easier than getting one," the pastor added. "You have to stay positive, but how will you do it?" He got prescriptive: "You have to read inspirational books that motivate you. You have to read the Word of God every day. You have to go to church. You have to meet people at church. You have to find a way to be motivated. You have to find people who will minister to your soul." The laundry list continued: "God has the power and authority to get ahead, and God is the one we need to get ahead."

Santiago began to look indignant.

"We're going to kneel," the pastor announced. "We are going to ask the Lord to help us. If you want to raise your hands to heaven, you can do so. If you want to repeat the words that I say, you can do so."

Santiago refused.

"Lord Jesus, today, this afternoon, I put my life in your hands," the pastor wailed. "I ask you, Lord, to forgive me. I have sinned against you, and I have done evil in your eyes. Today I put my life in your hands, and I ask you with all my heart, with all my strength, to help me." The pastor continued, "I give you my addictions, and I ask you to help me."

He then began to sob: "Have compassion and mercy on me. Forgive me. I have misbehaved with my mother. I have misbehaved with my father. I have misbehaved with my children. Forgive me, in the name of Jesus. Thank you, Lord, I know you're going to do a miracle in my life. I know there is rejoicing in heaven for every sinner who repents. In the name of Jesus, I receive my salvation. Thank you, Lord, amen!" Santiago shook his head, knowing that this would be his world for months to come.

Later that week, I sat down with this pastor. He told me about his own battles decades earlier with drinking and drugs, and then explained, "This is a year of liberation. The Lord has put the power of liberation in each of our hearts, and so hundreds of people are going to be released from slavery this year. They are going to be set free."

I asked what kind of slavery he might mean.

"I am talking about spiritual slavery," he said. "I am talking about people locked up in spiritual prisons. These are prisons made of drugs, alcohol, and delinquency. It's a prison made of vices."

But what about the center itself, I asked, isn't that also a kind of prison?

The pastor plowed past my question, again speaking directly into my digital recorder to yet another imagined audience. "The Lord is preparing his children. He is preparing their souls. He will give them liberty by freeing these sinners from their chains. The Lord is going to raise each of these sinners up. He is going to make each of them taller, spiritually speaking, and allow them to return to their families."

What is your responsibility? I asked the pastor.

He paused. "My role is to tell them that they must change."

TWELVE

Pedro issued a notebook to each captive once he entered the center. Sometimes it was a few sheets of paper, other times captives would share a notepad; a lucky few got an entire book all to themselves. This is because Pedro demanded that each of the men take notes when he or any other pastor preached. It was a fairly specific request, with Pedro insisting that captives catalogue every reference to scripture. The intention was for them to learn the Bible, chapter and verse. When a pastor gave a sermon, the captives would jot down each biblical reference and then afterwards, when there was nothing else to do, they would search the Bible for the full verse, copying it out word-for-word with pencil and paper.

Alejandro ascended to become the star student in this regard. His notebook was nothing short of pristine—a compendium of verses couched in disciplined penmanship that I came to admire. Never rushed in manner, Alejandro printed Bible verses neatly and with consistency; his *d*'s, *p*'s, and *o*'s often popped with a kind of optimism. The color of the script regularly changed too, with verses alternating between red, black, and blue ink. And still, the quality of the letters themselves bordered on the calligraphic.

Alejandro was also diligent about content. I would routinely find him amid a small group of men, flipping through a Bible and then copying the verse into his notebook. He paid great attention to even the slightest of details—spelling and the proper use of accents always mattered. He also shuttled between different translations and versions of the Bible, as the center always had several lying around the main room. Debates would erupt between Alejandro and the men about which verse had appeared in the sermon earlier that day, indexing a surprisingly high level of interest in getting the assignment right.

But Pedro never collected the notebooks. He had his huntsmen page through them from time to time, but Tomás and Bautista were never really in a position to assess biblical proficiency. They were less familiar with the good book than most of the captives and were at best functionally literate. Alejandro, on the other hand, seemed deeply committed to the practice, lining notebook after notebook with what would ultimately become Bibles transcribed out of order. One page in Alejandro's notebooks read:

Matthew 24:36—"But about that day or hour no one knows, not even the angels in heaven, nor the Son, but only the Father."

2 Corinthians 11:14—"And no wonder, for Satan himself masquerades as an angel of light."

2 Corinthians 11:16—"I repeat: Let no one take me for a fool. But if you do, then tolerate me just as you would a fool, so that I may do a little boasting."

John 3:8—"The wind blows wherever it pleases. You hear its sound, but you cannot tell where it comes from or where it is going. So it is with everyone born of the Spirit."

John 11:1—"Now a man named Lazarus was sick. He was from Bethany, the village of Mary and her sister Martha."

His notebook served as a model to the other men, about how to engage the sermons in ways that transformed stretches of captivity into open-ended Bible study. Alejandro and the other captives' notebooks evidenced a plodding kind of Pentecostalism that remained ever-committed to the word of God and one's ability to position the soul towards higher ground, but rarely did any kind of hermeneutical effort follow these citations. Pedro never asked the men to apply scripture to their own lives.

Alejandro could be excused, then, when amid his sea of scripture there appeared a half-written note to his aunt. She never visited and for the most had part cut all ties with him. She had proven unable to deal with her nephew's long battle with drugs and alcohol and knew that sustained contact would also mean having to pay for his captivity. Pedro was constantly on the lookout to monetize Alejandro's time spent inside the center, and so his aunt's inattentiveness made his note ever more wishful.

Bookended by a pair of verses, Alejandro's mind must have wandered beyond the confines of his own captivity when he wrote the following:

Matthew 7:13—"Enter through the narrow gate. For wide is the gate and broad is the road that leads to destruction, and many enter through it."

Aunt, forgive me for all the bad things that I have done. I am full of bitter thoughts. I once walked with a heavy heart through darkness, not understanding why God sent me to this country. I had to leave everything that I loved: my family, my wife and . . .

Matthew 7:14—"But small is the gate and narrow the road that leads to life, and only a few find it."

The note ended as hastily as it began—a frustratingly small window into Alejandro's inner world. It was in many ways a precursor to the letter that he would write to the National Police, as he cast about for someone who might be able to help him.

What else did Alejandro want to write to his aunt? The question could also be posed: What else did Alejandro want to write to himself? For he knew that his aunt would probably never read the letter. Perhaps he addressed the letter to her in an effort to work through his own feelings of being held captive by not simply the pastor but also by his own sin.[20]

The center produced no shortage of such letters. Captives often used their notebooks to pen messages to loved ones, holding the notebooks close to their chest while they slept and stashing them in knapsacks during the day. They became prized possessions in the rather austere center. The notebooks allowed men to extend themselves (even if only by way of imagination) beyond the walls of the center, and they contained notes to mothers and fathers; sisters and brothers; children and lovers. These scraps of paper were sometimes passed to visitors when no one else was watching, begging loved ones to bring basic necessities such as food, medicine, and toiletries. The notes could also be desperate pleas for freedom:

> Hi Mom—This is Javier, and I am sending you this letter to ask you to please come and get me out of here. I am better, thanks be to God. The thing is that they punish me here and they beat me and I do not want to suffer any more. Please help me. Only you can help me. I want to escape. Come quickly. I promise to change the way that I am. Please come and get me out because I want to continue living. I beg you. Mama, come here after you get this letter or you might lose me forever. I love you very much and I am waiting for you here. Love, Javier

Across the years, captives pressed an untold number of these letters into my hands without Pedro's knowledge, hoping that I might be able to deliver their message. Often making rather specific requests, the letters demonstrated how the epistle as a genre ensnares its addressee with the responsibility to reply. With every letter, I had to accept or decline a captive's request to engage not simply with his family but also with his life history—with the very politics of his captivity.[21]

> Dear Mom—The reason for this letter is to tell you that I want to get out of here. I beg you. I cannot stand it anymore. Please, mom, understand me because I understand you and I am sorry for bothering you with this letter but I cannot take it here anymore. Goodbye and God bless you. Yours, Tomás

> Mother—When am I getting out of here? You can tell me when you come to visit me on Wednesday or if you do not want to bother visiting me you can just send the answer with the man who is doing me the favor of giving you this letter. I love you. Your son, Andrew

I once found a letter on the sidewalk just outside of Pedro's center. Thrown from the second floor through a crack in one of the windows, it reads as if it were placed inside a bottle and then tossed out to sea:

> My name is Carlos Rigoberto Gonzalez M. They brought me here on the eleventh of November. They took me from my parents' house while I was sleeping. Today is August 13th and I have been locked up inside this

center for 9 months and 2 days. As much as I beg my parents to take me home, they say no.

One can read these letters not just as appeals for mercy but also as clandestine efforts at escape, written in the hope that an anonymous passerby would read the note and feel generous enough to call for help. That would be the work of luck, which these captives often held out for. Their letters were a practice of hopeful endurance as months stretched on.[22]

Of course, not all captives used their notebooks for such ends. During the slower moments, when afternoons felt like days, captives would lend me their notebooks, allowing their notes to structure our conversations about the Bible and salvation. But it quickly became clear as I thumbed through these books that many of these men would break from their assignments copying down biblical versus to drum up fantastic ledgers buried between pieces of scripture. They fashioned their own wish lists:

Psalm 18:41—They cried for help, but there was no one to save them—to the Lord, but he did not answer

5 pounds of beans, 5 pounds of rice, 5 pounds of sugar, 5 pounds of salt, soap to clean clothes, soap for the bath, soap chips, Clorox, cooking oil, toothpaste.

Proverbs 28:27—Those who give to the poor will lack nothing, but those who close their eyes to them receive many curses

Others would write their own scripture, folding their deepest desires inside of their notebooks and then hiding them as chapter and verse:

John 12:32—And I, when I am lifted up from the earth, will draw all people to myself.

Apocalypse 4:1—Positive words. Positiveness. Fun. Hard work. Realness. Honesty. Perception. Passionate. Knowledge. Wisdom. Happy. Love. Friendship. Sisterhood. Partnership. Obey, respect, Self-sufficient. Power of Will. Braveness. Joy. Serenity. True love. Red lips. Commitment. Pleasure.

Psalm 41:1—I swear to God I fucking miss you my little beauty. I miss you so much. No joke! Jesus Christ if I could have a moment with you. My God. I fucking adore you.

2 Peter 1:19—We also have the prophetic message as something completely reliable, and you will do well to pay attention to it, as to a light shining in a dark place, until the day dawns and the morning star rises in your hearts.

Most of the captives also drew in their notebooks, with each effort contributing to an expansive archive of images that shuttled between the surreal and the salvific. Santiago, for one, drew ghoulish ink drawings of hooded skeletons on the backs of horses racing through the night, sometimes with a spear in hand. These figures had almond-shaped eye sockets, drawn so compulsively that the paper rutted and bowed under the weight of the pen and its ink. Santiago would also sketch cityscapes and skylines, even rough drawings of what seemed to be weather patterns and thunderstorms. His notebook included anthropomorphized forests; trees had eyes, noses, and mouths, and thickets of branches that melded into some sort of trap. Flora appeared to be laughing with sinister intent as it struggled to pull its roots from the ground. Trees walked in the same way that someone might try to step out of quicksand: with high knees and snagged feet. They seemed to be on the run but were held back by their own form, quite literally rooted in place. Another drawing proved slightly less opaque. It featured an army of stick figures jumping out of a crack pipe towards a door marked "exit." Underneath, Santiago labeled the escapees with a single descriptor: "slaves."[23]

Many drawings by captives compressed multiple Christian metaphors. There were illustrations of hands folded in prayer atop roses in full bloom, all splayed across an empty cross. Muddled in composition but clear in intent, these images invoked the resurrection of Christ, if only to inspire the revival of the user. "I love you, Jesus," one drawing announced.

Other sketches trafficked in carceral imaginaries, of work camps and chain gangs. They tended to equate the time a captive spent inside the center with the emptiness of breaking rocks into pebbles. Lined with biblical passages, these sketches explored the absurdity of life inside the center alongside the optimism of renewal. "Is not my word like fire," asks an artist by way of Jeremiah 23:29, "and like a hammer that breaks a rock into pieces?" From the boulder fly pieces of alcohol, crack cocaine, liquor, LSD, cigarettes, and marijuana.

And then there was Michael the Archangel. His image often appeared inside Pedro's center, and one very memorable rendition hung in the morgue. A young man from the capital named Miguel depicted the angel with a muscular form, a wide set of wings, and flowing hair. Obviously midbattle, his sword pointed downward as if about to be thrust into a beast that sat just out of frame. The message was never lost on these men, as the angel is said to have commanded God's armies against Satan's forces in the Book of Revelation, hurling Satan and his angel to earth (12:7–9). Pastors such as Pedro often framed time spent inside a center as a battle between good and evil, with the very life of the user at stake.[24]

Miguel's drawings typically dripped with religious imagery. In one epic drawing, Jesus's bleeding heart breaks the chains of slavery while flying doves announce that man can be "free on the inside." All the while Christ stands crestfallen, too ashamed to face the materiality of mass incarceration. As with most of these montages, the artist represents himself somewhere in the piece. This one placed him in the bottom right corner of the page. Miguel depicted himself behind bars, in the shadows, and framed by scripture that he had invented: "One comes to understand through pain (Psalm 36:15)." The psalm actually doesn't say this; in the Bible, it reads: "Let their sword enter into their own hearts, and let their bow be broken."

"I didn't know that when I got out of jail in Guatemala," Miguel told me one day, "that I was chained up by cocaine. Because all I thought about when I was in jail was that I wanted to be free." Rolling a colored pencil between his fingers, he continued: "But I didn't think about my spirit, my soul . . . that I was chained up spiritually. Basically I got out of jail and came back to jail, again. And now that I'm in rehab, it's like I'm locked up again."[25]

Captives tried to render themselves legible through these drawings. Santiago's efforts were defiant, at least at first—a series of insults paired with scenes of escape—but they softened once he realized that no one was really watching. Left alone before God, his drawings eventually explored the more forgiving themes of solitude, loneliness, and remorse. He pieced together one image several months after his capture. It was of a child, maybe even a toddler, in overalls and a striped shirt. He may have set out to draw Chucky, the title character of the *Child's Play* horror film series. But rather than a murderous doll coming to life, Santiago depicted the toy sitting down, with shoulders slumped—as if it had been given a time out. The drawing seemed to be waiting for someone to set him free. An image frozen in time, the doll also lay in wait.

During the first week of Santiago's captivity, I asked to read his notebook. I had seen him studying in the corner with a Bible in his lap. He appeared to have taken notes during an earlier sermon and looked to be in the middle of his homework, diligently searching and writing down verse after biblical verse. His eagerness to engage the assignment seemed at odds with his initial feelings of resentment for having been hunted in the first place. Maybe, I thought, he was now keen to show the pastor his willingness to submit.

As he handed me his notebook, I carefully surveyed its cover, and then opened to the first page. Instead of finding biblical verses like I had expected, Santiago had written his name in tiny script on both sides of the first sheet, from top to bottom. The entire page was plastered with "Santiago." I counted the name 432 times on the first page alone. This was a solid block of script sculpted with a single word. The name was also written with an unnerving degree of consistency, the size and shape of each letter meticulously, almost mechanically, recreated with each movement of his pencil. The spaces between each of the words also proved steady. Without wanting to read too deeply into the effort, I found myself driven to contemplate its significance, and so I sat there silently trying to appreciate his work, fixing my eyes on the effort in the hopes of decoding its meaning. It looked something like this:

Santiago Santiago Santiago Santiago Santiago Santiago Santiago Santiago
Santiago Santiago Santiago Santiago Santiago Santiago Santiago Santiago
Santiago Santiago Santiago Santiago Santiago Santiago Santiago Santiago
Santiago Santiago Santiago Santiago Santiago Santiago Santiago Santiago
Santiago Santiago Santiago Santiago Santiago Santiago Santiago Santiago
Santiago Santiago Santiago Santiago Santiago Santiago Santiago Santiago
Santiago Santiago Santiago Santiago Santiago Santiago Santiago Santiago
Santiago Santiago Santiago Santiago Santiago Santiago Santiago Santiago
Santiago Santiago Santiago Santiago Santiago Santiago Santiago Santiago
Santiago Santiago Santiago Santiago Santiago Santiago Santiago Santiago
Santiago Santiago Santiago Santiago Santiago Santiago Santiago Santiago
Santiago Santiago Santiago Santiago Santiago Santiago Santiago Santiago
Santiago Santiago Santiago Santiago Santiago Santiago Santiago Santiago

Struck by his patience and even by the artistic potential of such a statement, and also egged on by the indeterminacy of the afternoon, I found myself floating towards some rather dreamy theorizations. My notebook from that day had some half-baked scribbles about subjectivity in the age of mechanical reproduction, an allusion to the philosopher Jacques Derrida's work on the signature, and even the performative nature of handwriting. With this in mind, I asked Santiago what it all meant. He took a moment to consider his intention and then decoded the letters for me. "Oh," he said in an offhand way, "it just means, 'Fuck this.'"

THIRTEEN

The true tyranny of captivity lies in the sheer unpredictability of events. Given fortuitous circumstances, some families would yank their loved ones out of the center at a moment's notice. Upon an order from Pedro, Alejandro would suddenly interrupt a sermon to pull a lucky captive from the general population, delivering the surprising news that it was time for him to leave. A person could find himself slugging through yet another testimony one moment and then packing his belongings the very next. The exit never took more than a few minutes. Any captive could be plucked from the crowd at any moment, not unlike the rapture.

This is because families could change their mind about captivity—for a price. After locking up their loved one during the heat of an argument, amid the very worst conditions, a family could then pay the pastor to have him released after only a few months in the center. This early release program had quickly become a second layer of income for Pedro, prompting the pastor to write these conditions into his contracts, such as the one Maria signed. The stakes of this political economy were serious. For if the hunt was central to the center and its business model, then the early release of captives also bolstered the center's bottom line. The contract elaborated this through two terms:

E. If I should stop treatment before the prescribed term I promise to pay the costs of room and board and waive any responsibility of this center in case of my death by natural causes and/or any other cause, including the use of alcohol or drugs or the abstention of either . . . I fully understand the circumstances under which I have arrived and the logical consequences of my intoxication. Because of this I will not hold the center accountable.

G. If I stop treatment before the previously specified length of time I promise to pay the fees associated with that lost time and what other costs that occur during my stay at a rate of Q55 per day. This covers the price of food, board, medicine, and miscellaneous purchases.

Given the unpredictability of captivity, Pedro's catch and release program proved to be lucrative. It also made the work of waiting a deeply fraught enterprise. In a clinical rehabilitation setting, one hitched to liberal notions of development, expansive apparatuses chart the progress of patients as they move from one therapeutic stage to another. Waiting is itself progressive. Programs like the famed Twelve Steps of Alcoholics Anonymous lay claim to an agentive, forward-moving plan of action, with each step building towards a full recovery. Given enough time, the logic goes, patients will progress. There are caveats, of course. Rehabilitation can be studded by holdups, delays, and setbacks. But even so, those conceits imply a progressive notion of time, however much progress is routinely held up, delayed, and set back.[26]

Conversely, waiting inside of Pedro's center never felt like moving onwards or upwards. Instead, Pedro's center aspired toward articulating a captive's before and after, which itself evidenced a commitment to the miraculous. Santiago could be held captive for months on end, with no signs of ever leaving, while the captive sitting next to him could suddenly walk out the door—often without rhyme or reason.

Pedro never preached about progress. When pressed, he would stick to the fundamentals of his faith. "I bring sinners here to wait for God," he said. "I bring them here to wait for a miracle." He insisted that he had no real power to help any of these men. His role was different. He hunted sinners so that the Lord could heal them. "All I can do," he said, "is pull them from the streets just long enough for God to save them." Pedro even downplayed the power of prayer, instead relying on the possibility of a miracle, of the grace of God to suddenly and without warning touch the heart of a sinner. "It's a miracle," he would say. "It's a miracle when these guys change. It's a miracle when they don't smoke crack or when they stop drinking." He had personally experienced this miracle. "I was in the streets," he told me "I was dying in the streets and God saved me."

Pedro's center operated through a paradigm of radical rupture and rebirth. The net effect was that Pedro never asked his captives to work harder but rather to wait longer. "They need to wait," Pedro insisted. "They need to wait until God is ready for them."

Christians have been known to wait. Following the death of Jesus, the earliest Christians waited for Christ to usher in a new order.[27] They oriented themselves toward a mindset of watching and waiting for Christ's imminent return, while at the same time evaluating their lives on the basis of Christ's first coming. This was a radical eschatology that contemporary Pentecostalism often assumes, with the end of the world not simply *near* but *here*. This makes the religion's relationship to history rather uncertain. The question becomes: What might progress look like at the end of times? Pedro's commitment to captivity provided one answer, as users were warehoused under the Pentecostal possibility of someday changing.[28]

"One of the hardest parts of this place is not knowing," Santiago admitted to me. "I don't know when I'm going to get out of here. Maybe seven months but maybe sooner." Santiago looked dispirited. "Or maybe I'll be here for even longer." The possibility of ever leaving Pedro's center largely amounted to a matter of waiting, which often proved terrifying. "I just don't know what is going to get me out of here," Santiago once confessed to me with tears in his eyes.

But the process of release was never clear, not even to me after years of fieldwork. "They don't get out of here until I say that they can get out of here," Pedro told me. "I need to talk to their families. They need to want the person back. But most of all, I need to see a change in the person. I need to see that they've changed. The way they talk. The way they dress. The way they pray. It all needs to change before they can go." Pedro then calmly laid out the consequences: "Or they fail and end up back here. Or worse, they end up dead." In Pedro's estimation, he had set far too many captives free far too soon. "Too many of them have died in the streets," he said, "not from overdose but from violence. They've been stabbed or shot. I don't want any of these guys to die in the streets." Given all the risks, very few families wanted these men out of the center.

Anxiety peaked among the captives when it was no longer obvious how exactly to perform the kind of change Pedro sought. Santiago seemed to have already given up. "I'm supposed to show the pastor that I'm better," he sniffed, "but how am I supposed to do that in here? Sitting through those sermons, next to all those guys?" All Santiago wanted to do was leave.

FOURTEEN

Alejandro also wanted out, and so he took matters into his own hands. As Santiago settled into the center, quietly tucking himself into a corner of the room, Alejandro began to hatch his own plan for escape. It took the form of a letter, one addressed to Guatemala's National Police, and it fell directly into my hands.

On June 2, 2016, Alejandro and I sat side by side as a visiting pastor preached about the love of God. "You have to know that God loves you," the pastor announced. "He loves you and he wants the best for your life. He wants you to get ahead." Alejandro suddenly got my attention by nudging me in the side. "No matter if you're using crack cocaine or marijuana or

whatever," the pastor added, "and it can even be the vice of sex, of prostitution. It doesn't matter. God has compassion for you. He loves you." Alejandro then pushed the letter into my hand. "God is going to help you, but you
have to ask him for help. Tell him that you have problems. Tell him your
limitations. Speak to God because God can change you. Only the Lord can
change you." The pastor straightened himself out, standing slightly taller
than before to punctuate his next point. During which, in the matter of a
moment, Alejandro got as close as he could to me.

"Get me the fuck out of here," he said.

Later, after the sermon but still on the second floor of the center, Alejandro explained: "You need to go to the police with the letter. Let me tell
you what it says." He looked over his shoulder to see if the coast was clear.
"It says that my name is Alejandro, and that I was born on such and such
a date. It then says that my mind is clear and that I am aware that I do not
want to be here." He told me all of this as the letter sat in my pants pocket.

Over the years, this had easily happened over a hundred times. Captives
would approach me, maintain eye contact, and then place a piece of paper
into the palm of my hand. They would also quietly tuck notes into my pockets during sermons or push a piece a paper into my bag, always mentioning
later that they wanted to me to deliver a message to a friend or a family member. Often it was just a phone number that I needed to call, and all I had to
do was to pass along as simple of a message as "please bring fresh clothes." In
this sense, nothing about this exchange with Alejandro seemed unusual. For
all I could tell, it was yet another moment in my fieldwork in which I would
connect captives to their families, either by phone or with a visit.

But then Alejandro grabbed my shoulder. He squeezed my arm in
some effort at creating intimacy while also conveying urgency, adding: "And
you know that I don't want to be here." Something had obviously changed
in him. Although he never wanted to be inside the center, it was not always
obvious that this disinterest outpaced the despair he often discovered in the
streets. For all of the abuse, humiliation, and near complete lack of freedom
that he endured inside the center, Alejandro knew that he lived relatively
well because of Pedro. He benefited not only from the food and shelter but
also from a sense of self that he cultivated through hunting. Rarely able to
hold down a job and forever struggling with his own dependencies, Alejandro could at times appear grateful for the center, but something had
changed.

"The letter says," Alejandro continued, "that on a date in April, I was
picked up by the pastor and by two of the main guys here. They held me,

beat me, and threw me in their truck. And on the way here, I told them that I do not want to be at the center, that I don't want to come here, that I don't need this place. It's all in the letter."

Alejandro took another quick look over his shoulder to see if Pedro was coming. "Look," he said, "the bottom line is that I don't want to be in this place and that I don't need this ministry. I don't need this help. I say in the letter that the pastor is very mean and rough. And then I describe the kinds of punishments that we get. We have to clean. We have to do exercises. We get no food. We get thrown into the morgue, and you know that the worst thing about all of this is that I have to tie people up."

This last part seemed to weigh on Alejandro the most. "If I leave to go pick people up, the pastor always tells me to pick them up rough-style," Alejandro explained. "He tells me to hit them." Over the past few months, Alejandro had become the center's main enforcer. He had always hunted, but now he had been tasked with disciplining the general population, which included tying people up with ropes. The hunts had also gotten more physical. Sometimes Alejandro would dominate the captive just enough to complete the task, to bring him back to the center, but increasingly he would play with his prey, working out his frustrations on the people he hunted.

Alejandro saw the long game. He thought past the most immediate of horizons towards life outside of the center. "The thing is," he said, "I have to pay the consequences for that stuff. For hitting people and tying them up. There are people in the streets who are mad at me." Alejandro looked scared. "I want to get out of here and I want to stop doing this stuff. I want to stop hunting." But he was trapped.

So why don't you just take off running the next time you go out for a hunt? I asked.

"I've done that so many times," he said, "and the pastor just finds me and brings me back. I need to send a message that I want out. Like I want to get out of here right now, and I don't want to come back."

Alejandro's letter would certainly send a message. Writing to the National Police, if they took the letter seriously, would trigger a raid of Pedro's center, effectively bottoming out the pastor's business.

I had sensed that Alejandro was frustrated, but I never anticipated that he wanted to escalate his plight to the National Police; and through me, no less. Again, I had become accustomed to delivering letters to loved ones. For years, I would travel throughout the city delivering notes to mothers and fathers, sisters and brothers. This created rapport between me and my interlocutors and allowed me to connect with their families—to hear the other side of the story. To speak with only Santiago about his captivity was to engage a story of Dickensian gloom, but then to hear the despair of his mother was to learn of a more robust struggle over freedom.

One time, in fact, not too long after his capture, Santiago sat in the back of the former family room as a visiting pastor delivered a sermon on the saving grace of Jesus Christ. "How many people here feel blessed to be alive?" the pastor preached. "Amen," the pastor answered—to himself, by himself. "Because life is a blessing." The pastor stood firmly behind the lectern. "And so I ask you, what is your intention?"

I then felt a piece of paper pushed into my pocket. "What is your purpose in life?" the pastor asked again. I turned to see Santiago settling back into his corner. "My purpose," the pastor continued, "is to tell you that Jesus has come to give all of us hope."

I fished the note from my pocket as the pastor extolled the struggles between hope and heaven and quickly realized that it was a letter written by Santiago. He had penned an apology to his family.

"Oh, you can tell," Pedro once told me. "When a person changes, there is a change in his physical status. His hygiene starts to change. He starts to fix himself, to change himself, to improve himself." We were sitting inside his office. "There are those who don't want to change. Their hearts are hard, but a fixed person is obedient. He follows the rules."

Later in the day, with that conversation with Pedro echoing in my ears, I opened Santiago's letter. It was addressed to his mother, brother, and sister.

"How are you?" it began. "I'm feeling better now that I am inside the center. I have begun to handle myself differently." The letter modeled the sincerity that Pedro had described, a sincerity that seemed to mark the beginning of real change. "I'm really happy because I'm not on drugs," the letter continued, "and I'm not drunk. This place has given me some time to think. I'm better now." Santiago's note worked hard to externalize things that would always be hidden on the inside: sincerity of faith, true conversion, maybe even radical change.

"The exterior reflects the interior," I remembered Pedro once telling me, infusing otherness with disorder and salvation with rectitude. "Did you know that? A person who is right with God is going to show it in his face. They are going to comport themselves differently."

"I hope," Santiago continued, "that you can forgive me for everything and for all the stuff I took from the house. Forgive me. Please. I'm really sorry."

"But there are people who just don't care," Pedro had said. "They come here and they act the same way inside the center as they do outside it, but the most important is the interior of the person. And if we can fix what's going on inside a person, then we can set that person free." Pedro quickly qualified his conditions of release. "Spiritually speaking," he said. "We can set that person free, spiritually speaking."

With physical liberation seemingly out of reach, Santiago's letter seemed an honest first step toward spiritual freedom. Regret, concession, and repentance—it all fit the genre. Santiago seemed to be doing things with words.[29] But then he suddenly slipped in slow motion, tumbling over himself.

"When you come," Santiago asked immediately after apologizing, without even a line break to mark a new thought, "could you bring some sugar and some bread?" The request was modest, but it also felt shallow. It was too soon, considering how much and for how long he had made his family suffer. Social theorists have long argued that the apology is a process through which a person symbolically splits into two parts: "the part that is guilty of an offense and the part that dissociates itself from the delict and affirms a belief in the offended rule."[30] Santiago seemed incapable of splitting himself into two parts. The ask also made him seem completely unaware. His requests rolled on.

"Could you also bring beans, coffee, soup, milk, ham, fried chicken and some French fries?" His apology suddenly became a grocery list: "and some juice, cookies, sardines, mayonnaise, a few of those muffins that you brought last time, ten pieces of fruit, and a cup of chicken broth?" At a certain point, the apology faded from sight entirely. One could even be forgiven for missing it. "Could you bring five pounds of rice. Five pounds of beans. A liter of Coca-Cola." Every item requested evidenced an interior in need of further rehabilitation: "Also could you get me some deodorant and some toothpaste, some floss, some soap to wash my pants, five tubes of glue, two razors, two tablets of aspirin, and two tablets of cold and flu medicine."

To Santiago's credit, the center's food was terrible. The men were chronically underfed, and Santiago had already lost considerable weight. But his letter as an effort at escape had obviously missed its mark. Santiago had misplaced his apology.

"But there are people who just don't care," Pedro repeated, as if having read Santiago's letter. "The way they comport themselves in the streets is the way they comport themselves here."

I remember arriving at Maria's home, where Santiago's brother eventually read the letter. He shook his head. It obviously upset him. With what seemed to be sincerity, Santiago's brother announced through gritted teeth,

"He'll stay there for another year. For another year." He turned to me to ask: "What do you think about that?"

A year sounded extreme, I remember saying. I also thought about how this conversation could not happen for a captive such as Alejandro, if only because he had no family to visit him or loved ones for me to engage. Nobody had ever signed a contract on his behalf, visited him inside the center, or paid Pedro for another month of his captivity. All Alejandro had was me and a postwar state that had proven to be as negligent as his aunt.

I knew that delivering his letter to the police would prompt a raid, and this made the missive a bold move. It would most certainly drag more than fifty families into his struggle, each with their own story of abuse and heartache. "Santiago stole the light bulbs right out the sockets," Maria once told me.

It was in such moments of moral adjudication that I most felt part of predation's pastoralism. I was poised to help Alejandro escape but unsure about whether his release should come at the expense of everyone else's suffering. It was a terribly uncomfortable position to be in because of the dead ends I knew we would find. Regardless, I felt compelled to act, if only because Alejandro had no one else to ask. Alejandro, a grown man with all of his faculties, was being held captive inside this center in ways that chafed against my own liberal assumptions about freedom and self-determination. While Maria assumed authority of Santiago, and while most other captives had families keeping them inside the center, no one in the city (except Pedro) gave much thought to Alejandro's life. And Pedro's interest in Alejandro had become so entangled with his bottom line that it was difficult to take his decisions seriously. Alejandro had been abducted and put to work, all against his will.

So what's the plan? I asked.

"You give this letter to the police," Alejandro said. "They'll come to the center, and they'll raid the place. Then they'll ask, 'who doesn't want to be here?' And I'll step forward."

Have you ever seen this happen? I asked.

"No," he said, "but I've heard that it's been done before."

ESCAPE

Free yourself, like a gazelle from the hand of the hunter, like a bird from the snare of the fowler.

—PROVERBS 6:5

FIFTEEN

Alejandro had been restless for months, often pulling me aside to build his case. In between sermons, with Pedro downstairs, we would sit and talk in a relatively unoccupied corner of the main room. He always asked me to turn on my digital recorder.

"The last time they picked me up," he said, "they were really mean. The pastor grabbed me and told me that I wasn't going to go anywhere." We sat together on the floor, our backs against a wall. Captives mingled. "But I told him that I don't want to be here," he explained, "that I don't want to be in this place."

He had not always been clear about this last point, expressing the contradictory feelings that often come with captivity. One day he would be grateful for the roof over his head and the relative power he held over other men, while the next day would bring waves of frustration for not being able to chart the course of his own life.

Alejandro liked to talk to me about this ambivalence, routinely confiding in me that he wanted out of the center but that he never really knew what life outside might look like. These were intimate conversations—slow, meandering, and at times playful. They were never rushed; there was literally nowhere to go. And so something akin to trust (maybe even friendship) eventually formed between the two of us. It took years, but it happened.

These discussions were one reason why Alejandro began to confide in me about his plans to escape the center. Alejandro had been the aggressor more times than he could remember, but our talks began to linger on his own experience of being hunted. "And even here, at the center," he told me, "I tried to get out and they came over and hit me again." Soon after his most recent capture, Alejandro had apparently made a dash for the front door, but they shut him down. "Pedro told me, 'You think you're so tough in here, but what are you going to do in the streets?'"

Alejandro once made an argument that stuck with me, that highlighted just how much Pedro had intervened in his life. "But I told the pastor," he said, "that it's none of his business what I do in the streets. It's none of his business. Who is he to tell me what to do with my life in the streets? I don't want to be in here. I don't want to be a part of his ministry. I don't want any of this." Alejandro spoke as plainly as he could: "I want to leave. I want to get a job. I want to make money."

So what did the pastor say? I asked. We were on the second floor of the center, our heads resting against concrete.

Alejandro gave me the short answer: "The pastor said that he wants me here."

Later that day, Pedro and I spoke in his office. I asked him point blank: Why do you care about what Alejandro does in the streets?

Pedro huffed in frustration, as he was always annoyed when I asked what seemed to him to be a basic question. Working toward his answer, he opened his Bible and began to read Matthew 18:12–14. "What do you think?" the passage asks. "If a man owns a hundred sheep, and one of them wanders away, will he not leave the ninety-nine on the hills and go to look for the one that wandered off?" He paused for a moment to have me consider the question, only to read on before I could offer an answer: "And if he finds it, truly I tell you, he is happier about that one sheep than about the ninety-nine that did not wander off. In the same way your Father in heaven is not willing that any of these little ones should perish."

I pressed him further: But is Alejandro one of your sheep? Is he yours to lose?

Pedro looked exasperated. "Alejandro is not one of my sheep," he explained in a way that demonstrated a practiced patience. "He is one of God's sheep, and I am the pastor. I am God's pastor, and I am Alejandro's pastor. I serve God as shepherd. I tend to all those lost sheep upstairs." Pedro closed his Bible. "Look," he said, "this is how I see it. All those other pastors with their churches, with their worship services and prayer sessions, they serve God by shepherding his sheep. But they shepherd the obedient sheep." I remembered the hundreds of services that I had been to in Guatemala City, with families swaying to the music and clapping in unison. One could easily take for granted the simple fact that all of those Christians traveled to church on their own accord. No one dragged them there. They walked with their own two feet.

Pedro then explained his mission more explicitly: "But I shepherd black sheep. I shepherd lost sheep. If a man owns a hundred sheep and he loses one of them, my mission is to find that lost sheep. My whole life is about finding lost sheep."[1]

Pedro's pastoral fantasies of hunting and holding captive lost sheep certainly departed from the liberal conceptions of human rights and freedoms that had floated around Guatemala since the 1980s. I reminded Pedro what he already knew—that the United Nations 1948 Universal Declaration of Human Rights works from the postwar premise that all human beings are born free (Article 1), that no one should be a slave (Article 4), that no one should be degraded (Article 5), that no one should be subject to arbitrary arrest (Article 9), that everyone has the right to freedom (Article 13), and that everyone has the right to work (Article 23). Since two historic truth commissions published massive reports in the late 1990s about the country's genocidal civil war, human rights have been common knowledge in Guatemala. Each of these commissions cast a long shadow into postwar Guatemala about the inherent dignity of the human being, making my impromptu lecture less of a pedantic sidebar than a somewhat unnecessary reminder of information that Pedro knew as well as any other Guatemalan.[2] But I wanted to see what he would say.

"Men wrote those words," Pedro responded, "but I answer to God." Although flippant in his demeanor, it was clear that Pedro pledged allegiance to a sovereign that stood outside (or possibly beside) the normative rule of law. Often railing against human rights activists while citing the theological clarity of his position, Pedro was quick to shoot toward an alternative universal. He also believed in an autonomous liberal subject, but his more utilitarian approach took into account society and family members when assessing the rights and responsibilities of individuals. The promise of Christ's return and the subsequent salvation of the faithful organized Pedro's life and his daily efforts to track down as many lost sheep as he could.[3]

Alejandro still questioned the sincerity of Pedro's intentions. A few weeks before handing me the letter, Alejandro became increasingly vocal in his criticism of the center. "From what I've heard," he said, "the pastor basically does not want me to go anywhere. He told Tomás and Bautista that 'I'm not going to let Alejandro go. Alejandro has to do his time. He's got to do his seven months.'"

This seemed standard, I told Alejandro. I had seen enough contracts to know as much.

"But yesterday," he said, "they let some guy out. Someone came and got him out. Just because the guy paid." Alejandro sounded upset. "Some guy showed up, talked to the pastor, and then paid him some cash. And the captive had only been here two months." It seemed unjust to me. "You see?" he said. "It's a bunch of crap. They let another guy go after not even a month here, and most of the guys who go out to the market or for the hunts, they don't even come back. They run off. That's what ends up happening. They just leave."

This constant turnover compelled Pedro to seek out long-term captives, as the center needed a certain amount of stability to stay afloat, and it was obvious that this interest in stability allowed Pedro to extract tremendous amounts of labor from men like Alejandro.

"What don't I do here?" Alejandro wondered. "I help with the cleaning. I got my crew working every single day. We clean the floors three times a day. We move the people from one side of the room to the other. I mean, that's my thing." Alejandro continued, "I also make sure that the bathrooms are clean. I make sure that everyone's taken a shower. You know?"

Displacing the brunt of this labor onto captives helped Pedro maintain his bottom line, and more importantly, it was the principal means by which captives were rehabilitated. Pedro referred to this work as occupational therapy, for it gave captives the only opportunity they had to prove to that they could handle life outside of the center.[4] But Alejandro then started to take note of all the work that Pedro no longer let him do: "Before he used to let me go to the markets and to hunt for him. We'd pray and then go out for a hunt. But he's not letting me do that stuff these days because he knows how I am." By this, Alejandro meant that Pedro knew how badly he now wanted to escape, that, in the words of the pastor, Alejandro was no longer sincere. He could no longer be trusted. "Because I don't want to be here," Alejandro said, "I've been kidnapped. And I have no say in the matter. I asked him the other day, and he says, 'Yeah, I'll let you go . . . with a big kick in the ass.'"[5]

In fact, before giving me the letter for the National Police, Alejandro disclosed to me that Pedro and his huntsmen "were all eating the other day, and the pastor was like 'Alejandro, do me a favor and tell your friend Kevin to get me some shoes. Tell him to get me some Nikes.'" Alejandro acted like he was offended on my behalf, as if the request was ignorant, but he then began to test the waters with me. Alejandro was obviously exploring every possible means of escape.

"It's different," Alejandro had apparently told the pastor, "when we go to the markets and ask people for food for the house, it's so that everyone can eat, but I can't just ask Kevin for shoes." He then explained that the food felt charitable because it fed the house, but the shoes seemed so specific to the pastor's desires that the very idea seemed to be offensive. He then added, "Then some other guy, I think it was Bautista, tells the pastor, 'Hey, why don't you tell Kevin to get you the shoes in exchange for letting Alejandro out?' And the pastor just looked at me with a look that was like: 'Don't put that idea in my mind.'" Alejandro feigned offense: "And so he's trying to get you to buy him some shoes for my freedom. That's crazy!" He then put his hand to his head to approximate something like disbelief, but Alejandro kept a close eye on my reaction.

It was crazy, I thought, to propose exchanging a pair of shoes for someone's freedom. At that moment with Alejandro, as we sat on the second floor of that center—in the middle of the city, behind three locked doors—I suddenly wondered how my fieldwork had brought me to this juncture. A number of reasons quickly came to mind, the most obvious being Alejandro's lack of family. At the same time, he had also begun to think with me about the morality of captivity and was actively shaping how I understood the industry as a whole.

During his time in captivity, Alejandro began to develop what could only be described as an abolitionist theology from all those Bible verses that he had collected in his notebook. He pieced together his insights into an argument against the very theology that informed his confinement.[6] I found it compelling.

"I just don't see the basis of religion with all that attitude," Alejandro once said. "If you're going to give someone the opportunity to make his life better, fine, but don't hold them hostage and make them do things that they don't want to do. That's what I don't understand." Alejandro then made some concessions: "Yes, I do live better than the other guys here when I hunt. When he lets me hunt, I get two plates of food, sometimes three plates, but I got to pay the consequences." And the consequences were real. The very people whom Alejandro had hunted, tied up, and thrown in the back of a truck now lay in wait for him to leave the center. In this sense, the entire industry had effectively bound Alejandro up within a set of social relationships that seemed impossible to disentangle. His resentment against Pedro had begun to bubble over.

"You know," he said, "when the pastor is preaching, I'm just like, how can you be preaching these words and expect me to do the complete opposite? Especially when it is according to your will?" He then made a theological argument. "The word of God," he said, "doesn't state that I have to serve my pastor. It states that I have to serve Jesus Christ according to his word and his will." Alejandro started to preach to me: "Jesus said that he didn't come to be served but that he came to serve. So what am I doing? I'm serving the pastor and all of his personal needs. He has people to wash his shoes, to wash his clothes, and to make his food. He has people to do everything for him. But I don't see why. If we're all users and addicts then why are we fulfilling all the personal needs of this one pastor?"

I had no idea what to say.

SIXTEEN

I took Alejandro's questions as well as his letter to the National Police. Inside a big, beautiful building located in the center of the city, I stood in line with citizens preparing to report crimes and file grievances. With tall ceilings and florescent lighting, the building was a supremely bureaucratic structure with long corridors studded with modular office spaces; its designers had obviously labored to replicate the aesthetics of North American corporatism. To travel from the margins of the city to the center of it, to speak with the state about the plight of one man felt so official, so formal, as I found myself swept up into lines that led to desks manned by office workers who then directed me to other lines and desks as well as more office workers. There was nothing intuitive about this building, nor about my relatively simple task: to tell someone of authority that a pastor was holding a man hostage for his use of drugs. The efficacy of appealing to the state was not assured. In a country in desperate need of judicial reform—where only three percent of homicides result in a conviction—what were the chances that Alejandro, a drug user held captive by Christians, would get a fair shake?

Years of fieldwork inside the centers and with law enforcement officials made this byzantine system seem somewhat familiar. Over the course of hours, I eventually shuttled from police officer to clerk to judge to lawyer and then back to judge. I told each person the same story—Alejandro has no family, the pastor kidnapped him, Alejandro wants out, but the pastor refuses to release him. I presented his letter to each of them. They all confirmed that the center itself was not an illegal enterprise, per se, so long as each person inside had been signed over to the pastor by a family member. I then stressed that Alejandro has no family here in Guatemala, and so it was clear that the pastor did not have the legal authority to hold him captive. Each of the authorities I spoke with confirmed that the letter provided enough cause to knock on the center's front door. Alongside my own testimony, it suggested a possible kidnapping, especially since Alejandro was alone.

"It's your decision," one official explained. "We can call a judge right now, and we can go to the center with you. We'll enter the center and ask the director for the names of every person that he's holding. And then we'll find out if everyone is there on their own free will." The official then explained that "everyone who wants to leave can then leave."

Every abolitionist instinct in me immediately committed to this plan. For years, I had argued with families in favor of releasing their loved ones sooner than planned, pointing out that their captivity was not providing them with the life skills necessary to avoid drugs. I had also battled with pastors, including Pedro, about the illiberal contours of extrajudicial incarceration. As I had explained to Pedro on numerous occasions, there are fundamental problems with the fact that the center has no formal intake process, no system of checks and balances or government oversight for new people arriving at the center. Never did I see a medical doctor, social worker, or lawyer participate. And the same was true with outtake. The process is murky at best, and families often bribed pastors for the early release of loved ones.

My concerns had also settled concretely on the perils of captivity itself. The vast majority of these centers, Pedro's included, were overcrowded spaces organized around improvisational therapeutics that often proved dangerous. Four locked doors separated those inside Pedro's morgue from their freedom. Of all the concerns raised by human rights and public health officials about the dangers of compulsory rehabilitation, one especially haunted me: What would happen in the event of a fire? How would these men claw themselves out of the center? It was not an unimaginable scenario. The men cooked with an open flame on the roof of the center. Hot embers often stumbled out of the oven and smoldered in the open air. It never took much effort to imagine how this would unfold—a stray ember might ignite a rag that then would catch an errant piece of furniture on fire. The entire roof would be set ablaze, with nearly sixty men scrambling under the flames. This very tragedy actually came to fruition at a different center in the spring of 2017, with at least forty teenagers burned alive.[7] Of all the horrific scenarios that these centers can provoke, it was fire that frightened me the most, causing me to recommit to basic human rights, the idea that imprisonment of any kind runs counter to upholding the elemental human dignity of individuals. I often muttered such bold pronouncements to myself as I mapped out my own personal escape plan should the building ever catch fire.

The prospect of setting Alejandro free, of kicking down the center's front door with a judge and police officer in tow, not only reconfirmed my most basic beliefs about justice, it also sent a jolt of adrenaline through my entire body.[8]

But the surge of emotion quickly faded, forcing me to remember that abolitionists can make for irresponsible anthropologists. The discipline has long accumulated an eviscerating set of critiques against the interventionist impulses of seemingly well-intentioned anthropologists.[9] The decision to help so often hurts. More than a decade of fieldwork inside these centers had taught me that the promise of freedom is often a trap. Centers will bait and gouge families on a monthly basis, locking up loved ones with a promise of freedom that is always just beyond reach. The entire industry rests on the possibility of truly escaping drugs and, in turn, the centers, but that very same industry structures itself around the inevitability of return.[10]

Michel Foucault argues that prisons produce prisoners instead of reformed citizens, and one can extend this insight to the centers.[11] By always forgiving the sinner again (and again and again), they produce sinners that forever need to be born again (and again and again).[12] This is one reason why the National Police so rarely raid these centers. Not only does this shadow carceral system benefit the state by effectively lifting thousands of chronically unemployable men off the streets, but families also need these centers to keep their loved ones alive. In fact, the person who kept coming to mind as I waffled on whether to greenlight the police raid was not Alejandro, with his desperate plea for freedom, but rather Santiago's mother, Maria, who knew better than anyone that Pedro's center was keeping her son alive. If the judge and a police officer addressed the captives, asking each individual whether he wanted to be held inside Pedro's center, Santiago would be the first to ask for immediate release. This would certainly mean returning to the very social networks that once got him shot while also forcing Maria to pay for another hunt.[13]

To focus only on Alejandro in making my decision would be to address a single instance of abuse and manipulation. At the same time, to tell his story at the expense of Santiago's—as well as the fifty-four other users held captive inside of Pedro's center—would be to ignore the severity of Guatemala City: the gangs, the drugs, and the violence. To kick down that door at Alejandro's request, I reasoned, would put dozens of lives at risk, Santiago's included.[14]

And yet the possibility of not acting—of doing nothing—was also no longer an option. While I had more than enough material to write a book, disappearing into the city felt unconscionable, morally unimaginable. I was in way too deep. Extended ethnography enables researchers to make otherwise unattainable observations, but it also tethers them to people and places that make both practical and moral demands.

Suddenly frozen in my tracks but also free falling into exceedingly uncomfortable territory, I told the judge that I would need to consider the decision in far more detail.[15]

SEVENTEEN

Alejandro was not the first captive to attempt an escape. Few users have chosen to enter a center of their own accord, and the vast majority of men spend their days inside scheming up ways to get out. Knowing this, pastors spent a considerable amount of their own time anticipating these plans, relying on very basic security measures.

"As long as the house is locked down," Pedro explained while we toured the center, "then I feel pretty confident." It was one of our earliest conversations. I didn't know Pedro well yet, but I knew the industry. I had been on dozens of similar tours up to that point, and so I found myself feeding Pedro standard questions that gave him the opportunity to explain his operation. I remember him pulling against some bars that capped a window to demonstrate the sturdiness of the construction. "The bars need to be anchored well," he explained, "and the doors need to be strong. I told you this before, but the doors need to be heavy and they need to be bolted down. They should be able to handle six or seven really hard stomps."

He toed one of the doors a little, drumming its surface to appreciate the echo. "Before opening the center," he recalled, "I needed to think about it from the sinner's perspective. I needed to walk through the house with their eyes to see if there was any possible way of getting out." He pointed toward the southern-facing windows inside the main room as we walked. "I didn't have bars on that window for a long time," Pedro admitted, "and I didn't have bars on it because we're on the second floor. Who is going to jump out of a second floor window?" The answer now seemed obvious to Pedro. "I'm pretty sure Alejandro jumped out that window once," he said, "but we hunted him down. We found him just a few blocks away, passed out in the streets." Pedro moved closer to the windows. "Anyway," he said, "this window became a problem. It was dangerous for the guys because they'd jump out, and it was bad for me because then I'd have to go find them."[16]

Pedro added bars. "But even with the bars," he said, "these guys would write notes to people walking by. They'd have little messages and phone numbers and just throw them at the people on the streets." This created problems with the neighbors. The sight of detained drug users hanging out of an elevated prison pitching desperate pleas to strangers upset an otherwise quiet street. So he covered the windows with a translucent sheet of plastic.[17]

Pedro then brought me back to his front office. I pulled up a stool and he sat down behind his desk. He opened one of his drawers and pulled out three objects.

"I keep these as reminders," he said. One was a metal clothes hanger that had been manipulated into something resembling a screwdriver. The straight edge had been filed to a point while a mash of metal formed what appeared to be a handle. Another was a metal spoon whose shallow oval had been sharpened to a point while a full spool of tape fattened the base into something that someone could actually hold. The third item was a long metal string bookended by two pieces of wood. The string seemed sharp to the touch, which is why the wood was so important. Someone could pull back on both handles without ever having to touch the metal. The first two objects had obviously been made for stabbing and the third for choking.

"I found all of these on the second floor," Pedro said, "and we search the place all the time. We flip the mattresses and strip everyone down to their underwear. We find weapons like these in their pockets or hidden in the walls. None of those guys can be trusted. None of them."

I asked why he kept these three particular weapons. He picked up the screwdriver and told me a story.[18]

"I was away at the store one day," he said, "and so Roberto was in charge of just checking in with the guys. He unlocks this door." Pedro motioned toward the heavy door that separated the front office from the rest of the center. "And everything was fine," Pedro said. "But then he climbs the stairs to the second floor, unlocks that door, and sticks his head inside." As he went on, Pedro rolled the weapon in his hands. "One of the guys sneaks up behind Roberto, grabs him around the neck, and stabbed him." Pedro exclaimed, "This son of a bitch pushes this thing into my son's back up until the handle." Pedro showed me the weapon again—the blade measured about three inches. "And so my son drops to the floor. He's stunned. He's not hurt very badly, thank God, but he doesn't know what to do. And while this is happening, that guy runs out the door and down the stairs." Pedro then turned to that same heavy door that separated his front office from the rest of the center. "The problem is that Roberto had locked this door and the front door. There were still two doors between him and the streets."

So what happened? I asked.

"He gets to this heavy door and starts trying to kick it down. But he can't and so he was trapped inside the center."

And Roberto? I asked Pedro.

"He was still on the floor," Pedro said. "He was bleeding and thinking the worst. He didn't know if he had been cut badly. He didn't know anything."

As Pedro spoke, I wanted to stop him to ask him questions about this failed escape. So many details didn't quite line up. The men seemed to know that Pedro was gone. At the very least, the assailant waited until Pedro was out running errands. He knew, as we all did, that Roberto carried far less weight inside the center than his father and that he lacked Pedro's decisive thinking. So it was no surprise that Roberto was the target, but then the story got difficult to decipher. The captive stabbed Roberto in the back just after he unlocked the first of three doors and then made a foolhardy attempt to muscle his way through the next two doors, which he knew were locked. Meanwhile, Roberto still had the keys for those doors in his pockets.

Weapon still in hand, Pedro continued: "Roberto is on the ground and this son of a bitch is trapped in between the general population and the front office. Because he doesn't have the keys to open the second door."

So what happened next? I pressed.

"Tomás and Bautista cornered the man. They wrestled him down and they tied him up. They used the straitjacket and threw him in the morgue. They kicked the shit out of him, but [overall] they took it easy on him. They didn't break anything and they didn't use the bat on him." Pedro seemed to be painting the punishment as a moment of Christian compassion. "I got back, took Roberto to the hospital, and kept that guy inside the morgue for two weeks. Tied up, with the straitjacket on."

Although Pedro could be reactive and come off as calculating, he seemed to harbor little contempt for the man who stabbed his son. "These guys don't know what they're doing," he said, gesturing toward the second floor of his center. "They think that they want to get out of here. They really feel it. Sometimes they scratch at the walls and pull at the bars. They want out of here, but then what?" Pedro put down the weapon and placed all three back in his desk drawer. "Maybe they stay sober for a week. Maybe a month? But then they fall back into sin and end up back here. They don't want to be here. I get that, but the streets are shit. The streets keep sending them back to me. My only job is to make sure that I catch them."[19]

I later asked Alejandro about the attack and why the rest of the captives didn't collectively organize an escape. Why had this guy acted alone?

"He wasn't acting alone," Alejandro said. "No way was he acting alone." He began to fill in some of the gaps. "Some of the guys were monitoring the front door. The pastor goes to the store every Saturday at about the same time, and you can hear him leave from up here on the second floor. And some other guys had made the knife. One guy stole the hanger and another guy knew how to make it. He'd been in prison before and knew how to make the thing." A roster of accomplices suddenly emerged. "And a few guys were supposed to get the keys off of Roberto and then open the next two doors. There were lots of guys in on that move. It was a big plan." Alejandro had apparently known all about it.

So why was this one guy left racing down the stairs all alone? Why did the rest of the captives let him just pound against the second door and not offer help?

"Because people lost their nerve," he said. "They didn't want to get into trouble with Pedro. They all know that they're going to end up back here. They all know that Pedro's going to get them again at some point."

Stories like these do circulate. At Jorge's center, Emilio, one of Pedro's huntsmen, had been in charge of laundry with another captive, which gave them access to the roof and front door, two obvious avenues for escape. As they gained Jorge's trust, the other captive convinced Emilio that they should escape the next time they found themselves in the front office with Jorge's clean laundry. There were always moments when the front door was open and people were distracted. They could just run. Though he knew simply making a break for the door would not give either of them enough of a head start, Emilio agreed, not wanting to be inside Jorge's center any longer than he needed to be. He then came up with his own plan. While standing with the man in Jorge's front office one day, he noticed the front door was ajar. Emilio subtly signaled to his co-conspirator to run, which he did. Emilio let the man get a small head start and then alerted the rest of the front office to the escape. As planned, every last person took off running in his direction. With everyone else distracted by the impromptu hunt, Emilio stepped out of the office and jogged in the opposite direction.

To some extent, Pedro was right about the nature of substance abuse. After Emilio successfully escaped, he ended up back at Jorge's a few weeks later. With nowhere to go and nothing to do, and without any real skills to manage his drug dependency, Emilio fell back into familiar circles. Jorge had him hunted a little less than a month later and then had Emilio hunting for him soon thereafter.[20]

Ultimately, within the dialectic of the hunter and the hunted, it is always possible for roles to be reversed, with the hunter suddenly finding himself hunted. Caught off-guard in a brief moment of near chaos, Roberto found himself at the mercy of the men his father held captive. It would have taken very little coordination or effort for those captives to throw Roberto into the morgue, straitjacket and all, and then quietly walk out of the center single file.

After telling me Roberto's story, Pedro spoke about a possibly more powerful sense of reversal: the sinner being saved. "This is what the center is about," he said, "letting these guys escape a life of sin, a life of drugs and drinking; it lets people start over. I want them to start over." Pedro's sermons about his own suffering at the hands of cocaine and heroin also buttressed the most powerful story of reversal known to this community: Christ's victory over death. He continued, "These sinners need to realize that I want them to escape this center, and I want them to get out of this place and stay out of this place, but not with weapons or with deception, but with prayer, meditation, and forgiveness. They need to be forgiven for what they've done to their families and they need to forgive themselves. Otherwise they're just going to run in the streets. They're going to try to escape their past through drugs." Pedro, at least as far as he was concerned, provided his captives with a clear plan for escape, but none of it involved jumping out of windows.[21]

Santiago entered the center cynical about his ability to escape. He knew that he didn't have the kind of charisma to lead a revolt, nor could he muscle his way past Tomás and Alejandro to make a break for the front door. Maria was not going to pay the pastor to release her son earlier than his contracted stay. With no real options, Santiago submitted.

To get out he needed to become a changed man, or at least act like one.

"The pastor and my mom are both looking for me to change," Santiago said, "to find Jesus and ask for forgiveness. It means that I need to act a certain way and be a certain way."

So will you actually change? I asked.

"I really don't think I can," he said, "but I'm going to work really hard to convince the pastor that I have." It seemed like a difficult act to keep up, and so I said so.

"You have a better idea?" he shot back at me.

I did not.

EIGHTEEN

The chase is central to Pentecostal theology, and not just in a literal sense. Each individual is expected to be in active pursuit of an ideal, aspirational soul. Inside the centers, the catchall term for this practice is called theological therapy. Theological therapy is an improvisational approach that, despite its name, has neither theological nor psychological systematicity, meaning that it doesn't have a historical legacy or disciplinary boundaries. Although it is used in almost every center in Guatemala, it lacks any common point of reference other than the Bible and can vary remarkably from center to center. Everyone seems to be making it up.[22]

"No," Pedro admitted, "it's not really an approach or a tradition or any-thing. The phrase just means that we all call on God for help." At its most fundamental, theological therapy sticks to a series of working assumptions. The first is that captivity will lead to conversion and that holding a user against his will for months on end will lead to rehabilitation. Captivity pulls the user off the streets, out of sin, and puts him in front of God. This pre-sumption is decidedly pastoral, and when pushed, Pedro justified his work biblically. He cited 1 Peter 2:25, "You were like sheep going astray, but now you have returned to the Shepherd and Overseer of your souls."[23]

While most mainstream approaches to drug rehabilitation, whether faith- or evidence-based, focus on incremental advances organized around a set of steps or stages, theological therapy assumes that a user can change, or convert, in an instant. Put differently, centers like Pedro's understand re-habilitation as a single, coherent event—a miracle. One does not get better or worse but is lost or found. "I've seen men change in a moment," Pedro said as he snapped his fingers. "The spirit entered their hearts and they just changed."

At the heart of this understanding of rehabilitation is the idea of re-demption, that a user can only walk away from drugs through the saving grace of Jesus Christ.[24] Without heartfelt repentance and God's uncondi-tional forgiveness, the user will always return to drugs. This assumption is especially pernicious as recidivism suggests that a user never sincerely con-fessed and, thus, never really changed. "Some of these guys are stubborn," Pedro said, "and so you have to keep bringing them back. You need to keep dragging them back here."

This faith in miracles justifies theological therapy's final assumption: that substance abuse is a sin and not a disease. While talk of pathologies and genetic predispositions do echo across some centers, theological therapy places both the etiology of drug use and the burden of change on the indi-vidual Christian. No one else is to blame for drug use but the user himself.

Taken together, these assumptions add up to a therapy whose principal aim is to drag the sinner in front of God to facilitate a miracle, which can take a single day or several years; only God knows. But the pastor's pri-mary responsibility is, in theory, to hold users long enough for this miracle to happen. Theological therapy simply relies on the pastor to provide God with a captive audience. "Theological therapy," Pedro said, "really just says that God will save the sinner, and this means that I need to keep him here until he is saved." He then sheepishly admitted, "It's really just about waiting and keeping these guys occupied until the miracle happens." Yet theological therapy also demands that the sinner hunt down his own sins, transforming self-rehabilitation into a kind of existential manhunt. "I drag these guys here," Pedro reflected. "But it's each of their responsibility to drag themselves to God."

Maria, for one, placed a tremendous amount of faith in theological therapy, hoping that after Santiago was captured, he would be guided toward God.

"He'll learn more about God inside the center," she said, "and the pastor will make sure that he prays to God every day." She sat on a chair, in her home. Santiago had only been inside the center for a few months, and Maria looked relaxed, and even spoke optimistically about the possibility of Santiago's salvation. She was sleeping well and visiting Santiago less often; I was convinced that these points were related. "He can use this time to find God," she said. "He can make the decision to change his life. Only he can make the decision, and with God's help he can start living a good Christian life." Even though Pedro's monthly fees made it almost impossible for Maria to keep a roof over her head, she was sustained by the promise of change. She was also encouraged by her new quality of life.

While users wait for divine intervention, a fairly random collection of reading material helps initiate them into the everyday dimensions of theological therapy. Many of the texts found in centers are secondhand, left by the itinerant pastors who move in and out of different centers across the city. Some come from captives themselves, as people arrive with books they later leave behind. Photocopied articles and missionary fliers also circulate throughout the general population. No two centers in Guatemala City ever share a core set of texts.

However improvisational, these texts play a significant role, as they are the only resources available to help users make sense of their situation. No other outside stimuli is ever allowed, including newspapers and televisions. Although never intended for their ultimate destination, these materials follow a long tradition of popular Christian writing by prompting the reader to "know thyself"—that is, to know one's own appetites, desires, and sins. They advocate a certain level of introspection. But in the context of these centers, Pedro's especially, these books take on a predatory quality, aiming to turn each captive in on himself.

Santiago entered the general population with a copy of Héctor Alvarado's *Escape for Your Life*, a self-published moral manual.[25] Alvarado is a Guatemalan pastor of modest success, with a reach that extends into southern

Mexico. The fifty-six men inside Pedro's center, however, paid little notice
to his reputation. Instead, what grabbed their attention was Alvarado's dic-
tum, the one that drives his book. He writes, in the introduction, that "man
is the sum total of all his decisions. You are who you choose to be."

The message echoed a familiar Christian attitude toward positive thinking, which places responsibility for living a Christian life in the hands of the
individual. A person's struggle over sin, Alvarado insists, comes down to individual decisions propelled by rational choice. This bootstrapping kind of
morality asks the Christian to ensure that his or her "inner speech" is positive,
to journal for hours over the decisions that he or she makes every day, and
to review the actions that he or she takes every six hours. It's a hypervigilant,
nearly compulsive ethics of living.[26]

In Alvarado's formulation, the sinner is effectively pitted against himself. "You have an enemy to overcome," he writes, "and that enemy is you."
His vision of the Christian condition divides every human into two halves.
The human, he writes, has been "created as a duality, with good and bad
residing in each of us. Our task consists of controlling, with the help of
God, the bad and developing the good that flows not only for our benefit
but for the benefit of others." Setting the Christian against himself, *Escape
for Your Life* frames the intimate relationship of self to self as a prolonged
chase scene, with the appropriate images.

The cover of the book depicts a scared young schoolgirl hiding behind
a tree. At the top, the title of the book, "Escape For Your Life," is written in
flames. In the introduction, Alvarado lays out his ethics of intentionality:
"if you say 'I am just like this,' what you are really saying is that 'I have
chosen to be like this.' Instead of saying 'I have always been like this,' you
should say 'I have always chosen to be like this.'" He then adds, "The intention here is to change the way you live your life, the way you think, and, by
consequence, the way you act." To escape a life of sin, the Christian must
escape himself—because the enemy that hunts the Christian, that puts him
on the run, is the Christian himself. Conversely, the Christian must also
hunt the part of himself that is evil. Works like Alvarado's shift the site of the
hunt from the streets to the soul.

Weeks into his captivity, Santiago gradually began to approach the
book with less cynicism. At first, he barely entertained it, often doodling
on its back cover. "In the end God does not need to listen to anyone,"
Alvarado writes. "Escape for your life. Nobody can do it for you. You have
the ability and the responsibility to do it." Santiago eventually read these

lines carefully, and his captivity suddenly seemed to make sense. "Will you make your own life productive," Alvarado asks, "or will you allow others to make decisions for you?"

Santiago, who once raced for hours around an open-air market to avoid captors, was now being told that he was still on the run. This time, he was learning that it wasn't huntsmen he was running from, or even the neighborhood kids who had shot him, but from himself—and that he had always been running from himself. It was a surprisingly convincing message. Through the conceptual bifurcation of the self, theological therapy proved eerily successful at grafting large-scale battles, such as the war on drugs, onto the soul of a single person. The effect was the awareness that making a change would mean making a break. "I sabotage myself," Santiago admitted late one night. I had stayed at the center well past sunset to hang out with the captives as they prepared the second floor for a night of sleep. "I trick myself into doing shit," he said. "I think I can handle a little weed or a few drinks, and then crack ends up grabbing hold of me for a few days or even a week." While still angry about his captivity, Santiago conceded fault for his drug dependency and had grown frustrated with everything, including himself. He seemed susceptible to theological therapy. "I can't stop smoking. I steal shit so I can smoke more," he confessed. "I make my mom mad. She's so fucking mad at me right now, and I'm the one to blame. No one is making me smoke or steal or whatever. I'm doing this to myself."

Alvarado's style of writing is exceedingly clear, leaving little room for multiple interpretations. Drawing on his own past sins, which range from masturbation to drug use, Alvarado argues that sin hunts the sinner and that it is every Christian's duty to escape its trappings. "In you is the power to avoid and prevent," he writes, "the power to repair, the power to modify and change. But it is not God that is going to change you. It is you who can change with God's help." His robust, deeply heroic staging of sin as a solitary social relationship conveniently aligns with the interests of Pedro's resource-strapped center and that of the anemic postwar state. Without paid staff or even sufficient living conditions, without a welfare system or even a functional formal economy to reenter, the idea of radical change was the best option. It asked little of anyone but the captive himself.

After only a few months of captivity, this call to arms was resonating with Santiago. "I want to get the fuck out of here," he had always said, but suddenly his "here" had shifted from the physical space of the center to a more abstract headspace of failed morality. The space to take flight from

was the space of sin—his soul. "If your life is in danger," Alvarado continues, "then it is time to escape. If you consider your life to be bad, then it is
time to escape. If your life is good, then it is time to escape to a better life."
Santiago desperately wanted a better life. "In you resides the highest power
of the universe," Alvarado insists. "It is the power of choice." Pedro would
often double down on Alvarado's message. "They need to make the choice,"
he would proclaim. "I bring them here against their will, but then they get
to choose to leave."

Santiago sometimes struggled to articulate what hunting his sins
would look like in practice, but Alvarado's proposal excited him—especially
its cry for the individual to be active in changing his life. He began to seek
what Alvarado's text advocated. "It is about taking control of my desires,"
Santiago waxed late at night, with us now pressed up against a wall as other
men mopped the floor. "It's about making some decisions about my life
and not blaming anyone for anything. It's about telling my desires to stop
and making sure I pray every day to keep my desires out of my mind." The
only problem was that Alvarado's practical advice on how to do this felt
awfully flat. It included "not letting yourself be curious about the world of
drugs," not looking "to drugs for a solution to your problem," not becoming
"friends with people who encourage you to do drugs," and "maintain[ing]
a solid relationship with God." These are his only directives, and they indi-
cate one of theological therapy's most troubling conceits: The power of transformation is placed in the hands of the sinner and yet is also dependent
upon the grace of God. This means that users like Santiago have little ability to contribute to their own salvation.

Sitting with Pedro in his front office, I asked him what autopredation
looked like in practice. "I don't know," he admitted. He stood up to stretch
his legs. "I don't know what it looks like," he repeated, "but I do know what
I look for. Because I can't really know what's inside any of these guys. I don't
know who is really being sincere and who is just fooling me." He leaned
against his desk, adding, "I know when someone has changed. These guys
start to look different. They start to clean up and take care of themselves.
They stand taller." Even after more than a decade of running a center for
drug rehabilitation, Pedro could not describe how to get from the problem
to the solution. Perhaps in a scramble to find some coordinates, 'theological
therapy' became a kind of shorthand for the mysterious transformation that
occurred once God granted a user enough grace to hunt his own sins. "Because when I see this change starting to take place," Pedro reasoned, "then I
can really start putting the guy to work."

NINETEEN

Pedro insisted that captives engage with the center. Each captive was expected to perform his sincerity of living a good Christian life by providing for the pastor, which meant going to work. Pedro's entire enterprise ran on conscripted labor. Captives did the cooking and the cleaning as well as provided each other with security and therapy. Those with formal electrical and mechanical training were even responsible for technical duties, like electrical and automotive work.

Placing work at the center of recovery made passivity both a problem and an opportunity. With so many captives coming and going, entering and leaving, Pedro quickly forgot about Santiago, who had a tendency to shrink into a corner with his hood pulled over his eyes. Pedro, in fact, would come to know very little about him over the course of his stay because neither Pedro nor any of his huntsmen ever really had any contact with him. Santiago rarely spoke to anyone, never really engaged with the sermons, and always shied away from contact with Pedro. When pressed by Maria about any improvements by her son, Pedro could not defer to a patient file or a progress chart because neither existed. Instead, he called upon his memory, in which he would always draw a blank. He had nearly no experience with Santiago. These gaps were one reason why he told Maria that her son needed more time—to change his life, he had to begin asserting himself inside the center. "I really don't know half of the guys here," Pedro once told me. "They come and go so quickly, and a lot of them just keep their heads down."

Alejandro was shrewdly aware of how to hustle his way through the center. "The trick with this place is that you need to prove yourself to the pastor," he told me during yet another empty moment inside the center. We lounged on the floor, feeling the cold concrete on our backs, our feet up against a wall. This gave our conversation the air of a therapy session. Alejandro reflected aloud about life in captivity: "The pastor needs to know that you can work and that you can be trusted." His plan for success always included an early start to the day. "When I end up in a center and once I'm sober," he said, "I wake up a little earlier than all the other guys." Alejandro framed the decision as a mix of self-care and strategy, yet it seemed to benefit Pedro the most.

"I like to be busy. I like to work," he said. "So I wake up an hour early, like at 4:00 a.m. I'll do some exercises, like push-ups and running in place, and then shower up before morning prayers." Alejandro always got a fresh start, both to clear his mind and to send a message to Pedro and the other captives. "There's always a guy who watches the general population during the night," Alejandro said. "He has to stay awake to make sure that no one tries to escape or attack someone while they're sleeping. He keeps a record book of all the stuff that happens." He paused. "Like when someone gets up to go to the bathroom," he explained, "the guy has to write down whether he took a shit or not." I expressed disbelief, and Alejandro called over Bautista to show me the notebook. There, written in pencil, was a long list of names accompanied by the exact time of their bowel movements. "Otherwise, there's really nothing to write down," Bautista said.

Alejandro continued. "And so I get up an hour earlier than everyone else," he said, "I work out and I bathe. This way the guard will always tell the pastor about it. Because it's the only thing that he sees at night. He'll pass along to the pastor that the new guy is a worker. That he's ready to make a change." Alejandro would then set a fairly aggressive pace for the rest of the day. "I never sleep during the day," he said. "You see these guys here. They don't have anything to do except sit through those sermons and just lay around." He sounded frustrated. "Some of them sleep like twenty hours a day. They just float in and out of sleep. I can't do that. If I sleep during the day, then I can't sleep at night. I need to go to bed tired, especially if I'm sleeping on the floor."

The optics of Alejandro being always on the move did help his image, as did his insistence on working. "What am I going to do?" he asked me. "I'm up early and I'm not sleeping during the day. I'll participate in the sermons and pay attention, but what I'm always trying to do is get out of those sermons by working. Even if I'm not part of the team that cleans, I still support them. I also help hand out the food during meals. I'm always showing people that I have skills, that I can be trusted. That I'm a worker." This was all part of a well-considered plan that had been crafted over years of captivity. "Because the sooner I can prove that I can work, the sooner the pastor pulls me from the general population." Alejandro knew that his hustle would never grant him a full release; Pedro seemed committed to having him inside the center indefinitely, but Alejandro was always trying to improve his living conditions inside the center. He never wanted to be on the second floor with the general population, listening to sermons and getting pressed up against a wall while someone mopped the floors. He wanted to end up in the kitchen and, eventually, to be tapped to go out on hunts.[27]

The kitchen was the perfect job for Alejandro. "Breakfast is easy," he said during another conversation. "We don't cook breakfast. We get some

bread or tortillas. That's no problem, but lunch is a lot of work." He started
to map out the logistics of cooking for almost sixty men. "The great thing
about cooking is that you need to start early in the day," he said, "You need
to start chopping vegetables and boiling water around eight in the morning." This schedule allowed Alejandro to leave the general population soon
after breakfast, just as morning sermons began. "When I'm in the kitchen, I
don't have to worry about any of that testimony bullshit or listen to visiting
pastors. I don't have to sit still or thumb through a Bible." As ambitious as
Alejandro was with his own study of the Bible, he resented the tediousness
of the center's daily schedule. He might not have been able to free himself
entirely from the house, but somehow existing outside of the center's routine delivered Alejandro a sense of purpose, of control.

In the kitchen, Alejandro called his own shots, which allowed him a degree of authority over the few captives who helped him. "We cook the same
thing every day," he said, "and it's not like I have a lot to work with, but it's
a whole lot better than having to be caged up all day." A big part of Alejandro's interest in the kitchen was the space itself. While Pedro's private family
kitchen was on the first floor, the second kitchen was on the roof. The former
had a propane stove and refrigerator, the latter a wood-burning stove and a big
black cauldron. The roof shared roughly the same floorplan as the center's second floor, but instead of more than fifty captives jockeying for position, there
were only three or four captives cooking in the open air. "It's so much better
in the kitchen," Alejandro said. "You can see the city. You get the fresh breezes,
and it's so much quieter." In contrast to the second floor, with its boarded-up
windows, "You almost feel free up there," Alejandro once told me.[28]

But the roof came with temptations. There were the cooking utensils,
which could be converted into weapons. At first, Alejandro got patted down
every time he returned to the second floor. "But at some point," he said, "the
pastor and his men stopped searching me for stuff. They started to trust
me and every day they searched me a little less." The neighborhood also
included a long row of houses, and the roof of Pedro's neighbor's house was
only a few meters away. In the past, people had taken running leaps to try
to land on the next roof. "But if you fall," Alejandro warned as we looked
over the edge, "then you're going to break your legs." It was a three-meter
fall to the ground. "You can escape from up here, for sure," Alejandro said.
"But it's not easy, and once you're up here, it's actually pretty hard to leave.
I can eat as much food as I want. No one is watching me. I have plenty of
space and it's peaceful up here. The guys who help me are pretty good. And
then there's the market."

Trust accrues with each captive, like a system of credit and debt.[29] Once Alejandro worked his way into the kitchen and had proven that he wanted to neither steal a knife nor jump to another roof, Pedro would let him go to the markets in the morning to beg for food. "I'm the one cooking," he said, "so it's better if I go to the market."

Donning business cards and badges with the center's information on them, Alejandro and three other captives would make a Christian plea to marketgoers in the hopes of winning the center a slightly better lunch.

I asked why he didn't simply run away.

"It would be pretty easy to take off running," he said, "guys do that all the time. But the market is so close to the center that it's usually hard to really escape. The guys just go back to the center, get the truck, and then start tracking you down." Alejandro mapped out the probability of getting away. "It's just hard to gain enough ground on the guys when you're on foot. Maybe you could hop a bus in time, but the pastor will get you. No doubt. He'd find you and then beat the shit out of you."

Alejandro knew the dismal prospects of escape, but that didn't mean he never tried to flee. In one heroic run, Alejandro was in the kitchen when he had a realization. He simply could not spend another night inside, on the floor, next to another user. "Sometimes I get to a point," he said, "that I just can't be inside anymore. Even if I'm in the kitchen and on the roof, I'm still on the floor at night, pressed up against some guy. I'm getting yelled at for having to take a piss in the middle of the night. Sometimes I don't want to be a fucking slave." So he made a move.

Having been inside the center for three months, he took a knife from the kitchen and put it to the throat of a visiting pastor. "I grabbed his arm and pinned it behind his back. He was an old man so it wasn't that hard. And then I put the knife up to his throat. So I'm pulling him into my body, with the knife poking him in the neck." Alejandro walked out the front door, his hostage providing him safe passage through each of the center's locked doors. "It was all pretty smooth, I wasn't working with anyone. I hadn't even really planned it too much. I just snapped. I just needed to get out of the center." Yet those last ten meters to freedom tripped him up. Terrible timing placed a hunting party at the front door just as Alejandro was making his break.

"Tomás and Emilio saw me coming out the front door, and I didn't really see them. Because I had my back to them." The pastor, out on errands, was nowhere to be seen, and so Tomás and Emilio acted fast, tackling Alejandro to the ground and safely separating him from the visiting pastor.

What happened next? I pressed.

"They beat the shit out of me," he said.

Alejandro routinely rose and fell within the ranks of the center, making it to the kitchen and the coveted hunts, but then usually slipping back to the very bottom with an attempted escape.

"When they catch me and bring me back," Alejandro said, "it starts all over again."

This includes the early morning workouts, modeling attentiveness at sermons, and giving personal testimonies.

"I've done this a few times with this pastor," Alejandro said. "I've worked really hard and then fucked up somehow." I asked Pedro why he trusted Alejandro, even when his track record suggested he shouldn't.

"This is the point," he said. "You have to trust that people can change. That they can find their inner strength and make the decision to take charge of their lives." Pedro also seemed at a loss for talent. "Plus," he said, "I know Alejandro. I know how hard he can work and I've started to know when he's about to screw up. I can start to see some of the signs."

I asked Pedro to give me examples.

"He'll start talking less," Pedro said, "he'll start thinking more, being really quiet. Like he's planning something."

Couldn't he just be in prayer? I asked.

"No," Pedro said from experience, "prayer looks different than this. Prayer is peaceful. This is a deceptive look. It's a scared look. When Alejandro is not at peace, I know that he's starting to make plans to escape." Pedro could read Alejandro so well that he would reduce his privileges once he suspected something. He would keep Alejandro out of the kitchen, bar him from going to the market, and never let him out on a hunt. Rescinding these privileges forced Alejandro to work harder to prove himself again.

It was a delicate game; Pedro needed to tease Alejandro with enough freedom to make him work, but not give him so much that it would invite an escape. "The problem is that I need Alejandro," the pastor admitted. "I need him to keep this center running."

By the time Alejandro handed me his letter, he had tested the pastor's patience one too many times. Pedro was suspicious. Alejandro had successfully been working in the kitchen and visiting the markets every day. He had also been hunting with the rest of the crew most nights. All seemed to be going well, but Alejandro had his eye on leaving and had let this slip to Bautista.

"He asked me about a friend of mine that works in the market," Bautista later told me, "and whether he could get him a job unloading trucks." Bautista shook his head, adding: "I knew that he was up to something."

"Yeah," Alejandro admitted to me, "I was making plans. I was trying to figure out what I would do once I got out. Because I don't have family here. I don't have anyone to help me out once I leave. So I want to make sure that I have some work." He added, "I need Q30 [$5 USD] to pay for a hotel and then Q15 [$2.50 USD] to feed myself. I can make Q50 [$8 USD] the first day that I'm out of this center, but I need a plan. I need to know that I can start working immediately or I'm going to be back on the streets." Bautista apparently told the pastor about Alejandro's query, and Pedro read it as part of some larger plan. Because he relied so much on Alejandro, he immediately pulled Alejandro from the kitchen.

"That was fucked up," Alejandro said, "because then I had to listen to all those testimonies and sermons and sit with all those people." Pedro then stopped letting Alejandro go to the market. "So I lost any chance of getting a job," Alejandro reasoned. He was even replaced on nightly hunts. "The new guy is not as good as me," he insisted. "The pastor will figure that out." But Pedro seemed steadfast in keeping Alejandro inside his center, hoping he would commit himself anew to rising through the ranks: from the kitchen to the market to the hunting fields.

"He's not leaving this place," Pedro told me. "Alejandro is here, and he's going to stay here."

It seemed that Pedro had pushed Alejandro a little too hard this time. Every previous effort at escape had been a duel between Alejandro and Pedro, a private affair. Alejandro's letter, on the other hand, now expanded the frame to include everyone inside the center as well as me and the police. It was a bold and desperate attempt at escape that put multiple people at risk.

TWENTY

"I'm telling you," Alejandro said, "I want to get out of here. I don't care anymore. The pastor can't keep me locked up here. It's not right. It's not legal. And it's not Christian. Take this letter and go to the police. They'll come here and let us all go."

Having lived most of his life in the United States, Alejandro had few relatives in Central America. The only two people that he ever spoke about were his aunt in Guatemala City and his ex-wife in the United States. His aunt proved to be completely unresponsive. She often refused to answer his phone calls and they would erupt into arguments when she did. She lived in a respectable, middle-class community on the other side of the city and wanted nothing to do with her nephew. I first approached her with Alejandro's letter, but she refused to get involved. She insisted this was a matter between Alejandro and the pastor.

Alejandro also spoke of a close friend named Manuel, whom he called his cousin. I had met Manuel inside a factory-turned-rehab five years earlier, where a different pastor was holding him and Alejandro against their will for alcohol and cocaine use. The two sobered up together and worked their way out—by getting up early, never sleeping during the day, and eventually getting the chance to collect food from markets, which was when they escaped.

"Once we were out the door," Manuel remembered, "we just kept walking away." While Manuel got back to work, kept his drinking under control, and moved into a house with his wife and child, Alejandro could not do the same. He went back to the streets, worked day jobs in the market, and bounced between hotel rooms.

The realities of life inside the center made it nearly impossible for Alejandro to sustain lasting relationships. Drugs and alcohol did not help, and the practicalities of constantly entering and exiting centers caught up to him as well. Alejandro would disappear for months on end, only to reappear after escaping yet again. Though gregarious and well liked, his acquaintances rarely became trusted friends, largely because his presence never proved to be permanent. He was a good person to drink or smoke with, but Alejandro had trouble establishing intimacy. He did not know anyone well enough to stay with them while he got back on his feet.[30]

Alejandro's hunting had also made him enemies, which turned city streets into a minefield. Although some could forgive the fact that he had tied them up and dragged them to the center, others could not. "I get it," Alejandro said. "I'm cool with it because I do it all the time. The guys who hunted me were just doing their job. So I don't hold a grudge, but some guys do. They really don't like me."

Once, in a different center across town, I met someone whom Alejandro had hunted. "Fuck that guy," he said. "He didn't have to be so rough with me. He didn't have to punch me or tie me up. I would've gone to the center without all of that shit." A good ten years older than Alejandro, this captive remembered him with real anger. "Tell that motherfucker that I'm looking for him," he said. "Tell that fucker that I'm going to kick his ass."

In the end, this confluence of pressures and neglect made Alejandro absolutely alone in Guatemala. He was never lonely, per se, but he was most certainly alone. Pedro knew this and exploited it. He was aware that Alejandro needed him as much as he needed Alejandro, and the pastor often acted as if he had the upper hand, which he usually did.[31]

"If he leaves," Pedro said, "he'll be back here in a week. He can't last out on the streets for more than a week without crawling back here."

A few days after he handed me the letter, I asked Alejandro what he would do if he left the center.

"I told you," he said, "I have a plan." He explained it to me again: "I know a guy at the market, and he'll let me work for him. I'll unload trucks for him and that will give me enough money to find a place to sleep. That will keep me off the streets until I can find some better work, like with a construction crew or something. I'll also need to get my papers." Alejandro had lost his government-issued identification card when the pastor last picked him up. "The papers will let me apply for a [formal] job," he said, "so I don't have to work in the markets or do construction." Alejandro imagined himself waiting tables, something with a steady paycheck and regular hours. "Then I'll be able to afford an apartment," he said. "I can buy a stove and maybe get some furniture."

The plan seemed completely reasonable to me. Given Alejandro's work ethic inside the center, with his early morning workouts and ever-mounting levels of responsibilities, his strategy seemed doable, perhaps even modest. "And my ex-wife in the States," he added. "She'll send me a few hundred dollars to get me started. She's done it before."

I pointed out that she rarely answered his phone calls and instructed me—the last time I contacted her on his behalf—to leave her out of his life.

"She's upset," he said. "But when she knows that I'm on the streets, she'll come through."

In light of the letter and the hundreds of conversations Alejandro and I had had over the previous five years, the possible success of this plan put me in an awkward position. For years, I had observed family members and pastors gauge a captive's sincerity while the person strived to demonstrate to both parties that he had changed. Sincerity always existed for me as an object of study, something I observed others performing and interpreting. As an anthropologist, the fact that sincerity was the means by which so many sought freedom made for compelling ethnography; facial expressions and bodily comportment became media through which the sincerity of a sinner's soul could be laid bare. Alejandro exploited this with his early morning workouts and incessant work ethic. All he wanted was to reach the roof, to spend his days in the fresh air, and so he outwardly performed the interior conversion that Pedro desperately sought for his captives. Captives would comb their hair, tuck in their shirts, and sit up straight—all to suggest that their souls were doing the same. But Alejandro had now caught me on a personal level, pulling me in to participate in this assessment and determine his freedom.

Was he being sincere with me?

I had known Alejandro for more than five years; I had seen him both inside and outside of centers. I always knew him to be running some kind of scheme, be it at the market to make a little extra money or inside the center to improve his quality of life. But he also seemed to confide in me, often making himself emotionally vulnerable when he didn't have to. We would speak about his life, his past, and his future and digress into conversations about the challenges of family and the pain of failed promises. And it troubled me to know that Pedro was taking advantage of him, extracting his labor at all hours of the day and night. I knew Alejandro had no real family in Guatemala, and I reminded myself that his aunt did not want to get involved. I reasoned that Alejandro needed a chance at a new life. At the same time, I also knew that initiating a police raid would put everyone in the house at risk, as the captives would run out the door and end up back on the streets.

Guatemala City did not have the kind of social services that could adequately absorb fifty-six more men. They would live on the streets, without support of any kind. Keeping Santiago inside Pedro's center was a matter of life and death for him, although he did not want to stay. Alejandro, however, seemed ready to leave, even if Pedro refused to see it. He had given years of his life to this center and finally wanted to make a move. I thought he had the skills to put his plan into action. But then, did I fully believe this? Years earlier, after Alejandro had escaped a different center, I loaned him some money. I remember how he shook my hand, pledged to pay me back, and then insisted that we meet the next day—just to talk. I ended up waiting on a street corner for the better part of an afternoon and didn't see Alejandro again for months. And so I found myself doubting Alejandro's sincerity.

Had he been playing me this whole time? Could I really trust Alejandro to stick to his plan? Was he really ready? And did any of that even matter when it came to questions of self-determination? Alejandro had been held captive for months, and he wanted out. Now in the position to make this decision, it became radiantly clear just how arbitrary these judgments actually were. The timeline also felt incredibly rushed. Alejandro had simply handed me the letter one day, and I immediately began to weigh the possibilities. In trying to exhaust all avenues before making a decision of my own, I brought Manuel to the center to speak with Alejandro.

"Just get my cousin," Alejandro had said soon after handing me the letter, "and he'll tell you that I'm ready to get out of here. Shit, bring him here! Bring him here, and he can talk to the pastor."

I tracked down Manuel living not far from the center. He seemed pleased to hear from me and wanted to know how my fieldwork was going. I had last seen him inside a rehab, in rather bad straits, and he was excited to show me his new life. He now had a job, new clothes, and a stable relationship. He rented a house in an upwardly mobile part of the city. His entire existence emanated sincerity, and he was proud to show it off. He also seemed concerned that Alejandro wanted to get out. As we drove to the center, spending an hour negotiating city traffic, Manuel suggested that Alejandro might be better served by staying inside the center for a few months more.

I shot him a look of disbelief and asked why, especially since Manuel had not been in contact with Alejandro for close to a year. He had no idea what Alejandro was like these days.

"I know what Alejandro is like," Manuel assured me. "He's not sincere. He's never been sincere. He'll say anything to get out of a center, but then he's never ready for life on the outside. He doesn't have anywhere to sleep. He doesn't have a job. He'll be smoking and drinking the day he leaves the center."

I suddenly felt compelled to defend Alejandro, feeling that my own ability to discern sincerity was somehow now in question. At a stoplight, I turned to Manuel and peppered him with observations. But Alejandro does have a plan, I asserted. He wakes up early every morning, I added, and he works all day. The pastor, I continued, just wants him for his labor. He's a prisoner! I finally blurted out.

"But he's *not* sincere," Manuel retorted. "You can't trust what he says. He believes what he says, but he's not even being sincere with himself. He's lying to you, and he's lying to himself." Frustrated by the conversation, we both went silent. After another half an hour in traffic, we finally arrived at the center to find a giant padlock hanging on the front door. Pedro had left the building, locked the door from the outside, and taken the key with him. We would have to wait for him to return. The fact that Pedro had made it impossible for any of his men to escape during an emergency only bolstered my case about how unsafe the center was. I gestured to the locked door to impress this point and then asked Manuel if I should go to the police. Locking people inside a center puts people at risk, I said.

"Don't be an idiot," he told me. "You're really putting people in danger if you call the police."[32]

Pedro returned about an hour later, welcomed us in, and arranged some stools for us and Alejandro. He then left to preach to the general population.

As soon as Pedro was out of earshot, Alejandro began to make his case to Manuel. He laid out his plan: the market, then construction, and then a restaurant. He would stay in a budget hotel and find an apartment. His wife would send him money. Manuel listened. Having been sober for more than a year, he looked healthy, especially when seated next to Alejandro. Manuel had a fresh haircut and clean clothes, a far cry from when I saw him five years earlier. Back then, he had a black eye and needed a shower.

The man sitting in front of Alejandro had undergone a remarkable change. But this worked against Alejandro by making Manuel seem morally superior.[33] Manuel's freedom and apparent transformation enabled him to speak at Alejandro rather than with or to him. What I witnessed was not a conversation between two equals but a lesson delivered from teacher to student.

"You should stay here," Manuel told Alejandro. "You need to complete three more months." Alejandro looked betrayed. "I did it," Manuel lectured, "I did my full time inside a center and then I got a job. If I can clean up, so can you."

Alejandro corrected Manuel, reminding him that he knew as well as anyone that the centers are not useful. Committed to his own conversion, Manuel doubled down on the power of change.

"I did it and so can you," he said.

Alejandro suddenly started to cry, which made Manuel even colder. He was not going to budge, even after Alejandro confronted him with a list of the abuses he had suffered at Pedro's hands.

"That happens at every center," Manuel reminded him. "It's not just here. It's everywhere."

Upset that the conversation had not gone according to plan, Alejandro told Manuel to "get the fuck out of here," which he did with Pedro's assistance, leaving Alejandro and me alone on the first floor.

"Go talk to the pastor," Alejandro told me. "Just go talk to the pastor and see what you can do to get me out of here." At this point, Alejandro was clearly unnerved. He had not left the center in weeks, with the pastor's suspicions keeping Alejandro out of the kitchen, away from the markets, and off the hunts. "Just see what he says," Alejandro pleaded.

At his request, I asked to speak with Pedro in his front office. It was a quick pivot on my part. Alejandro's meeting with Manuel had gone so poorly, between Manuel's moralizing and Alejandro's tears, that my reluctance to engage was wearing thin. As Pedro locked the front door with what seemed like a light spirit, I thought that a conversation could not hurt. At the moment, there was no one to advocate for Alejandro. Neither his aunt nor his ex-wife would answer the phone. His close friend had just walked out the door. How could I abandon him, too?

With Pedro behind his desk and me again on a flimsy stool, I offered my opinion of Alejandro and his situation. I stressed that he did not have any family in Guatemala and that he had been holed up in the center off and on for years. He deserved an opportunity at a fresh start.

As I spoke, I began to notice Pedro looking at me. He was studying me just as I had seen him study not just users but also their families. Suddenly, my sincerity was also under scrutiny. I found myself forming sentences more carefully so as not to sound too confident or too casual. I modulated the tone of my voice to strike the right tenor. Though I was knowledgeable about both Alejandro's situation and how these centers worked generally, I tried to maintain a deferential posture. I slumped in my chair, posting my elbows on my knees so Pedro could look down on me. The conversation felt like supplication.

"He'll be back here in a week," Pedro said with complete confidence. "I give him a week."

Holding firm, I contended that Alejandro had a plan. I floated the idea that the Holy Spirit could have taken hold of his heart, and suggested that Alejandro may have grown weary of street life.

Pedro listened, and I waited for an answer.

"The contract," he reminded me. "The contract says that Alejandro needs to be here for seven full months." Almost impulsively, I fired back that no family member had signed this contract and that Alejandro had been clear about not wanting to be inside the center. I stopped short of saying that the contract held absolutely no legal weight in Guatemala. The piece of paper was at best a contrived agreement between two unequal parties, with signatures and thumbprints collected under duress. I didn't think that

Pedro had even written a contract the last time he hunted Alejandro and had just dragged him to the morgue.

"The contract says that he stays here for seven months," Pedro said.

I asked if there was another option.

"Well." He cleared this throat. "The contract says that if someone leaves before the seven months, then someone needs to pay."

For what? I asked.

"For the time not spent," he said. He paused. "For Alejandro," he said, "Q800 [$100 USD]."

The suggestion of my paying for Alejandro's freedom ended my inclination to be sincere. I suddenly found myself sitting up straight on the stool. The jig was up, the performance over. The new atmosphere seemed to have the same effect on Pedro. We were suddenly negotiating a payment instead of an offering. With Alejandro's freedom now a financial matter rather than one of the heart, he stopped studying me. I was a customer and Pedro a seller. Alejandro's freedom had a price tag.

And if I pay, Alejandro can go? I asked.

"Alejandro can walk out this door right now," Pedro answered. "He can do whatever he wants. Someone just needs to pay."

Overwhelmed by the ethics of this exchange, I suddenly needed fresh air. I also didn't have that much cash on me. I told Pedro that I needed to think about it, but I would be back later that afternoon.

"It's your decision," Pedro reminded me. "You can pay me the money or he can spend another four months here."

Now ensnared by his proposition, I walked with Pedro to the door.

RETURN

"Return to me, and I will return to you," says the Lord Almighty. But you ask, "How are we to return?"

—MALACHI 3:7

TWENTY-ONE

To walk out of a Pentecostal drug rehabilitation center is to be struck by sunlight. Inside, there is no natural light. The few windows that these centers have are typically lined with bars and covered with corrugated metal. One pastor even went so far as to plug each of his center's windows with cinder blocks. During power outages in that center, when the fluorescent lights failed to turn on, the captives used candles to illuminate the room.

Pedro's center was dark. It was also cold and shadowy. To ascend and descend the center's staircase, to reach the second floor or to return to the first floor, I would palm the wall, my foot groping toward the next step. After Pedro walked me to the center's front door, carefully unlatching and relocking its padlock, I squinted until my eyes adjusted, feeling like one of the captives from the allegory of Plato's cave, having suddenly emerged from darkness into the sunlight for the first time.[1] In the wake of our conversation, I felt like I needed guidance. I was both blinded by knowledge and completely in the dark. I was offended by Pedro's ultimatum. After years of conversation and what seemed like mutual admiration, I really thought we had a strong rapport. Yet our relationship had so quickly descended into a fee-for-service transaction. I was also overwhelmed by the responsibility that suddenly sat on my shoulders.[2]

How did I get myself into this situation?

At one level, the answer was obvious: longitudinal fieldwork often binds an ethnographer to his or her subjects in ways that extend well beyond simple exchanges of information. Walking with the hunted (as well as with those who hunt) was an intimate activity that demanded trust, sincerity, and, sometimes, money. I never paid for access, but when I look back across my years of research inside these centers, and even to earlier projects in Guatemala, I had offered the occasional meal or taxi fare and also given handouts for lawyer fees, bail money, antipsychotic medication, a coffin, rent money, and tuition fees. I passed captives antibiotic skin cream, sticks of deodorant, and rolls of toilet paper. I once bought a secondhand bicycle helmet for a man who suffered from epilepsy. His family insisted on keeping him inside the center, for lack of anywhere else to put him, but the young man risked cracking his head on the floor during a seizure. The helmet was his idea. How could I say no? I was engaged in a long-term research project, and these were gestures of reciprocity to people in obvious and immediate need. Marcel Mauss would have seen these gifts as part of a moral economy. Pedro would have called them offerings.[3]

The problem was that while Alejandro needed an offering, Pedro seemed to want a payment. I tried my best to recruit more perspectives before making my decision, even attempting to shift responsibility to a family member, but Alejandro's aunt would not answer my calls. Nor would Alejandro's former wife in the United States. The lawyer I had previously spoken with about Alejandro's situation suddenly had no opinion on the matter. Instead, he seemed increasingly ambivalent about provoking a raid on the center, knowing as well as I did that there would be little help available to the newly released. He finally suggested that a payment might be the most expedient solution, but then he questioned even this advice.[4] Manuel also proved to be less of a resource than I had hoped. Unbeknownst to me, there was bad blood between him and Alejandro.

"One of the reasons Manuel was so mad," Alejandro explained, "is that when we were both inside another center [a few years earlier], I started treating people mean. The pastor didn't like that, and I told the pastor to then let me leave or else I was going to beat people up every single day." Alejandro strategically disrupted the sheepfold, which forced the pastor to cut his losses. "He let me go," Alejandro said, "but Manuel had to stay there for another six months, and so Manuel got mad at me."

Manuel was apparently prepared to let Alejandro sit inside a center as Alejandro had once made Manuel do. "When Manuel got out he was like, 'Why didn't you come and see me?' And I was like, 'So they could stick me in there again and not let me out?' I told him, 'You're lucky I told your wife where you were.'" Alejandro's insistence on escaping had come back to haunt him. "You're crazy," Alejandro had told his cousin. "If I had gone back to the center, they'd never had let me leave."

Alone in my decision, I began to use a hypothetical as a kind of ethical compass: What if I did nothing? What if I let Alejandro sit inside the center for another four months? I had used this speculative method before—to decide whether I should post bail, pay for a coffin, or buy that bicycle helmet. To refuse any of those requests always felt like a failure to sincerely engage with the moral economy that I had made my object of study.[5]

A few days before, Alejandro had confronted Pedro. "I got mad," Alejandro said. "I told the pastor that I don't want to be in the center. I told him the other day that I don't want to be here, that this is kidnapping. 'Open the door!' I yelled. 'Let me go!'" Alejandro then returned to the question of self-determination. "It doesn't matter to you what I do," he told Pedro. "If I want to go drink and sleep on the streets, then let me do it. It's my life. I'm the architect of my life. And the scriptures say that God gives us that choice. Everyone has dominion over themselves. It's there, in the Bible." Again, Alejandro turned toward scripture to litigate his life. "Who are you," he interrogated Pedro, "to steal my freedom?"

What did he say? I asked.

"He didn't tell me anything," Alejandro replied. "He just punished me. He tied me up, took my food away, and threw me in the morgue." Alejandro sat in the morgue for four hours with a straitjacket on. "Bautista then comes over," he continued, "and was like, 'Look, the pastor says for you to give me a thousand sit-ups but just do two hundred and I'll tell him that you did a thousand.'" Alejandro complied, for the food. "But to get the jacket off," he added, "I had to do the sit-ups." Of the hundreds of captives I had met over years of research, I had never known anyone who had been so clearly caught by the industry, so obviously ensnared largely for the sake of conscripted labor. Turning my back on Alejandro for a relatively small amount of money made me more uneasy than the prospect of just paying it.

Ethical deliberation, at least philosophically, tends to stress the decision-making process as an exclusively logical procedure. I was tempted to think, following the tradition of Immanuel Kant, that moral obligations should be unconditional—that is, moral judgments should be binding in all circumstances and not dependent on a person's inclination or purpose. In this vein, extrajudicial incarceration is not and will never be just.[6] Yet my fieldwork routinely forced me to confront the many instances in which captivity kept people alive. While Maria had reservations about Pedro's methods, keeping her son alive was more important to her than refusing extrajudicial incarceration on ethical grounds. Keeping Santiago inside the center offered an alternative to him running the streets, with captivity a better option than death. Neither Maria nor Pedro would describe their ethics as wholly dependent on the anticipated effects of their actions. Within these webs of predation, the ethical choice always proved to be a moving object—a target constrained by context. Paying Pedro would give Alejandro a sure way out of the center, but not paying him would certainly mean more months of captivity. Would this be all that different from handouts I had previously given people? Ultimately, the idea of Alejandro trapped inside that center for four more months felt wrong.[7] I paid Pedro the Q800 ($100 USD).

TWENTY-TWO

I returned to the center later that day to sit in Pedro's office. I had my digital recorder on his desk, its little red light signaling the machine's readiness to record every detail of the exchange. The transaction, though, was banal, eerily everyday. I tried to provoke a conversation about Alejandro's next steps, to get Pedro to offer some advice about how Alejandro should proceed. But Pedro proved unemotional, observably unaffected by the transaction. Just like that, he called Alejandro to the front office, made sure he had his belongings, and promptly walked us toward the front door. As we approached, with Pedro fishing the keys from his pocket, I noticed for the first time a sign that hung over the doorframe. It read: "I command you to strive and to be brave." Pedro unlocked one last padlock and held open the door just long enough for Alejandro and me to step into the midday sun.

Pedro said not a word to either of us.

Alejandro was immediately elated, thrilled to be outside after so many months of captivity. We walked to the end of the street and onto a busy thoroughfare. The noise of traffic and the smell of diesel fumes immediately enlivened Alejandro—he was out. Finally. But as we settled on a place to eat, to gather our thoughts and make a plan, Alejandro suddenly looked crestfallen. I prodded him for an explanation, and he gave me several.

"This is the rule," he said, "when people leave, the pastor calls him to the front office and he talks to the guy with his family. He says stuff like, 'your son needs this. Your son needs that. He needs to join a church. That's what he needs to do.' And he talks to the family about stuff like that." Alejandro then added another fact. "And he calls everyone together. All the guys and he has them pray for the person." Captives huddle around the soon-to-be-released man, lay their hands on him, and pray along with the pastor—for a new life, for the man's strong will, and for him to have the good sense to seek help before falling again into sin. These prayers were often joyous events, full of laughter and comradery.[8]

There was also the outtake form. Had Alejandro agreed to the standard contract—the same one that Maria signed for Santiago—the back of the paper should have contained the following language:

On this day at 3:45 p.m., Miguel Alejandro Gonzalez has been discharged at the request of his family because he has served his previously agreed upon seven months. He has been delivered in perfect physical, mental, and spiritual condition.

Upon release, the captive signs the statement, then a family member, and then Pedro. Taken in concert, the conversation, a group prayer, and the outtake form constitute the ritual of exit.

Alejandro received none of this, and he felt slighted. If the study of religion establishes anything, it is the power of ritual to bind people together. Émile Durkheim argues that the collective effervescence known as religion emerges through social practice—through ritualized conversations, prayers, and texts. By way of predatory pastoralism, Pedro had bound his subjects together too tightly, not simply taking lost souls by the arm but also holding them down in the dead of night. The intensity of this captivity, with all of its aggression and violence, continued into liberation. In the case of Alejandro—who had been pulled from the streets and tied up in the name of love—release prompted ambivalence. He had been let go without going through the established rites of passage, and this agitated him.[9]

"He just opened the door," Alejandro said about an hour after the fact, "and just let me go. No prayer. No nothing."

Alejandro was dejected. Durkheim called this sensation anomie, the feeling of no longer being a part of a group. Anomie names the breakdown of social bonds, the fragmentation of social identity, and the rejection of self-regulatory values. Immediately after his release, Alejandro felt untethered, nostalgic for the forced sociality he had just escaped.[10]

"Trust me," Alejandro said, "I feel good. I feel free, but I feel sad for the guys that I left behind." He held his head in his hands. "Because who's going to be there to protect them?" he wondered. "To take care of them? Especially the old men who are there? I was the one taking care of them. I was the one who made sure they learned how to read scripture. I was the one who made sure that they took a shower and had clothes. Because I had authority to do that."

Alejandro started to cry. In the middle of a busy roadside eatery, with traffic creeping past us, Alejandro wiped tears from his face, adding, "Who's going to write down all the verses for them? I even got one of the old men to sleep next to me on the floor. I told the pastor, 'Send him over here with me. And I put him next to me. I will take care of him.'" Amid the abuse and the violence, the humiliation and the failed promises, Alejandro had found warmth and purpose.[11]

We continued this conversation as we finished our meal and traversed the city, hopping a bus to another part of town. Alejandro wanted to stay in a particular hotel that he'd long had his eye on. It was modest and close to the market where he had been promised work. The sun was already starting to set when we arrived, and Alejandro was looking forward to sleeping in a bed for the first time in months. As I paid for the room, we agreed that he would devote the next few days to securing work and getting new state-issued identification cards. He had lost his cards the last time he was hunted, and those documents were crucial to finding work in the formal economy. We also planned to connect Alejandro with his ex-wife for a possible infusion of funds. Alejandro seemed excited as the hotel manager (with a gun fixed to his hip) unlocked the front door. As we parted ways, Alejandro began laying out his vision of what he hoped was to come.

"When I start working," he told me, "when I start dressing nice, I'm going to go back to the center. I want to see the look on their faces." He took some pleasure in the fantasy of showing the pastor that he had changed, adding, "Romans 12:17–21 says that if you find a man hungry, then give him food. If there are people who talk bad about you, then help them out. Do all of this," Alejandro ad-libbed, "so you can see the shame on their faces for having once hurt you." He squared himself to me. "And that's what I want to do. Because before I left, Bautista was joking around, like 'Alejandro's going to be drunk in a few hours. He's going to be high once he gets some money in his pocket.'"

Alejandro looked me in the eyes and said, "Fuck that guy."

TWENTY-THREE

The odds were not in Alejandro's favor. Guatemala provides close to no services for the treatment of what the international public health community calls "substance use disorders" (SUD). Nor does the country host many nongovernmental organizations that work on the issue. The World Health Organization's World Atlas tells a rather bleak story. Its profile of Guatemala's health resources appears incomplete, as if someone failed to do the assignment:

Is there a national epidemiological data collection for drugs? No.
Is there a national epidemiological data collection for alcohol? No.
Is there a special legislative provision for treatment and rehabilitation? No.
Is there the presence of drug courts in the country? No.

Are there programs that divert clients towards treatment programs? No.

Is there a government unit responsible for treatment services for SUD? No.

Is there a line in annual budget of government for SUD treatment services? No.

What is the financing method for treatment services? Out-of-pocket.

What is the most common treatment used for alcohol use disorders? [Blank]

What is the most common treatment used for drug use disorders? [Blank]

What is the availability of treatment services and estimated coverage? [Blank]

Are there specialized treatment services for patients with drug use disorders? No.

Number of outpatient treatment slots for alcohol and drug use disorders? [Blank]

What is the total number of beds for alcohol and drug use disorders? [Blank]

Is there screening/brief intervention in primary care for alcohol? No.

Is there screening/brief intervention in primary care for drugs? No.

Top three health professionals for treatment of persons with SUD? [Blank]

Are there NGOs in the country focusing on alcohol? No.

Are there NGOs in the country focusing on drugs? No.

What is the government unit responsible for the prevention of SUD? None.

Is there a line in government's annual budget for prevention of SUD? No.

What is the financing method for prevention services of SUD? [Blank]

Are there prevention services available? No.

Are there harm reduction programs available? No.[12]

Alejandro left the center and entered a city with no support apart from my commitment to getting him back on his feet. This was a problem. I felt capable of floating Alejandro for a few weeks, maybe even a few months, but this was not a solution. These centers were the only resource available to vulnerable individuals such as Alejandro.

A few years after the World Health Organization published this profile, the Guatemalan government opened its own drug treatment center. Run by the National Antidrug Commission of Guatemala (SECCATID), the center employed three psychologists and one general practitioner to serve an outpatient population that arrived weekly for group therapy sessions. Modest in scope and limited in resources, the center struggled to provide a counternarrative to the city's Pentecostal centers. I once proposed the government center to Maria, thinking that Santiago might be able to commit to treatment while pursuing fulltime work, but she scoffed at the entire enterprise—not simply its commitment to evidence-based treatment programs (for Christ was the answer) but also the freedom. "Santiago needs to be locked up," she told me, "or they will kill him."[13]

As a form of outreach, SECCATID sent psychologists to some of the city's Pentecostal drug rehabilitation centers for weekly talks. For a short period, until SECCATID ran out of funding, Pedro's center hosted a psychologist every week. These informal conversations between a psychologist and the captives often lasted for less than an hour, but the captives proved thirsty, positively parched, for an alternative understanding of their appetites.

A few months before Alejandro walked out of Pedro's center, more than fifty men sat on the floor as a young psychologist aggressively lorded over the group. He wore a black leather jacket and distressed blue jeans, with close cropped hair that looked almost military. "I'm here to talk to you about the physical and psychological effects of addiction," he said with some swagger. "Because drugs and alcohol affect our neurons and, as a result, they affect our entire nervous system. Drugs and alcohol affect the way that we think and feel." He pointed to his head and spoke much more loudly than he needed to. He also enunciated each of his words as if wanting the men to read his lips.

It is difficult to describe the effect that these statements had on the captives. Confined to a single narrative while inside the center—that sin haunts their soul—this psychologist seemed to offer a different vision. "And when your thought patterns change," he continued, "your conduct also changes. I want you to understand this relationship—because if you understand this relationship, then you have the chance to change your habits. And if you can change your habits, then you can change your thought patterns."

The psychologist pulled a marker from his coat and boldly began to write the word "PERCEPTION" in all caps on the wall. "Drugs and alcohol make us perceive the world differently," he said. "They make us perceive ourselves differently. So we need to work hard today to consider how our thoughts and our conduct are related to each other. Together they form perceptions. All of this changes our way of thinking. Because if we can change our way of thinking, then we can change how we act." He underlined the word "PERCEPTION" for effect.

Driving this psychologist's discourse was a clear idea of progress. Never did he mention a miracle, nor did he celebrate the virtues of waiting. His tone proved impatient for a change that could only be achieved through a plodding kind of labor.

"Your body," he almost yelled, "produces symptoms. These symptoms emerge when you start using drugs and when you start drinking alcohol. When you start to consume, you start to have symptoms. And before you start to consume, you have symptoms. You consume because of these symptoms." He peppered the crowd with questions.

"What are your symptoms before you start using?" he asked a young man.

The captive had no idea how to answer. He stared at the psychologist, and then smiled and tried to form an answer, but nothing came out.

"How do you feel before you start consuming?" the psychologist clarified, dropping the medical language for a moment.

"Terrible," the young man offered.

"We need to work on understanding how we think and how we feel," the psychologist declared. "We need to get to know ourselves. We need to start looking for symptoms before we start consuming drugs or alcohol." The novelty of this approach piqued everyone's interest, with even Tomás and Bautista leaning toward him curiously. I too was taken aback by the approach. It seemed to mark such a bright departure from all the other pastors who preached about the virtues of a positive attitude. And yet at the same time it seemed very similar to theological therapy, down to its very performance. I tried to dismiss the feeling as a professional hazard, as the result of an overactive anthropological instinct toward two realms of thought with much in common. Behavioral psychology has a recognizable and well-documented genealogy that courses through the history of North American Protestantism and was eventually exported to every corner of the world by missionaries and nongovernmental organizations. To know thyself is an imperative as psychological as it is Christian.[14]

"How many people have been inside this center before?" the psychologist asked the group. "How many? Show me your hands." More than half the captives raised their hands. "And how many have been inside a different center than this one?" He again asked to see a show of hands, with all but a dozen people responding. The psychologist gasped to feign surprise. "Do you know why you keep coming back? Do you know why you keep returning and returning and returning?" I saw Santiago look out from under his hood. "You keep coming back here because you do not know yourself. You do not know your temperament. You do not know your perceptions. And you do not know your symptoms." He ticked each of these observations off the tips of his fingers. "Do you hear me?" he asked. "You do not know your symptoms." He pounded his palm against the wall: "Change your thoughts and you will change your actions; change your actions and you will change your life. I promise you, but you need to first change the way that you think." He kept slapping the wall to hold the men's attention.

The psychologist suggested that the minds of these men were labora-tories. "Take marijuana," he said. "What you want is the highest concentra-tion of THC to get high, right? THC stands for tetrahydrocannabinol." He repeated the word three times, as if it held some kind of magical power. He even went so far as to dissect the word by syllables, and then wrote it on the wall with his marker. Tomás practiced saying it to himself.

The psychologist then drew circles signifying molecules. "The mol-ecules of THC carry the effects to your brain through your neurons." He connected the circles with straight lines, forming the vague contours of chemical compounds. "You smoke the marijuana and then the chemical inside the seed changes the way that your brain works. This means that it changes the way that you think and the way that you act. It determines your conduct and produces symptoms in your body."

And then, something happened that made the entire intervention feel like an elaborate trap. The session suddenly turned toward more familiar terrain. Without warning, the psychologist pulled a Bible from his bag and began to flip through its pages. With "tetrahydrocannabinol" written on the wall behind him near an assortment of chemical compounds mapped out with a black marker, he called out both chapter and verse: Matthew 13:13. He then began to read: "Though seeing, they do not see; though hearing, they do not hear or understand."

I first thought that he was using scripture as a bridge, a kind of rhe-torical device, to advance another insight. Maybe he was using the Bible as a kind of vernacular to articulate his earlier comments about molecules and neurons? But he was not. He instead angled his entire talk, more than thirty minutes of scientific explanation, into a Christian parable about the authority of God.

"It is your responsibility," he said, "to know the authority of God. It is your personal responsibility to hold yourself accountable to God." He was now in lockstep with theological therapy. His apparent departure gave way to an uncanny return. Even his earlier commitment to thoughts and action suddenly aligned with a previous sermon by another pastor on having a positive attitude. "The reason you keep coming back to this place," he said, "is because you do not truly understand that God has authority over your life." His style of presentation took on the rhythm of a sermon. "The door is open," he said. "The door is really open and we are telling you to go, to get out of here, and to never come back, but you do not understand. You will not be able to leave until you change your understanding of yourself. You need to understand that God has complete authority over your life."

The psychologist checked his watch, noticed his hour was almost up, and started to career toward a conclusion. He softened his voice, out of either exhaustion or empathy. "The point," he said, "is for you to change, but you need to know yourself so that you do not return to using drugs. You think that drugs have power over you, but it is God that has power over you." He made eye contact with a few of the men as he spoke, approximating the kind of intimacy that pastors try to create. "You know what happens," he concluded, "when you don't realize that God has power over you? You look to change yourself, but you keep coming back here. And then you look to change yourself again, but you keep coming back here. You know what happens? You never leave this place."

It was a haunting conclusion for a population that often struggled to imagine a life outside of the center. And so I followed the psychologist down the stairs, past Pedro, and out of the center after Bautista unlocked the doors for us. I needed to talk to him about the relationship between his understanding of psychology and Christianity. It was absolutely unclear how he related one to the other—until we reached his van. It was parked in front of Pedro's center, quietly nestled under a tree. Oversized and without any rear windows, the van was painted with camouflage splotches of green, black, and brown. Huge black letters lined both sides of the vehicle, announcing: "Warrior for Christ."[15]

"What are we going to do?" the psychologist asked me as we stood next to it. "How are we going to defeat the devil in this great war for Christ?" I did not have an answer, but this exchange confirmed for me that even the most earnest efforts to disrupt the hegemony of theological therapy often returned to the familiar tropes of sin and salvation.

How come this psychologist was a pastor? I later asked an administrator at SECCATID.

"The only psychological training in this country, at least the only kind that we can afford, is ministerial counseling," she said.

I meditated on that moment as Alejandro entered the hotel. As he went on about how excited he was to fall asleep on a bed rather than the floor, I worried that theological therapy would not let him go. One small misstep might send him into a spiral about his inability to live a good Christian life. I was also worried that being a repeated target of predatory pastoralism had not only left him with few practical skills to manage his desires but had also made him understand himself as an object of Pentecostal intervention. Alejandro had escaped the center, with my help, but could he escape a cycle that always seemed to return him to a center?

TWENTY-FOUR

I met Alejandro the next morning, in front of the hotel, and he was drunk. I was so uncomfortable with this outcome, so ashamed that I had subscribed to the belief that Alejandro could power through his addictions in a mere instant, that I pretended as if he were sober, even though he did a better job of acting the part than I did believing it. I remember asking how his night went and Alejandro reported that he had gone to sleep early. The conversation turned awkward as we both found ourselves scrambling to act like nothing was wrong, that we had not fumbled Alejandro's first night out of the center. So we kept talking about absolutely nothing until we hailed a taxi to take us to the offices of RENAP, Guatemala's National Registry of Persons, where he was going to reapply for a national identification card.

"The Bible says," Alejandro had told me a few weeks earlier, "that people who believe in the word of God but aren't sincere with their thoughts and actions get twice the punishment from God than the guy who drinks." He was making a case for his own sincerity and the ability to live his life on his own terms. "Because they know the word of God," he said, "they know what they're doing. So someone might believe the word of God, but his intentions are for self-pleasure." This biblical logic had somehow caught me as well. Backed by Alejandro's confidence, the Christian coordinates of right and wrong resonated inside the center, often bouncing beautifully against those four walls. But now, outside in the open air, that logic seemed to float away with no sign that it would ever return.

Confusion mounted as we arrived at RENAP, an anonymous government office tucked in the basement of a middle-class shopping center. We took our place in line to enter the building, where we would sign forms, take pictures, and submit fingerprints, even complete a brief interview. And Alejandro was thoroughly intoxicated.[16]

Freshly showered and very high functioning, he did not immediately stand out from the crowd. The dead giveaway was his scent—he smelled of alcohol, which caused several people to turn their heads and furrow their brows. Gesticulating in ways that he never did while sober, Alejandro's booming voice also made clear his inability to appropriately project in an office setting. The contrast between him and everyone else in line recalled Pedro's sermons on bodily comportment. Pedro's entire enterprise relied on documenting such failings in the starkest of terms. His office was covered with evidence to this effect: a photograph of a user who had been on the streets for months would be placed next to a photograph of that same person after time in the center, having showered, gotten a fresh haircut, and been dressed in a clean shirt.[17]

While Alejandro's comportment inside the center was often impeccable—he almost always outperformed his fellow captives, down to his knowledge of scripture and verse—behaving correctly in the RENAP office proved an entirely different task. Amid a sea of middle-class individuals, Alejandro flailed while trying to send the right signals. In an effort to establish a little comradery with those in line, he huffed at the long wait, in the end just encroaching on people's personal space. He then tried to draw on his own cultural capital of having lived in the United States, announcing in a voice slightly too loud that the government offices in the United States open earlier in the day than those in Guatemala. This too backfired, attracting another set of uncomfortable scowls in our direction.[18]

We waited for close to an hour to be seen by a clerk, and as time passed, it became patently clear just how many barriers Alejandro would have to overcome to reenter society. This is why family proves so very important— ideally, they would have shuttled Alejandro from a warm bed to a government office and stood with him as he negotiated middle-class socialities organized around muted notions of respectability. Eventually, they would have directed Alejandro toward self-sustaining lines of work. Never had Pentecostal drug rehabilitation centers appeared so thin, so narrow in scope, as when I stood in line with Alejandro. All I could do was point him in the right direction, which at that moment meant moving him through a series of bureaucratic conversations. This included submitting the requisite information for a new birth certificate.

Alejandro finally arrived at the front of the line and approached a woman sitting at a desk. She had positioned her computer in such a way so that we could all see the screen. She asked Alejandro to press his hands against a sensor that would collect his fingerprints. Still drunk, Alejandro was playful with the clerk. When she asked for his digits, he offered his thumbs, and showed his thumbs when she requested his digits. I couldn't tell whether he was horsing around or just plain confused. The woman, however, had no reaction, obviously not wanting to participate in Alejandro's games. I nervously stepped in, engaging Alejandro in conversation in an effort to distract him. All the while his fingerprints generated a screen full of information, collected when he had been repatriated seven years earlier.

Much of the data was similar to the information that rehabilitation centers gathered: name, date of birth, education level, and so on. Also archived was a signature from Alejandro, squiggly lines authenticating that he was really who he said he was.

The most stunning thing, however, was a government-generated photograph taken moments after Alejandro's repatriation. Having spent some of his life in the United States, bouncing between the streets and prison, Alejandro usually carried himself in Guatemala like a big man. He had a bluster to him, a confidence that suggested he knew how to handle himself. His frame also suggested that he might have carried some weight at one time, yet the man standing before me was skeletal. The reason was clear. In one of our earliest conversations, held at a different center at least five years before we sat inside that government office, Alejandro explained in detail the punishment that the center doled out to its men. It ended up being the same kind that Pedro delivered to his captives.[19]

"When people don't sit inside the center and be somber," he said, "it's a problem. When a parent wants his children to behave, the parent's going to take a belt to them and beat them. Well, they can't take a belt to us all the time, but they can take away the little privileges that we have. Like they tell everybody in the morning to bathe and whoever doesn't bathe doesn't get breakfast." I remember Alejandro looking upset. "How cruel is that?" he asked. "We eat dinner at six o'clock. We don't eat breakfast until eight, sometimes nine o'clock in the morning, and if you don't eat breakfast, you've got to wait until two o'clock to eat lunch. That's almost twenty-four hours without eating. And what? No protein? Just that soup and those tortillas? That's why everyone looks like a zombie."

The repatriation photograph before us did not depict a zombie. Alejandro's face was full, even round, with a broad mouth and strong cheekbones. He had a goatee, which helped fill out his face, as well as broad shoulders that covered the entire frame of the photograph. He looked strong. He explained that life inside a US prison helped him beef up. He had been eating three sizable meals a day and lifting weights. The solidity of this image became starker when he posed for his updated photograph. He stood in front of a white backdrop, his shabby T-shirt pulled to one side and his glassy eyes fighting to maintain some kind of focus for the camera.

This second photograph, taken seven years after the original, depicts a man fifty pounds lighter, with a face riveted with wrinkles. In that span of time, Alejandro had seemed to age twenty years, his shoulders in no way filling out the frame of this photograph. It was a violent contrast. The life that Alejandro had lived over the last seven years had robbed him of his youth and dignity. His body had suffered, for sure, but so too had his soul.

In fact, the distance between the "before" and the "after" of these photos did not instill confidence in centers so much as invoke images from a work camp, of prisoners with sunken faces and unresponsive eyes.[20]

In some effort at a thought experiment, I stood in the RENAP office and held printouts of each of these photographs in my hands. The recently repatriated Alejandro gave way to the zombified ex-captive. It was heartbreaking to look at. And so I rearranged the images, essentially pretending that the narrow-shouldered, glassy-eyed man had become a broadshouldered survivor. But this wasn't true. More tragically, when we exited the office with a new birth certificate and government identification card in tow, it became clear that Alejandro was now largely on his own.

Alejandro later told me he had spent the previous night at the market. He went to look for work, he said, but then he saw some people he knew. They got to talking and to drinking. "But I left before they started smoking crack," he insisted. Alejandro did not have the money to smoke, and he said that he did not want to go into debt so soon after his release. It's also very possible that these people did not trust Alejandro to pay them back. Having just left a center, they might have sensed that he seemed destined to return to one.

TWENTY-FIVE

On our way back to the hotel, which was just blocks from the market where Alejandro wanted to work, we ran into a set of his acquaintances. Alejandro presented his take on his situation. Yet instead of receiving sympathetic suggestions about what to do next, his friends began to lecture him about his life choices.[21]

"Look," one said, "you need to think about it. Why can't you just think about your choices?" He looked at Alejandro, discerning that he had been drinking. "Yesterday you leave the center and then hours later you're doing the same shit?" His friend seemed fed up. "You don't have a future doing this shit," he said. "Your only future is going back to that center! And when you're back in that center, reading that fucking Bible, you'll be back in the same place, thinking about what is good and what is bad." Alejandro's friend spoke from years of experience inside similar centers. "But right now you're free," he reminded Alejandro. "You have a chance to move forward, but you're doing the same old shit."

By now Alejandro had sobered up, and the midday sun had made him parched and short-tempered. Alejandro dug in: "I'm going to throw two verses at you right now." The two men squared up. "Matthew 18," Alejandro announced. "Peter came to Jesus and asked, 'Lord, how many times shall I forgive my brother or sister who sins against me? Up to seven times?' And Jesus said, 'I tell you, not seven times, but seventy-seven times.'" Alejandro was impressed with his ability to cite the verse word for word, but then he began to fumble. "I can't remember the other one," he admitted, "but it's about Jesus's mercy and about my own ability to make my own decisions." Alejandro was adamant about this last part. "That's why God sent his only son down from heaven to be killed," he said. "So that I can make my own decisions, so that I can decide between right and wrong. And even if I fuck up, Jesus Christ is full of love and forgiveness. He is full of mercy. He will forgive me seventy-seven more times. If I sin today, he will forgive me tomorrow."

As traffic squeezed past us in the busy street market, Alejandro's friend stood firm. "Look," he said, "you know all of this but you don't do any of it. You know the Bible but you aren't living the Bible. Clearly you know the shit but you can't do the shit." This assertion pleased the small crowd that had begun to form around the exchange, and giggles quickly became chortles. "And the only stuff that is really good," the friend said, "is the stuff that we can do all the time. And you aren't living like a Christian all the time."

While seeming to buck the Bible, Alejandro would also return to it as a proof text. "But like I told you," he said, "this is my life. No one else gets to tell me what to do. I get to choose the kind of life I want to live." This message always made an impact on me, but it failed to compel Alejandro's friend, who shook it off as totally false.

"I'll show you where it says that in the Bible," Alejandro added, "I'll show you where the Bible says it. We can read it in the Bible, if you like." But his friend wanted nothing to do with the Bible. He only wanted Alejandro to know that he needed to start living a better life.

"But this is my life," Alejandro said again. "This is my life. Christ came for people like me. And he died on that cross for people like me." He had now stumbled into a new line of biblical reasoning. "Listen," he said, growing fatigued. "I could throw Bible verses at you all day but I don't want to do that. I just want you to know that Jesus will forgive me. That I will be with Jesus in paradise someday. It's just that I don't have it in my heart right now to be better. I don't have it in my heart. I pray every day but for what? To be some false prophet?" He paused. "I can't do that," he said. "I don't want to be a false prophet. I could go on that corner with my Bible and announce the saving glory of Jesus Christ, but why? I don't want to do that. I can't go do that. Because my heart is rotten. Look, man, my heart is black. My heart has turned black and that's why I am the way that I am."

As Alejandro continued to fight with his friend over scripture, an acquaintance I knew in the crowd pulled me aside to ask about Alejandro's next steps. I said that he was looking for work. Unconvinced, he suggested that I bring Alejandro back to the hotel, and that I pay the doorman a little extra to keep Alejandro inside his room all night.

I asked how he would do that.

"Does the guy have a gun?" he asked.

I said that he did.

"Then just have him hold Alejandro inside the room all night," he reasoned.

Or else he'll shoot Alejandro? I said, baffled by the plan.

"Yeah," he said. "People pay for that kind of service all the time." The man assured me that this approach was Alejandro's only bet, which sent me reeling. Had Alejandro left captivity in the center only to be held at gunpoint in a hotel? I could not and did not do this to Alejandro. We started walking back to the hotel with the intention of a fresh start the next morning.

TWENTY-SIX

On the way back to the hotel, we walked past open-air drug markets. Men loitered about, selling crack and killing time. It had become an increasingly familiar scene in Guatemala City. While incarceration rates for drugs escalated in the United States across the 1980s and 1990s, forcing drug markets underground—or at least inside apartment blocks and store fronts—Guatemala's National Police rarely patrol the streets with an eye toward the purchase or distribution of drugs. While Guatemala's prison system stood at roughly over 250 percent capacity when Alejandro left Pedro's center, far less than one percent of its prisoners had been convicted on drug charges. The prison system's official statics do not even list drugs as a significant factor for incarceration. There is no cat and mouse game between users and the police.[22]

Instead of National Police patrolling the streets, pastors walk the beat, often leaving in their wake sheets of paper known as evangelical tracts. These are small pamphlets that were produced as persuasive religious literature after the advent of the printing press and were deployed throughout the Protestant Reformation.[23] They have survived into the digital age because of their relative durability and because they provide a trace of evangelical intention, a sign that a pastor or a missionary passed through at one time or another. They can be tucked into pockets, folded into Bibles, and traded among friends. While I have seen men use these tracts to roll joints or wipe themselves, they do provide a glimmer of hope in atmospheres that otherwise often feel like dead ends.

Authored for the functionally literate and designed to attract attention, these pamphlets tell stories of predation, captivity, and escape. They also foreshadow return. The tracts self-consciously set their sights on wayward souls with the intention of dragging them back home.[24] "God is looking for you," threatens one of the most common tracts to appear in the drug markets. It depicts a lonely sinner wandering through a busy city, within a crowd but absolutely alone. It advances its message with a series of simple sentences: "God is looking for you even in the deepest moments of your rebellion. Many times He has called out to you: in moments of anguish, perhaps at the foot of a tomb or during a sleepless night, but you have failed to hear Him because you are running away from Him." The predatory dialectic then grows stronger: "God is looking for you! Stop running away!" The message evokes the very anomie that Alejandro experienced after leaving Pedro's center. "I'm just completely alone," Alejandro had told me earlier that day.

Other tracts depict this chase in more apocalyptic terms. "Escape for your life," pleads another, drawing on the visual aesthetics of mid-twentieth-century horror films. The image is cartoonish in its depiction of crisis, with young teenagers fleeing the scene of an accident or attack. It is difficult to tell what happened, but a car has been turned on its side and is in flames. A wide-eyed young woman screaming for help runs away from the scene. "The angels say you cannot stay in the city of sin," the tract reads. "You need to escape to the mountain." The biblical idea of seeking higher ground is one that haunted Alejandro. "You cannot continue being the person that you are," the tract insists, "passing one day after another, waiting until it is too late for you, until it is too late for all of eternity." The time to act is now. "Escape to the mountain to save yourself!"

Rather than escaping, Alejandro understood himself to be running away—from the center but also from his sins. He was constantly on the run. The most pernicious part of the centers had always been their ability to ensnare a user's body and soul, to have a man struggle against the physical confines of a space only to then have him realize that he was enslaved by sin itself. Alejandro was caught both physically and affectively. He had been trapped by barred windows and locked doors and by the nagging sensation that he was letting down both God and himself.[25]

"Are you free?" asks another tract. With an image of hands cuffed, the flyer warned that freedom is "the great illusion of man." The tract even mocks individual freedom: "I do what I want, when I want, as I want, and where I want." Was this not the logic that Alejandro advanced to me and that I, in Alejandro's name, advanced to lawyers, police officers, and judges? The tract rendered juvenile the principle of liberal democratic justice, interpreting individual freedom as a mode of personal slavery: "I act out of fear or arrogance. I do not have control over myself; I frequent places that are harmful to me. I do all of this against my own free will. I am so bad to myself." So much of this mirrored Alejandro's internal dialogue.

The tracts reminded Alejandro about the difficult tension that exists between freedom and slavery within the Christian tradition—that freedom from slavery can also mean slavery to freedom. This dynamic often emerged inside Pedro's center, as Pedro preached about how everyone must submit to Christ. A sinner may be free but nonetheless a slave to sin. True freedom, he would intone, happens when sinners such as Alejandro become slaves to Christ. The tracts celebrate the virtues of spiritual slavery: "Receive Jesus into your life right now as your personal savior!"

In this spirit, Alejandro was certain that his appetites were more restrictive than Pedro's straitjacket. "Put me in the jacket," he once told me while inside the center. "I don't care about being inside of the jacket. It's the sin that I can't get out of. It's the sin that has me tied up." The blame always landed in Alejandro's lap, his apparent failures serving as evidence that he needed to be inside a center rather than on the streets. By mobilizing his guilt in this way, the entire industry set Alejandro up to fail, or at least return to a center. The pamphlets provided a subtle drumbeat for drug users in the city's markets.

A single image appears on all these tracts, and this image also hangs inside every Pentecostal center, Pedro's included. Thomas Blackshear's *The Forgiven* is a Christian classic, an internationally recognized work by a contemporary African American evangelical artist whose diverse oeuvre includes black heritage portraits and classic movie monsters. The painting depicts a young man in jeans and a purple T-shirt collapsed into Jesus's arms. Completely unconscious with legs buckled, the young man's head slumps to one side. With his back pressed tightly against his savior's chest, Jesus hoists him upright by wrapping one arm around his waist and another under his shoulder. Jesus's slightly oversized hands bear the signs of the crucifixion, with puncture wounds marking his flesh. A small rivulet of blood trickles from underneath his feet toward two patches of Easter lilies. Brought to life by Christ's blood, the flowers signal his resurrection.

The Forgiven is a deeply ambiguous image. Its portrayal of Jesus strongly diverges from other evangelical depictions of Christ, which present him amid sheep, children, and clouds. Jesus is often seen treading lightly in ways that emphasize his ethereal combination of humanity and divinity. Going against this, Blackshear's image presents an intensely physical scenario, a complicated mix of Good Friday and Easter Sunday.

The story that Blackshear advances here is as compassionate as it is brutal. The young man has been caught at his most vulnerable. Yet he is not the victim—with a mallet in one hand and a railroad spike in the other, the unconscious man is apparently the one who nailed Jesus to the cross. We are led to believe that this young man held Jesus down and drove nails into his hands and his feet, that he plunged a spear into Jesus's side. But following the resurrection, Jesus embraces the sinner in front of an audience of Easter lilies. It is a powerfully redemptive scene, to which these centers obviously aspire, but one that's also messy, with streaks of blood on the ground and the sinner's eyes rolled back in his head. The more one stares at this image, the more unsettling it becomes. While at first glance it looks as if this young man has collapsed into Christ's arms, it could also be the case that Jesus is taking him away. This could be a rescue, but it could also very well be a kidnapping.

"God didn't come for the righteous or the saints," Pedro once told me. "Jesus came for the unclean." The idea that Jesus came to Guatemala City in search of certain people—to either catch them as they fall or to pick them up off the floor—framed the way Pedro and his clients saw this image. The Forgiven is as predatory as it is pastoral. It is a moment of empathy presented in the form of an abduction.[26]

Pedro adored Blackshear's image and had Roberto paint it on a wall inside his center. But instead of the young man dressed in jeans and a purple T-shirt, the mural portrayed Pedro himself as having fallen into the forgiving arms of Jesus Christ. "The real testimony," Pedro explained, "is about how God intervened in my life. It's about the role that a drug and alcohol rehabilitation center played in my life." Pedro took some additional artistic license with the mural. Rather than a mallet and a spike in either hand,

Pedro holds a pistol and joint. Both, he insisted, played a role in Christ's crucifixion.

Outside of the center, this image was pasted onto pieces of paper in the hopes that sinners would find them at their moments of need.

People tend to engage with these tracts when they are in the middle of a crisis, when a user is at his lowest. "Escape because of your eternal life. Escape to secure your place with the Lord Jesus who washes away your sins and mine." The verticality of this morality, with Christ on the mountain and the sinner in the pits of hell, resonated with Alejandro. "Those [tracts] are everywhere you go," Alejandro once told me. "They follow me everywhere." Only hours after having walked out of Pedro's front door, he spotted the papers out of the corner of his eye. He did not pick any up, because he didn't need to. He had already read them. "Yeah, I saw those [tracts] in the market," he told me. "They just reminded me about God. That's all they did. They just reminded me about God." I later discovered that he left his hotel and went back to the market roughly an hour after we left his friend on the street and said goodbye. That night, Alejandro found himself walking the streets and the drug markets of Guatemala City, scrambling for some sense of liberation.

But none came.

TWENTY-SEVEN

Alejandro left the hotel before I arrived in the morning.

The young man behind the desk, the one with the gun on his hip, informed me that Alejandro checked out of his room at 6:00 a.m., exactly three hours before we were scheduled to meet. Was this the end of it all? I was tempted to take this as Alejandro's silent exit from our relationship. He had always been clear that he wanted to have complete control over his life, to answer to no one, and his departure seemed to be a rather straightforward sign that he wanted a clean break. How many times had I heard Alejandro rail against the pastor, or ask that singularly haunting question: Why does the pastor care about my life? And how many times did I recoil at the pastoral ideal that Alejandro's life was not entirely his own, that God, the devil, and Alejandro himself competed for control over his body and soul? The pastor, rejecting Satan and serving God, took it upon himself to control Alejandro, which chafed against my own concerns about individual rights. Alejandro's disappearance suggested that he was done with not only the pastor but also with me.

Where did he go? I asked the man at the hotel.

"He didn't say," he answered.

I stood in front of the hotel completely dumbfounded by my failure to accurately discern Alejandro's sincerity. I grappled with feelings of foolishness for having been part of his escape. I had known Alejandro for years, and I thought I understood his tendencies. I had total faith in his ability to turn it all around. But those assessments proved false.

I left the hotel to try to find him. I had no specific ideas about where he might be, but Alejandro was a creature of habit. He often returned to the same neighborhood. This is one of the reasons why he wanted to find work in that particular market. Seamlessly transitioning from captivity to freedom in a familiar space was a fantasy that appealed to him. While the city seemed to stretch out onto the horizon, Alejandro had most likely limited himself to a half dozen city blocks.

I began, as the pastor always would on his hunts, in the middle. I started in the center of the market and explored the terrain in outwardly expanding circles, making sure not to retread already studied ground. I looked under tables, behind stalls, and inside of stores. I asked workers if they had seen Alejandro. I told them to call me if they did, giving these newly acquired informants my phone number. The chances of spotting Alejandro outright seemed unlikely, but there was the possibility of stumbling upon a fresh set of tracks.

Carrying out this hunt shifted my perspective entirely, occasioning me to engage with the city as if for the first time. My head sat on a swivel. I read the city streets differently, taking notes about what I saw. "Not under the tables," I jotted down after searching some stands at the market. "Not at either bar," I added after scouring two popular drinking spots. I also mapped the neighborhood in my mind. It was exhilarating and dispiriting, as the prospects of spotting Alejandro decreased with every moment.

After spending a full morning circling only a few city blocks, I eventually found Alejandro on a street corner. He looked absolutely defeated. Freshly showered and well rested, he was still very drunk. I sat down next to him and he barely nodded to acknowledge my presence. I asked him if he was all right.

"God knows all about my life," he said. He then looked away and raised his hand in my general direction. "Look," he said, "I want to thank you for everything that you've done for me, but I'm worse than what I told you. I haven't been sincere with you."

I told him that I did not care, that I just wanted to know that he was well.

"I mean, what am I supposed to do?" he exclaimed. "What am I supposed to do?" It was the most important question and one without any obvious answer. Alejandro knew, by way of his Christianity, that he struggled toward something that he could never achieve on his own: redemption. And my support had unintentionally facilitated his relapse. While it had offered Alejandro the freedom he so deeply desired, I had failed to provide him with any of the skills necessary for living on the streets. In this sense, both the pastor and I were at fault for offering simple answers to the exceedingly difficult problem of addiction. When it came to Alejandro's situation, both captivity and freedom ironically represented two failing alternatives.

As we sat on the street corner, Alejandro told me that he was absolutely convinced his aunt would come to help him. He explained that they had made arrangements and he was now waiting for her to pick him up. "My aunt is going to bring me back to her house," he clarified. "She lives in an enclave, with security guards. It's real strict. They don't let people in or out without permission." Alejandro developed the story with some poetic license. "Those guards are *kaibiles*," he said. Kaibiles are members of the Guatemalan military; they are agents of the army's jungle commando crew who became infamous during the civil war. Guatemalans often use the word as slang to denote people who are murderous, disciplined, cold blooded, and brutal.

"The entire enclave has been militarized," he said, "and my aunt is going to pay the guards to keep me there. They won't let me out unless my aunt tells them that it's ok." Alejandro continued to fill out what was clearly a fantasy: "And in the enclave there is nothing to do. I'll just walk around and watch television. I'll make myself food to eat. But I won't be able to drink or smoke crack because all of that shit is outside of the enclave."

I asked him when his aunt was going to arrive. "She said she would come," he said, glossing over any specifics about time. "Four kaibiles are going to come with her in a big pick-up truck and take me back to the enclave."

As he spoke, it became clear how limited his horizon of possibility had become. Alejandro knew he was in trouble, but he could only imagine a more spacious version of the pastor's center. Rather than a barred house, he wanted a compound. Instead of Tomás and Bautista, he wanted kaibiles.

I stopped Alejandro to tell him that Pedro probably knew that he was drinking. Although unstated at the time of his release, it was implied that my payment only released Alejandro from the center at that time. The amount I

had paid was too small to fend off a future hunt. And I wasn't even sure that
a much larger amount would keep Pedro off his tracks for good. In a sense,
I had not paid for Alejandro's release so much as his indefinite probation.

My speculation sent Alejandro into a panic. "Who told you that?" he
asked.

Absolutely no one, I said, but it was a logical assumption. Alejandro
had been drinking and smoking with the very people that the pastor hunted,
in the very neighborhood in which the pastor hunted. How long would it
be before Pedro learned that Alejandro was back on the streets? It had been
less than forty-eight hours since Alejandro had left the center, and I was
certain that the pastor knew about Alejandro's whereabouts.

"No," Alejandro concluded. "They aren't going to come looking for
me. They're scared because I got these." He looked down at his arms, which
had once been able to intimidate almost anyone. Many times in the past I
had seen him wrap men up and pull them into the center. But now, as he
slumped over, depleted from alcohol, he seemed worn. His arms looked
gray and spindly.

"If he comes looking for me—" he puffed up "—he'll have to bring six
guys. That's how many it will take. I'll grab that tree right there and I won't
let go." He pointed to a lone tree that poked out from the sidewalk. We both
knew that such efforts never worked. Alejandro had years of experience
peeling fingers from trees, lampposts, and door frames. He would rabbit
punch the target in the stomach, forcing him to contract and release his
chosen anchor. It was an easy move, and we both knew that the pastor could
have any of his huntsmen do it.

"But the pastor loves me," Alejandro finally said.

He was right. Pedro did deeply care for Alejandro. It was obvious that
Pedro appreciated Alejandro's personality as much as his labor and was offended by Alejandro's desire to escape the center. These kinds of attachments and subsequent offenses were precisely what fueled the pastoral cycle
of capture and release, with every failure in the street justifying yet another
hunt. Before he set Alejandro free, Pedro had worried about Alejandro falling right back into his old ways.

"I just don't think he can do it," Pedro had warned me as he counted
my money. "He doesn't know anybody out there except for sinners. He
hasn't found a church. He hasn't found a new community."

I reminded him about the work that waited for Alejandro.

"That work will kill him," Pedro said. "When he has money, he can't
stop himself from drinking and smoking."

But he deserves a chance, I insisted.

"A chance at what?" Pedro asked.

I answered—freedom.

Pedro rolled his eyes.

Back on the corner, Alejandro and I continued to wait for his aunt. "How'd you find me?" he demanded.

It wasn't that hard, I answered. You're just sitting on the corner. It was kind of obvious.

Alejandro laughed a little, but he then shifted the conversation to his failed ambitions. "Everything I promised went to shit," he said. "Yesterday, when we were getting the identification card, I was making all these promises to work and to find a job. But look at me right now." He struggled for answers, shrinking his social circle to the limits of his body.

"Look," he said, "I'm in this alone. You've been helpful. Really, I thank you, but I'm in this alone. I need to do this myself. And if I fall, if I fall twenty more times, then it's my fault. It's my sin." Alejandro looked up, only to add in a dark, oddly optimistic tone: "In two weeks, I'll be in an apartment. I'll be working for a restaurant, making money and living well. And I'll call you just to tell you how good I'm doing. Just to tell you that I'm free, that I escaped my Egypt, just like the Jews." His eyes turned defiant, as if wanting to prove me wrong. "I'll call you just to show you how well I'm doing." He wanted me to understand. "You know why I'll do that?" he asked. "To show you how much God loves me. To show you that I might have fallen but that God got me back up on my feet."

I asked Alejandro what the next step was. "I have to wait here. My aunt told me that I have to wait here."

On this corner? I asked.

"Yeah, right here." I then handed Alejandro a card with my contact information.

"What did you tell that hotel guy?" he asked.

Nothing, I said. I didn't tell him anything because there was nothing to tell him. The front desk clerk turned out to be completely unhelpful, only telling me the direction Alejandro had walked out of the hotel. It was obvious, however, that Alejandro could feel Pedro on his back. As he grew increasingly paranoid, he began speaking in hypotheticals.

"If I don't see you . . ." Alejandro started to say.

I cut him off. I'm going to see you, I said.

"But, look, I know what's going to happen. My aunt's going to come in the truck, with the four guys, and they're going to bring me back to her enclave."

You don't think they'll bring you to another center? I asked.

"No, they're not. They're going to kick my ass first," he said. "But, you know what? She's the only one who can take care of me. And I need it. I need it more than you think."

I asked if he meant his aunt's care or getting his ass kicked. Alejandro said both.

With that, I said goodbye to Alejandro, leaving him on a random street corner in Guatemala City. I knew, just as he did, that the pastor had already started his hunt. After only forty-eight hours outside of the center, word had indeed reached Pedro, and Pedro's love for Alejandro made him a target of pastoral affection.

TWENTY-EIGHT

Yet Pedro did not end up catching Alejandro. Christ did. I eventually learned that Alejandro had sat on that street corner all day and through much of the night. At some point, he sobered up, grew restless, and then hungry. At about the time his restlessness morphed into hunger, a local church group approached him. They routinely spent the early evenings ministering to men and women from their neighborhood who, like Alejandro, found themselves on the streets. They were the ones who distributed the tracts.

I later spoke to the young man who first approached Alejandro. Gerardo was twenty-something and earnest, with a tightly cropped haircut and smart glasses. He mentioned that when he approached Alejandro he looked lost in thought, either unwilling or unable to move from that corner. Gerardo spoke to Alejandro about the Bible and, to Gerardo's surprise, Alejandro shot back Bible verses of his own, providing a counterinterpretation to each of Gerardo's efforts. This banter went on for a few minutes, Gerardo explained, until other churchgoers joined. With the street corner suddenly transforming into a kind of makeshift revival, Alejandro found himself swept away by the effervescence of it all, ostensibly called to join the congregants at their nearby church for a meal and more Bible study. Maybe for the faith but most certainly for the food, Alejandro followed along. Gerardo considered it a victory over Satan.

"When we can be a vessel for Christ," he told me, "then we have found our purpose. We were meant to meet Alejandro that night. God sent him to us."

Gerardo's church is located only a few blocks from Pedro's center in a garage that has been transformed into a place of worship. It has an elevated stage, oversized speakers, and a lectern that announces: "Jesus Saves!" The entire operation was so earnest that it was difficult to question their motives. Gerardo even brushed off the idea that feeding the hungry might be a form of Christian charity. Instead, he referred back to biblical moments in which Jesus enticed crowds with food, multiplying loaves and fish in order to capture their attention. "We just want people to listen to the Word of God," Gerardo said, "and this might mean providing the hungry with a little food."

While eating and listening to the sermon, Alejandro mentioned that he had recently left Pedro's center. This piqued Gerardo's interest. Encouraged by Alejandro's vibrant knowledge of Christianity and intrigued by his experience in the center, the pastor persuaded Alejandro to deliver his testimony—to confess his life to the entire congregation. As early evening careened toward midnight, Alejandro started from the very beginning, with his life in the United States, and ended in the present, with the impossibility of his current situation. The group decided, Gerardo and his pastor remembered quite clearly, that Alejandro should return to the center. He should ask Pedro to take him back.

"We felt like he should return to his community," Gerardo said. "He should return to the place that needed him and that he needed." He paused. "The other thing," Gerardo said, was that "it was getting pretty late and we don't have the resources to have anyone stay here at the church." As the Bible group yawned past midnight, with most attendees needing to wake up the next day for work, the group suggested to Alejandro that Pedro's center was the only available option.

"It must be better than the streets," Gerardo reasoned. "And, like I said, we really don't have the capacity to have people stay here."

Gerardo walked Alejandro to Pedro's center a little after midnight. During those hours Guatemala City is a quiet and desperately dark city. Street lamps are rare and the roads are often empty. Alejandro knew his way around the neighborhood and would not have been scared by the journey itself. Yet knocking on the center's front door must have been terrifying. A few knocks would not have done the trick: he would have had to knock harder and harder to get Pedro's attention so late at night. He would have woken up most of the house with his banging.

I have witnessed many similar scenes of return. The sight is uncomfortable to watch. Its brightest manifestation comes after an escape. The user returns, some days later, of his own accord, either in search of help or to sober up. These are desperate moments, but Pedro rarely let the escapee reenter the center straightaway. He would instead make the user wait outside the front door—sometimes for days on end.

One young man stood out in my mind as an extreme example. Physically strong and with a long history of hunting, he had escaped the center. He returned days later only to be denied reentrance and so he waited outside the front door for the pastor to let him back in. The process took days. The scene was harrowing and especially so each time I crossed this poor man's path while entering the center. He would grab my arm, pull me close, and ask or beg me to take him with me—to somehow sneak him into the center. "*Antrópologo*," he would call to me, "talk to the pastor. Talk to him for me. Get me inside." It was in those moments that a parable Pedro often preached seemed perversely prescient: "Once the owner of the house gets up and locks the door," reads Luke 13:25, "you will stand outside knocking and pleading, 'Sir, open the door for us.' But he will answer, 'I don't know you or where you come from.'" The more desperate this man became the more stubborn this pastor proved, and the tighter this man would grab my arm.

Reeling from withdrawal, these men would sometimes squat in the threshold of freedom, pleading for the pastor to drag them inside—to unlock his steel door and let them in. "But the gate is narrow," Pedro would preach, referencing Luke 13:23–30, a parable that places the sinner just outside the gates of heaven. "Make every effort to enter through the narrow door," the passage pleads, "because many, I tell you, will try to enter and will not be able to."

Pedro relayed this parable in explicitly apocalyptic terms, provoking a kind of impromptu passion play that brought to life yet another Pentecostal tract. "Where will you spend eternity?" both the pastor and a mass-produced pamphlet asked. Embedded in this question is a moral imperative. On one side of the abyss is an earthly city. It is a debauched, flaming hellscape, literally pouring over the edge of a cliff. On the other side of the abyss is the City of God, with ordered streets and tree-lined green spaces. Christ's crucifixion bridges these two worlds together and enables the faithful to choose a side. Or so it seems. Upon further reflection, one can ask, Is this really a choice? Who would pick flames over freedom?

The real question, it would seem, is not whether one prefers the earthly city or the City of God but whether the center is heaven or hell in this scenario. Are the streets of Guatemala City on fire? Is the center itself up in flames? Conversely, is the capital city Christian, or does the center represent some kind of salvation? There are no clear answers to these questions, at least from Alejandro's perspective. The streets, the center, and his addictions all kept him on edge, in a near constant state of anxiety. Desperation is how Alejandro became both huntable and hunted: he was huntable because Pedro had him on the run and hunted because the pastor had Alejandro right where he wanted him. Only days after leaving, Alejandro was outside Pedro's front door, frantic to reenter, and splayed out on a cross of his own making.

TWENTY-NINE

After Pedro called me to say that Alejandro was back, I went to speak with him the very next day. We sat on the second floor of the center. Alejandro was again slumped over, his head resting in his hands.

You're back? I asked.

"Yeah," he said, "because I had nowhere to go and I didn't want them to come and get me."

What did your aunt say? I asked.

"She said, 'No. I'm not going to help you.' That's why she was making all those excuses about coming to get me. And then she got mad and said that she'd come and get me when she's ready." I had last seen Alejandro when his aunt had made just such a pronouncement. "I called her back three times," he said in despair, "and she finally said that she wasn't ready to come pick me up and that I should just see what I can do to survive."

Alejandro then told me about what happened back on that street corner. "Gerardo bought me some bread," he explained, "and he asked me what I was going to do. And everyone I ran into was like, 'We don't want to see you on the street. We don't want to see you on your own.' Everyone said that I should just go back to the center."

Alejandro told me more about the street ministry, how they plied him with soft drinks and regaled him with biblical quotes. "And so I came back and talked to the pastor," he said. "I told him that I had fallen, that I couldn't live on the streets by myself, that I needed his help." This was a monumental, if violent, moment of humility for Alejandro. "I told him all of that. I just couldn't be on the streets. I mean, what's the point of being on the streets? If I had somewhere to go, trust me, I'd go, but I don't and so I am here." Alejandro sat in the back of the room where Santiago once hid his head. He had obviously plummeted from grace. "I mean, I don't want to be here. I don't want to be here but to sleep on the streets? I don't want to sleep on the streets. There's no point to it. That's why I came to talk to him."

Although Alejandro had submitted to Pedro's will, he negotiated a few things before reentering the center. "The pastor told me before I came back inside that he would move me to another center." This, I thought, was a promising development. "It's four hours way from here," Alejandro said. "I know the pastor who runs it and I like him. The place is bigger and nicer. It has more room. Things are more relaxed. And so the next time that the pastor is going out there, he's going to take me. This new pastor will let me go to the markets and work in the kitchen. It's more relaxed than this house." Loosely connected by ministerial associations, the two centers regularly exchanged captives in the hopes of balancing out their population. When one center needed a mechanic, they might trade for a huntsman.

"It's a good place and I think that I can be there for a long time," Alejandro added. "There are beds, hot water. It's not like here. So I came back inside the center because the pastor promised to move me to another center."

And he's open to you leaving? I asked.

"He said that we'd talk in a couple of days," Alejandro explained. "I'm not going to ask him today or tomorrow. I'm going to give it a little time. But I need to get out of here. I mean, the last thing I want to be is a discipline problem. Especially since not too many people like me because I used to be the person bossing everyone around."

So have you started over? I probed. Are you now at the bottom of the system here?

Irritated, Alejandro replied, "I'm not in charge of shit now. I don't think I'll be in charge of anything here. Look, I don't want to be here."

Alejandro returned to the basic facts. "I have a lot of friends but they don't have any place to go either. And so when I leave here I'm back in that circle of people who just smoke and drink. And for what? I looked at it and did it for a few days and I was like, no, I can't do it." Alejandro was fed up. "If I had somewhere to go, somewhere to be, then it would be different. I thought my aunt was going to help me. She would have given me discipline. She would not have let me out of the enclave. But she didn't come." Alejandro's aunt even refused my phone calls. "And the therapy here isn't therapy. It's just discipline. So when I get out of here, I just go do the same shit that got me here in the first place. Look, there's no charm. There's no sentiment to this therapy. There's no sincerity. It's just us doing shit all day and that doesn't help me when I get out. I mean, Bautista was up here this morning and he was treating me like a rag doll. He was like, 'Look who's back.' He got everybody's attention and pointed at me. He was like, 'This guy used to be so important here. He used to hunt and go to the market and stuff. And now look at him. He's sitting at the back of the group with his head down.' And then everybody looked at me and I didn't say anything. I just looked at Bautista and was like, 'All right. If that's how you want to be.'"

The realities of confinement pummeled Alejandro. His sobriety and familiarity with the house kept him out of the morgue, and instead he was sent directly to the floor. "I was sleeping last night, next to all those guys, and it got hot. I was sweating with all those bodies. And I already had to do the cleaning again. I did the bathroom and the floors. I did that shit again. But you know what? I don't care. That keeps my mind occupied. I know it's the shit work but it keeps my mind occupied. Instead of just sitting around thinking about why I came back. I mean, these guys are asking me why I came back. They're all like, 'Why did you come back?' I told them the truth. I told them that they all have families. That they all have families that can help but I don't have anyone. I mean, what am I supposed to do? Sleep on the streets? So I can get shot or something? I can't do that."

Without missing a beat, as if he hadn't just recommitted himself to the center, Alejandro turned to me to say: "There's a window in the pastor's room that he sometimes keeps open. If I can just get past the first locked door, I bet I could leap out of that window."

THIRTY

Six days into captivity, Alejandro had a conversation with Pedro. "The pastor brought me into his room," Alejandro said, "and he asked me, 'What's going on?'" Pedro wanted to know why Alejandro wanted to leave so quickly and why he came back just as fast.

"I have nothing against your home," Alejandro told him. "I have nothing against you, but I need to take some time to get better. It's going to take a few months to get back on my feet, and I don't want to be on the streets." He then asked a question that pertained not only to his life but to the entire industry: "What's the point of getting out, if I'm just going to end up back inside?" Alejandro was frank with the pastor. "I don't want to be here," he said. "If you can't get me to another center, then just tell me now."

"What's wrong with my place?" Pedro prodded.

"You," Alejandro said, suddenly emboldened by having nothing else to lose. "I didn't come to this place like this," Alejandro said. "You made me mean. You put blackness in my heart. You took everything that you preach about away from me. Look, I asked you one simple question. I heard that you're taking people to the other center on Tuesday. I want to be one of them."

"You really want to go?" he asked.

"Do I have your word as a pastor that you'll take me to the other center?"

Pedro looked at him and said, "Yes."

The transfer happened that same day.

Before he left, we had one more conversation. "I don't want to hunt anymore," Alejandro told me as we sat together. He had had enough. "That part of me is over," he said. He wanted to make a clean break with predation. "I did it for years, and that's what made me so mean."

And so we made a plan. I would return to Guatemala in three months. This would give Alejandro some time to work on himself. "I'm going to take that time for reflection," he said. "To pray. To change myself. To try to build a little bit of sincerity with this new pastor." He had a goal.

The only thing that Alejandro asked of me was to get his paperwork back from Pedro. The pastor had apparently taken Alejandro's new identification cards.

"That shit is personal," he said. "I don't want him to have that stuff. I mean, why does he want stuff like that? Does it give him power or something?" We debated Pedro's motives as I handed Alejandro a bag of clothes that I had brought for him. His most coveted item was a gray hooded sweatshirt that seemed thick enough for the new center's cooler location. "Now this is what I'm talking about," Alejandro said, pulling it on.

It would be the last time I would speak with Alejandro, though not the last time I would see that sweatshirt.

HUNTED, A CONCLUSION

Like a hunted gazelle, like sheep without a shepherd, they will all return to their own people, they will flee to their native land.

—ISAIAH 13:14

Alejandro was never one to wait. I landed in Guatemala City on December 4, 2016, and traveled the next day to Xela, the country's second largest city, to visit him inside his new center. We had not been in communication for three months, which was not unusual. Pentecostal drug rehabilitation centers rarely allow phone privileges, and we had agreed that he would take three months to think through his life. Over the previous five years our contact had been sporadic, with Alejandro often floating in and out of my research, so this silence seemed inconsequential.

Before I left Guatemala City in August, Alejandro had assured me that he was going to spend his time inside the new center preparing for the future. "I'm going to take the next three months," he said, "just for reflection and to build myself up in the word of God and just calm down. And get somewhere with the [new] pastor. And when you come back we'll talk about phase two." By somewhere, he meant that he wanted to secure a certain set of privileges, such as working in the kitchen and possibly leaving the center on occasion to beg for food in the markets. And by phase two, he meant moving on to the next stage in his life, which involved another attempt at living on his own. He again imagined a series of small jobs that could lead to self-sufficiency. His new plan involved joining a church and, to remind him of the life he was trying to escape, maybe even preaching at centers on occasion. All of this made good sense to me.

Xela is a squat city, with a quaint town square and ever-expanding industrial sprawl around the periphery. Framed by green mountains and distant volcanoes, the city looks gray, with cracked streets and uneven sidewalks. Alejandro's new center sat on the outskirts at the end of an alleyway, behind a row of concrete buildings. There was no sign out front, and the center had no direct access to a main street. This three-story building, which held some sixty men, could easily have been overlooked, maybe even mistaken for an apartment building or a warehouse. To reach its front door, I had to park on a main street, snake through a series of lanes, and trudge across unpaved patches of ground. The front door of the unremarkable building was a gray slab folded into a jumbled row of gray slabs.

I had been given a shopping list ahead of time naming the supplies I was required to bring. The pastor, a congenial young man with an eye for business, made these offerings a condition for hour-long visits. They were allegedly redistributed across the population, as some captives never received visitors and others received them constantly, but there were whispers that the goods never made it to the captives. I later noticed that in the pastor's front office, alongside at least fifteen diplomas, three of which had been issued by the United States Embassy, was a sign informing guests that to visit someone, you must bring:

Salt	Clorox
Sugar	Floor cleaner
Rice	Detergent
Beans	Hand soap
Noodles	Body soap
Corn flour	Sponges

After an uneventful car ride and a trip to the grocery store, I knocked on the center's front door with my supplies and Alejandro's identification cards in tow. I was eager to see how Alejandro was doing in what immediately appeared to be a more hospitable center. The windows were fortified with bars and a heavy metal door capped the building's front entrance. Another heavy metal door separated the front office from the rest of the center, but the house was easily three times the size of Pedro's. The air even seemed lighter, if only because the entire operation sat well outside the noisy and polluted capital city. This young pastor was also less aggressive than Pedro. While he was quick to fleece visitors, his interest was in manipulating hearts and minds rather than overpowering bodies and souls. I could see why this house was an opportunity for Alejandro. In our last conversation before his transfer, Alejandro told me that he was "supposed to be rehabilitating with the word of God. Showing peace and love. I don't want to hunt anymore. I don't want that. I want peace. Calmness." All of that seemed possible here.

When the pastor opened the door, I handed over the bags and asked to speak with Alejandro.

"Haven't you read the newspaper?" he asked me.

I arrived yesterday, I said.

"Here," he mumbled, "take a look." The pastor handed me a newspaper published on December 1. The pages had already started to wilt from sitting in the sun.

The headline announced: "Unidentified Man Killed by Car" next to a full-color image that took up more than half the front page. The photograph was taken at night, moments after the accident, and the flash from the camera made the entire scene appear a bit shiny, with patches of bright light next

to stretches of darkness. The editorial team, as per custom, blurred the victim's face, but the man's body—its size and shape—were dreadfully familiar,
and so were his clothes. The man on the ground wore a gray sweatshirt very
like the one I had given to Alejandro before he left for his new center.

Have you been to the morgue? I asked the pastor with some panic.
The article said that the man had no identification on him and had been
struck by a speeding car while trying to cross a busy street late at night. The
man, whom the article identified simply as "XX," had an exceedingly high
blood-alcohol level. It also said that he appeared to be about sixty-five years
old, a comment that spoke volumes about the toll that Alejandro's time on
Guatemala's streets and in these centers had taken on him. Adding insult to
injury, the paper then turned the entire affair into a morality story, twisting
the tragedy into a grizzly reminder that pedestrians should use overpasses
when crossing busy highways. A handful of bystanders gave quotes insisting that the victim should have known better.

The pastor feigned ignorance, claiming he wasn't sure if it was Alejandro.

Then why haven't you checked? I asked, both angry at this man's callousness and disappointed in his character. The pastor explained that Alejandro had escaped the center a week earlier after earning the privilege to
collect donations at a nearby market. When Alejandro took off running, the
pastor told me that they had done their best to hunt him down but couldn't
catch him. He was too fast, and maybe too smart.

The pastor also stopped short of stating the obvious—that the center he
ran was entirely off the grid, with little to no contact with the Guatemalan
government. Identifying a body from the morgue could trigger a series of
questions that the pastor was not prepared to answer. It also seemed clear
that this young man did not have the same attachment to Alejandro that
Pedro did. While Pedro had cultivated an appreciation and obvious love for
Alejandro over the years, prompting him to hunt Alejandro down whenever
he was on the lam, this young pastor apparently had other lost sheep to seek
out and secure.

I drove to the city morgue. The newspaper article accompanying the
image stated that the body would be held for one week and that if no one
identified him, it would be slid into a mass grave known as an ossuary.
This is a deep pit where the state disposes of unidentified bodies. Imagine
corpses atop of corpses, all slowly decaying into one another. Driving to
the morgue was a liberal impulse on my part to defend Alejandro's dignity,
or, to paraphrase Michel Foucault, to provide Alejandro "a right to his own

little box for his own little personal decay."[1] Alejandro deserved far better than ending up at the bottom of a pit, and I hoped that the morgue had not expedited the burial in an effort to clear out paperwork before the holiday season.

I presented myself to the receptionist with both the newspaper article and Alejandro's identification cards in hand, and I asked to speak to the morgue's lead anthropologist. Over years of working in Guatemala, I had shadowed enough forensic anthropologists to know that my status as a professional anthropologist might garner me some privileges inside the morgue. The forensic anthropologist I met seemed grateful that I had stepped forward to identify the body. She was also relieved that I too was an anthropologist, which allowed her to speak more freely about the state of the body and to share technical details about its recovery.

Alejandro was indeed only days away from being buried in complete anonymity. With his official identification card in hand, she asked me to identify the body, a process that began with forensic photographs.

We sat huddled over a computer screen in a bleached white office as she opened the first image. It was of Alejandro's tattoo, the cartoon character on his shoulder. I winced. This was enough for me to identify him with absolute certainty and to lose any hope that the body at the morgue might not be Alejandro.

She continued with the full battery of photographs. There was one profile shot, and another showing the length of his body. The forensic anthropologist also documented each of Alejandro's wounds, including those on his skull, which had split open upon impact with the windshield. He had died instantly.

The final image, which the director suggested I give to his aunt, was a shot taken above his head and angled down toward his feet. It was a very long photograph, requisite for the process but also somewhat artistic. The image trained the viewer's gaze from the top of his forehead to the tips of his toes. Alejandro's eyes, frozen in a distant stare, looked upward toward the camera, eerily making eye contact with the viewer.

I called Alejandro's aunt, who answered on my third try, and I told her about the accident, trying to cushion the tragedy with the serendipity of my arrival and Alejandro's rescue from the ossuary. Had I pushed my trip to Xela forward by a week or scrapped it altogether, Alejandro would have disappeared, and all we would have known was the pastor's story of him escaping sometime in late November. To listen to his aunt's reaction, to hear her raw grief, was to witness someone pushed to the brink by a person she loved. I explained to her that only a family member could claim the body for burial. She began to make plans.

Alejandro had been hunted at many different levels. He had last been hunted for escaping his new center, but pastoralism had also put him on the run from himself. Autopredation had long been a part of Alejandro's interior world. The goal had always been for Alejandro to chase down his sins rather than the other way around. Even literal hunting seemed to involve a kind of metaphorical hunt for Alejandro. When I once asked him about it, he told me, "Yeah, hunting is fun and interesting because I get out of the house and stuff like that, but after a while picking people up, bringing them back to the center, knocking them around, making them clean, taking their food away, tying them up, yelling and screaming at them, twenty-four hours a day—what does that make a person?" Perhaps because of his seeming inability to break from his own patterns, Alejandro was always keen to consider big questions about personhood and self-determination.

Pentecostalism asked Alejandro to escape for his life while also demanding that he refuse his temptations, which he never could. "I've picked up too many people over the years," Alejandro admitted while still inside Pedro's center. "I just want to get some of that blackness out of my heart. I feel like the pastor mentally programmed me to be a certain kind of person." He was always hunting down his sins in an effort to be a better person, and even I never let him rest, following him until the very moment of his burial to learn as much as I could.

One lesson here may be that the imperative to make live rather than let die is not always voluntary. The shepherd often decides not simply *whether* but more importantly *how* the subject is to live. And the shepherd decides this whether the sheep likes it or not. Amid the language of individual choice and personal autonomy, Alejandro's struggle over various freedoms routinely pierced his fantasy of free will. I was reminded of when he grabbed my thumb inside of Pedro's center. Standing on the tips of my toes with my arm locked, I can still hear Alejandro explain in a cool, calm voice: "I then tell [the hunted] that 'you either walk out of here with me quietly, or I'll break your arm and drag you to the car.'"

Pentecostalism enables predation in Guatemala, and every hunt distinguishes the active technologies of tracking and capturing from the relative passivity of letting die.

But to conclude that Alejandro had either hunted or been hunted is to commit too quickly to predation's dialectic—to the idea that one is either giving chase or on the lam. Alejandro often found himself pivoting between these roles, but this bifurcation misses the more powerful, more abstract point that Alejandro often occupied both subject positions at once. Pentecostalism made this possible. It was, in fact, when Pedro pressed Alejandro to hunt his own sins by hunting down sinners that the dialectic collapsed in on itself, making it unclear who could be considered the hunted and who the hunter. For there were moments when Pedro plucked men from his general population to hunt, explaining that the privilege was a reward for their sincerity and a recognition of their ability to subdue their desires by rescuing others in need. During these moments, the lines between the pursuer and the pursued became entangled.

As Alejandro learned, the prey escapes predation's dialectic by internalizing the hunt. For being "hunted" does not only denote a social relationship between two or more people, such as a pastor and his prey; it is also a subjectivity, a sense of self that implies expansive interior worlds that press people to do things to others as well as to themselves. As a subject position, being hunted can boil down to a single scenario: To be on the run with nowhere to go.

This situation literally took place when Alejandro took flight one last time from the market. He most likely knew no one in Xela. He didn't have a dollar to his name and could never have cobbled together a plan while held captive inside a new center in an unfamiliar city. But he ran with no destination in mind. In the market he broke free without any safety net. Most likely drunk after working a few shifts in the market, he eventually stumbled into a four-lane highway. He wasn't on his way to anywhere in particular. He was just on the move.

In Pentecostal Guatemala, life has become one extended manhunt, and Christianity is not the sole cause. For reasons beyond tradition, Pentecostalism improvises a set of imperatives and practices that stand in for a criminally negligent state. One could romanticize the privatization of state services by recalling a not-so-distant past when the Guatemalan government hunted its own citizens. During the civil war (1960–1996), the state used a combination of military soldiers, intelligence agents, and police officers to disappear tens of thousands of student leaders, trade unionists, and human rights activists. They set out to quash a leftist insurgency but in the end abducted a generation of citizens.[2] Officials pulled civilians from the streets, sometimes from their beds, and dragged them into cars. They were never seen or heard from again.[3] The stories salvaged from this era are chilling, as the state compiled thick files on the most intimate aspects of victims' lives.

But today, free from the long arm of the law or its murderous intent, Pentecostal drug rehabilitation centers scour the streets for sinners—not to disappear them, per se, but rather to render them human to a society that would rather let them die. The hunt is reframed as an act of Christian love. While Pedro called his evangelical efforts hunts, he understood them as rescues.

This dynamic resonates because so many people remain stuck. Santiago, for example, would spend years inside of Pedro's center. From the moment Alejandro hunted him to the day I completed this book, Santiago had spent forty-four out of forty-eight months inside Pedro's center. His only respite came after his father died—Maria took him out of the general population to attend the funeral and offered to let him live at home, to try life one more time. Soon, he began to drink and smoke crack. Maria had him hunted again, and then seemed to forget about him.

During those three years, I often spoke with Maria and occasionally brought her to the center to speak with Santiago. Although he was a grown man approaching his thirties, Maria still held the power to decide her son's fate. As Santiago became increasingly aggressive toward Maria, Pedro used these encounters to encourage Maria to keep her son for just a few more months. Without any real ability to win his mother's confidence, Santiago eventually resorted to passing me letters. The first, from August 2017, was addressed to Maria.

> From your son Santiago:
> How I miss being close to you, Mom. The truth is that no one loves me as much as you do. But why do you keep me here for no reason. It's one thing to put me here for a month. I can even understand being here for three months. But I've been here for almost 33 months. I hope you come soon. Please come and get me out. I'm going crazy here.
> Your son, Santiago

Santiago signed the letter, inexplicably, with a pen drawing of a devil—either to further antagonize his mother or to perform the very craziness that he feared had started to take ahold of his mind.

A second letter, from that same month, was addressed to the National Police. Santiago had started the letter in blue ink and switched to pencil halfway through, showing off all the resources he had garnered to escape. The letter reads, in part:

> *Dear National Police,*
>
> *I have been held inside this center since February 2014. It is now August 2017. This is almost 33 months. It is either a kidnapping or a violation of my human rights. The pastor holds me here. I do not know who signed to have me stay here for so much time. I have been here from February 2014 until December 2014. I was locked up from March 2015 to April 2015. I was locked up from October 2015 until August 2017. It is not right. It is like I have been killed.*
>
> *Santiago*

The second letter had been written on a scrap of paper torn from an evangelical tract. On the opposite side of the note is commentary about the Apostolic Letters of the New Testament. The tract reads: "For the most part, these letters are not addressed to particular individuals or communities, but to larger groups. In them they reflect the challenges that confronted the first Christians amid hostile pagans. The Epistle to the Hebrews must also be considered here as a sermon of exhortation which invites Christians to remain faithful to Jesus Christ, in the midst of an adverse place."

It would be imprudent to overextend a coincidence and draw too much from this commentary. Santiago said that he never considered there to be any relationship between this passage and his desperate pleas to his mother and the police. For him, the commentary was just printed on the other side of a blank piece of paper. But inserted within a robust tradition of letter writing, Santiago's letter invites a conversation about how letters are able to interrupt the dialectic of predation—to move beyond the overlapping cycles of hunting and being hunted toward a broader conversation about the conditions that enable hunting to happen.

I delivered Santiago's letters to Maria and the National Police. The police reminded me what I already knew, that only Maria had the power to decide her son's fate. Maria, meanwhile, remains unwilling to risk her son's life for his freedom. And so Santiago is still there, even now.

Guatemala City, March 2018

EPILOGUE

I SAID GOODBYE TO GUATEMALA CITY in summer 2016 not knowing what lay ahead. Near the end of August, as I prepared to return to Toronto, I stopped by the center to wish Pedro well. He looked terrible, and I told him so. His skin was gray, and he moved slowly. Pedro had always made a point to send me off with a meal and a bit of fanfare, but this time he pushed the honor off to the next time we met.

He had looked tired for months, and I figured he was wrestling with diabetes, a condition he had struggled with for as long as I had known him. He thought the same, and I encouraged him to see a doctor, even offering to get him in front of a medical professional within an hour. Pedro declined, insisting that he didn't need any help. He wished me safe travels and nudged me out the front door.

The next week I was told that he had suffered a severe stomachache. After tossing and turning for more than twenty-four hours, he began to cough up blood. These were not specks of dark spittle but deep patches of bright red that coated his handkerchief and then the toilet bowl. He finally agreed to see a doctor and was promptly diagnosed with stage four cancer. A tumor had engulfed his liver. The doctor said that the mass was so huge that he must have been physically uncomfortable for months, maybe even years. But until his body began to shut down, Pedro had kept his pain to himself. Two days after speaking to the doctor Pedro was in a hospital and, hours later, on a morphine drip. He died five days after his diagnosis.

Pedro was not a saint. His life before finding Christ was raucous. Street life in Central America is treacherous, and Pedro met it head-on, with drinking and drugs and carousing. Sometimes I felt like questioning him about his descriptions of life before salvation, as they seemed to conveniently serve his conversion narrative, but the tracks on his arms did suggest that he had lived on the edge.

Pedro's life after Christ never came together so neatly. While his life before conversion fit perfectly with Pentecostal profiles in sin, his time inside Jorge's center and later in his own complicated notions of Christian compassion. Predation proved to be the most ambiguous part, as expressing love for a neighbor was compromised by also engaging in gratuitous amounts of violence. Why beat men with a bat? And why have a bat at all? The handcuffs and the straitjackets also begged questions, as did the morgue and the barred windows. Why did Pedro's affection make him hold his captives so tightly? Why did he need to constantly anticipate every effort at escape? It all seemed brutal, falling far short of what many consider to be Christian.

This was not just Pedro's vision of pastoralism, but also the entire industry's. Hunting down a sinner in Guatemala is perhaps the most material manifestation of the Christian commandment to love thy neighbor as thy self. Pedro's contribution to Christianity could very well be seen as an appreciation of the fact that sometimes sinners choose Christ, and other times Christ chooses the sinner.

Others have pushed predation too far. For years, the director of the city's most notorious Pentecostal rehabilitation center held over one hundred men captive inside a frighteningly small space, clearing a sizable amount of money every month through his cohort of brawny huntsmen. "We go anywhere," the director once told me. "We'll chase guys up rooftops. To the edge of cliffs. We'll even hunt them in the middle of the night." His aggressive brand of predation eventually caught up to him.

On August 7, 2017, two young men on a motorbike knocked on the center's front door. A huntsman answered. One of the men on the motorbike shot him in the stomach four times, and the director, startled by the gunshots, went to the door to see what had happened. The gunmen then shot the director eight times before driving off into the night. Within minutes, as both the director and the huntsman bled out, the captives inside the center began to riot. They pulled at the locked doors, kicked at the windows, and began to tear at the ceiling, doing anything they could to find a way out. A group of them used a massive concrete block that plugged the house's underground cistern system to ram one of the locked doors separating them from the street. When this got them nowhere, they took one of the huntsmen hostage and threatened to beat him to death if he did not hand over the keys. The men in the front office quickly complied. They unlocked the doors and eighty captives streamed into the night, stepping over the director and huntsman's bodies on their way out.

I landed in Guatemala about eight hours after the attack and spent the day inside this center, stitching together the story and noting the evidence left over from the revolt. There were the dents in the doors and holes in the roof created out of sheer desperation, which let in patches of light. There were also twenty remaining captives. No one had stopped them from leaving. Much like Frener, from Jorge's original center, they simply couldn't make it through that front door. Perhaps they knew that the center was a better option than the streets. Or, maybe they figured that they would be back inside this center within a few days, so why bother fighting?

The center, soon under the management of the most senior huntsman, slowly tracked down as many of the missing men as they could. It continued even after the director of another center suffered the same fate a week later, with a gunman on a motorbike entering the building and shooting him dead. These two directors had likely been hunted for having gone after the wrong sinners at the wrong time, but their deaths nevertheless sent a shock wave across the capital. They were feared and hated enough to be assassinated, yet they also enjoyed the love of their city.

My clearest memories of Pedro are of driving from his center to a family's house, often to discuss the details of a possible hunt. As he would get a block or two away from his center, neighbors would recognize him and cheer, pumping their fists and clapping their hands in ways usually reserved for celebrities and beloved politicians. To drive with Pedro was to be at the center of a predatory world. Pedro would always return the affection with a series of quick honks and a balled fist, sometimes commenting to me about how much they loved him. And they did. For Pedro had saved so many of their sons, brothers, and husbands from the streets. He had kept young men alive when everything suggested that they should be dead.

It is not surprising that Pedro's death sparked a public mourning that started inside the center and spilled into the streets. Only a day after his death, his son requested that Pedro's body lay in state inside his center. At first this meant inside the front office, but this proved impractical. There was no way that the office could handle the hordes of people that had already begun to descend on the center. So they moved Pedro's body outside, in front of the center, and built a memorial around his casket. Flowers were layered atop flowers, and a white sheet hung from a wall so as to provide an angelic backdrop. It was an open casket, and Pedro was dressed in his favorite soccer jersey. A neighbor lent the center a kneeler so mourners could pay their respects a few feet from his body.

Pedro looked restful, but there was nothing quiet about the event. A mob came out to mourn his death. Thousands occupied the streets. Former captives and their families came to say their goodbyes. Neighbors mingled with police officers and judges, and vendors sold fruit juices and bottles of water as if the event were a street fair. A mariachi band played for hours, guiding a motley crew of mourners through a series of dirges. People openly drank and smoked joints in the streets. The event was rowdy, and hunters shared stories with the very people who had hunted them. As day turned into night and the early morning burial approached, the crowd held strong, and people began to weep for the man they had lost.

As all this happened, the nearly sixty captives held on the second floor of the center overheard the festivities. None had been allowed to participate. With only bars on the windows, the center had always been a porous cage, the sounds of street life and the smells of food serving as reminders of the life left behind. The captives heard the mariachi band; they listened to the speeches and the prayers; those near the windows could even see a bit of the casket and perhaps get a contact high from the weed, but they were not allowed to attend. None could be trusted. The arbiter of their sincerity now lay in state.

And so, the captives wept. They did not weep because they had been excluded from the party; nobody seemed to mind this too much. Instead, they wept because they too cared for Pedro. They appreciated the love he had extended to them—often by surprising them in their sleep and dragging them to his center. Even Santiago, who at that point was approaching almost three years of captivity, wished Pedro peace and mourned his loss. Santiago noted that he felt doubly sad when, at exactly 7:30 a.m., the party stopped and the streets grew quiet as the National Police escorted a caravan of mourners to the cemetery for the burial. Santiago described the moment as akin to turning off a very loud television. One moment there was noise and the next, nothing. The captives sat in silence.

Pedro's center did not have to stay open. His death provided an opportunity to reconsider the mission and possibly pivot toward new activities, or to just close entirely. Roberto had not been keen on continuing the business, given that he had never struggled with substance abuse and had no motivation to take over. But Pedro's death came with a surprise. Unbeknownst to Roberto,

Pedro had amassed a tremendous amount of debt. Pedro had been caught many times pirating electricity from a power line, but even after reconnecting his house to the meter he still never paid any of his electric bills. Roberto was left with a debt of about $10,000 USD from that and other failed commitments, and over the course of the funeral, people emerged from the crowd to let him know that Pedro also owed them money.

Roberto had a job that paid an hourly wage, one that allowed him to keep a roof over his family's head but not one that would let him earn enough to begin to pay back those debts. And so an additional layer of predation formed atop an already complicated web of hunting. Collectors kept an eye on Roberto as he found himself forced to keep the center going. Always the sensible one, Roberto focused on efficiencies: he raised the price of captivity by 25 percent and began to enforce payments. Pedro had grown lax over the years, often accepting hardship cases and going easy on families who came up short every month.

Roberto's upgrades are also part of the reason why Santiago stayed inside the center for so many years. The most successful centers in Guatemala City follow a model that keeps a close eye on the deeply interrelated variables of stock (i.e., long-term captives) and flow (i.e., short-term captives). While the centers' populations are in constant motion, in an effort to shepherd the herd and stabilize the flock, most pastors negotiate with families over contractually obligated lengths of captivity. Canny pastors are especially interested in captives who do not need three, six, or nine months of lock-up, but instead require years. And so, because he could count on Maria's monthly offerings, Roberto likely saw the advantage of keeping Santiago inside the center for years at a time. Maria wanted her son captive so he could live another day, and Roberto wanted Santiago captive so that he might one day climb out from under his father's debt.

And until that happens, the center hunts.

ACKNOWLEDGMENTS

I FIRST WENT TO LATIN AMERICA in 1999 to study the politics of Christianity; a decade later, I completed an ethnography of a Pentecostal megachurch in Guatemala City. The church's vision of Christian citizenship seemed to inspire optimism in this postwar country, but as I documented in my book, gangs and drugs gradually undermined that hope. While my twenty-year engagement with Guatemala City has offered me moments of great joy and purpose, there have also been stretches of deep sadness: I have seen prayer circles form at crime scenes, young bodies prepared for burial, and drug users hunt each other for salvation. I often considered leaving. Guatemala never needed another anthropologist, but at some point, turning away no longer seemed like an option. And so, *Hunted* is a study of predatory pastoralism, of the war on drugs from the perspective of Pentecostalism, but it's also an ethnographic reflection on no longer being able to turn away.

Alejandro never let me leave. He was a fighter in every sense of the word, scratching out a life against incredible odds. During one of our last interviews, I remember him mentioning a story he had read. "These guys are on an island, and they're hunters," he said. "But they aren't hunting animals. They're hunting men." He was describing the plotline of Richard Connell's 1924 classic *The Most Dangerous Game*. As we argued about whether hunting any human could ever be justified, Alejandro signaled that he was thinking with me about my fieldwork's most basic categories. Thank you.

I remember the first time I met Pedro. He answered the front door of his center in a black tank top, billowing soccer shorts, and a pair of flip-flops. He stared blankly at me as I jumped into a script about my research. He interrupted me to see whether I wanted to talk to his captives. He then shepherded me into the center, walked me up a flight of stairs, and locked me inside with the general population, leaving me alone with a few more than fifty men. Pedro had nothing to hide, and his unflinching confidence in his mission made my work possible. It was a tremendous gift that I hope that this book can repay.

I failed Santiago. My extended conversations with his mother and brother got him nowhere. He spent years inside Pedro's center. When I returned to visit him, sometimes after having been away for months, Santiago would remind me that time had stood still for him. With Maria never able to imagine Santiago living outside of the center and me never being able to convince her that he could, Santiago sat there for years. I am sorry.

Alejandro, Pedro, Maria, and Santiago are not composite characters, but they do function (at least for me) as archetypes of an industry. Pentecostal drug rehabilitation centers present such patterned relationships that Alejandro and Santiago could stand in for the thousands of Guatemalans trying their best to escape not just the centers but also drugs. Pedro and Maria approximate the other side of this equation. My fieldwork for this book stretched across more than a decade and over fifty centers, and I want to thank the dozens of pastors and hundreds of captives who helped me conduct my research.

Outside of the centers, I did my best to cultivate thought and debate around this subject. With Benjamin Fogarty-Valenzuela, I curated a series of photography exhibits in Guatemala City on the theme of compulsory drug rehabilitation centers. With Tomas Matza, I co-organized a workshop on "the will" at the University of Toronto. My thanks to the participants: Peter Benson, Jon Bialecki, Naisargi Dave, Pamela Klassen, Tania Li, Kathryn Lofton, John Modern, Bethany Moreton, Andrea Muehlebach, Laurence Ralph, Daromir Rudnyckyj, and Mariana Valverde. I also co-organized a pair of workshops on "captivity" at the University of Toronto with Jatin Dua. Thank you Melissa Burch, Susan Lepselter, Darryl Li, Juno Salazar Parreñas, Rhacel Salazar Parreñas, Padraic Scanlan, Judith Scheele, Andrew Shryock, Rachel Silvey, Caleb Smith, and Noah Tamarkin.

For several years now I have hosted very informal writing workshops at the annual meetings of the American Anthropological Association. One gathering in Denver turned this book around. For their honesty and enthusiasm, I want to thank Lucas Bessire, Angela Garcia, Tomas Matza, Amy Moran, Laurence Ralph, and Harris Solomon. Through editing a book series, Atelier, I have been inspired by its contributors: Sarah Besky, Lauren Coyle Rosen, Laurie Denyer Willis, Namita Dharia, Jacob Doherty, Jatin Dua, Anthony Fontes, Kate Mariner, Nomi Stone, Christien Tompkins, and Marina Andrea Welker. Finally, I hosted a book workshop at the University of Toronto in September 2017 for a final conversation about this manuscript. Thank you to Edward Escalon, Basit Kareem Iqbal, Ayan Kassim, Kathryn Lofton, Amira Mittermaier, John Modern, Graham Denyer Willis, and Ato Quayson for their enthusiasm and insights.

Others hosted me for invited talks. My many thanks to hosts and audiences at the University of Toronto, Harvard University, Columbia University, University of Cambridge, the London School of Economics and Political Science, Oxford University, Duke University, Yale University, Cornell University, Stanford University, University of Texas, the Ohio State University, University of Virginia, University of North Carolina, Washington University, Universidad del Valle de Guatemala, Open Society Foundations, and Guatemala's Secretaría Ejecutiva de la Comisión contra las Adicciones y el Tráfico.

My thoughts on this book were sharpened through writing essays about Guatemala's rehab centers. These essays appear in the journals *Social Text* (32:3), *Public Culture* (29:3 and 30:1), *Critical Inquiry* (43:3), *Cultural Anthropology* (33:3), and *Environment and Planning D* (34:4). Those essays, and this book, draw on fieldwork supported by the Open Society Foundations, the Social Science Research Council, the Social Sciences and Humanities Research Council of Canada, the Wenner Gren Foundation, the American Academy of Religion, and the Jackman Humanities Institute at the University of Toronto.

I have long been in the habit of hiring exceedingly bright research assistants and copyeditors—not to sift through archives or transcribe materials, although they sometimes get stuck with that, but, more importantly, to think with me. Edward Escalon and Fizza Joffrey read a penultimate draft of the book with me page by page, and then Jessica Loudis edited it with a fresh set of eyes. Years before, Ayan Kassim helped me transform an idea into an actual draft, encouraging me to think more daringly at every turn. And before all of that, Benjamin Fogarty Valenzuela helped me recognize the potential these centers could have for a full-fledged book project, and Basit Kareem Iqbal talked me through the intellectual terrain.

I know very few things for certain, but one of them is that the University of Toronto is the preeminent place to work on the anthropology of religion. I am grateful to have had the support of my colleagues—from the Department for the Study of Religion and the Department of Anthropology but also the Centre for Diaspora and Transnational Studies. Innovation is atmospheric in Toronto, and insights emerge in the hallways, at seminar tables, and over drinks. They also, of course, materialize in classrooms, and I reserve special thanks for the members of two reoccurring graduate courses who read drafts of this book with unparalleled eagerness: Theory and Method in the Study of Religion and Predation.

Kathryn Lofton and John Modern are what's right with religious studies. Their vision for humanistic inquiry has made their book series Class 200 an absolute gift. The support I received at the University of Chicago Press was outstanding, with my deepest appreciation to Priya Nelson and Kyle Wagner as well as Caterina MacLean and Mollie McFee for all their work.

Finally, my in-laws have supported my work in the most practical of ways, from asking engaged questions to coparenting when I travel. None of my fieldwork could happened without them. Thank you. My brother is also an anthropologist. He works in a different part of the world on entirely different themes, but our training is so similar that we're able to talk out our ideas at the earliest stages, pushing each other to be clearer and more creative. Our conversations are invaluable. My wife deserves a special acknowledgment. Early on in my career I told her that I planned to write only one book. As I write the acknowledgments for this book while knee deep in the next, it is clear that her flexibility has been essential to our marriage. All of it has been worth it, I hope, because our son has been such a joy. Ignatius came into consciousness as this book progressed, often developing faster than the manuscript. While the details of my fieldwork were never appropriate for a young child, he could follow the themes of chase and capture, and we often talked about how complete freedom could never really be the ideal. Who would want to be completely untethered? I would ask him. For it is our love of him that binds us all together.

NOTES

1. There is an expanding social scientific literature on compulsory drug rehabilitation centers in Latin America. While its arguments and insights vary from scholar to scholar, the literature generally approaches these centers as a recognizable genre of captivity. Some key characteristics of these centers include little to no state regulation, the renovation of abandoned or unwanted spaces, a for-profit business model, an affiliation with either Roman Catholicism or Protestant Christianity, forced captivity, and a reliance on confessional therapeutics. This reliance includes approaches adapted from Twelve Steps or even more improvisational efforts at therapy. See Hansen 2012; Wilkinson 2013; K. O'Neill 2014; Garcia 2015.

2. This turn of phrase comes from a 1995 essay titled "Human Vulnerability and the Experience of Being Prey." The essay recounts, with great philosophical insight, the experience of Val Plumwood being stalked, attacked, and left for dead by a crocodile in the Australian Outback. She writes, "When I pulled my canoe across in driving rain to a rock outcrop rising out of the swamp for a hasty, sodden lunch, I had experienced strongly the unfamiliar sensation of being watched" (1995, 29). With great literary skill, Plumwood narrates her experience of canoeing through lagoons and marshlands until a crocodile attacked her vessel, tipping her into the water and then rolling her toward death. "For the first time," she writes, "it came to me fully that I was prey" (30). Her reflections then bend toward the affective: "The human species evolved not only as predator, but also as prey, and this has very likely given us capacities to sense danger which we cannot now recognize or account for" (30). Unwilling to concede too much ground to such evolutionary assumptions, I am nonetheless intrigued by the hunt's affective conditions.

3. Grégoire Chamayou makes a provocative argument in *Manhunts*. He announces that pastoralism and predation have "parallel and opposed" genealogies. "Christian pastoralism," he writes, "was opposed . . . to cynegetic powers: fishing for souls rather than hunting for men, persuasion rather than coercion" (2012, 18). The only predatory practices that Chamayou attributes to Christianity are what he calls pastoral hunts:

"To protect the flock sometimes one has to hunt down certain sheep, to sacrifice a few to save all the others. Here we are no longer in a logic of predatory appropriation but rather in a rationality of salutary ablation and beneficent exclusion" (20). My ethnographic observations lead me to fundamentally disagree with these philosophical distinctions. Predation upsets an increasingly bundled set of images about pastoralism not because the two modes of governance are opposed but because they are interdependent in their everyday function.

4. It is important to note that Christianity can be "not good" and yet it can still be Christianity. While the faithful may debate the virtues of hunting and may even dismiss the pastor's hunts as a failed or perverted kind of Christianity, I argue that these hunts are indifferent to such normative evaluations. Neither good nor bad, they are Christian. Further, if we take into light certain Protestant tenets, including the fall, the total depravity of humanity, and the necessity of God's grace, one could argue that hunting's preoccupation with the bad makes the practice particularly Christian. In a fallen world, there are no truly moral or good actions, only a series of compromised choices and faith in God's grace. Hunting is one such choice that seeks to create a forced encounter between the hunted and God's grace.

5. Pastoralism is a mode of power modeled after the Christian image of the shepherd who cares for his flock and yet would risk the herd to save even one lost sheep. Michel Foucault develops this Christian metaphor to name four aspects of pastoral power. They are: "(1) [Pastoral power] is a form of power whose ultimate aim is to assure individual salvation in the next world. (2) Pastoral power is not merely a form of power which commands; it must also be prepared to sacrifice itself for the life and salvation of the flock. Therefore, it is different from royal power, which demands a sacrifice from its subjects to save the throne. (3) It is a form of power which does not look after just the whole community but each individual in particular, during his entire life. (4) Finally, this form of power cannot be exercised without knowing the inside of people's minds, without exploring their souls, without making them reveal their innermost secrets. It implies a knowledge of the conscience and an ability to direct it" (Foucault 1982, 783).

6. Scholars deliver steadfast portraits of neoliberal withdrawal. This includes the privatization of state enterprises, the liberalization of trade, and the relaxation of government regulation. As mentioned in the main text, while each of these approaches advances an analytically distinct proposition, each also contributes to an image of the failed shepherd. For those approaches referenced in the main text, see Bales 1999; Petryna 2002; Harvey 2004; Li 2010; Povinelli 2011; Standing 2011; Sassen 2014.

7. Biopolitics, as articulated in the work of Michel Foucault, is a set of strategies and mechanisms through which human life processes come to be managed. Foucault first developed the concepts of biopower and biopolitics in his *History of Sexuality, Volume 1*. In the broadest of strokes, Foucault understands biopower as encompassing a modern form of governance that turns from a sovereign's ability to "take life or let live" toward its power instead to "foster life or disallow it to the point of death" (1978, 138). Two bodies organize biopower for Foucault. The first is the politics of the individual body (anatomo-politics). The second is the politics of the species body, or population (biopolitics). Yet, after a brief discussion at the end of *History of Sexuality, Volume 1*,

Foucault never returns to the concept of biopower. Nikolas Rose has since provided an excellent definition in *The Politics of Life Itself*, where biopolitics refers to "the management of life in the name of the well-being of the population . . . and of each of its living subjects" (2006, 52). See Foucault 2003, 241.

8. The point is that while scholars often organize today's literature in ways that prize narratives of abandonment over acquisition, a so far uncoordinated conversation about predation has the power to pull the practice of critical inquiry to the very edges of the pastorate. From this perspective, what becomes clear is that it is hunting season, and maybe it always has been. Drones with their kill lists (Chamayou 2013), minutemen on the Mexican-American border (Shapira 2013), and Somali pirates in the Indian Ocean (Dua 2019) all lie in wait, and they are not alone. Extortionists across Central America (Fontes 2018), kidnappers in Iraq (Al-Mohammad 2012), and eviction notices stapled to front doors across the United States (Desmond 2016) are all additional examples of hunts employing the active technologies of tracking and capturing in contrast to the relative passivity of letting die.

9. Richard Nixon, "Remarks About an Intensified Program for Drug Abuse Prevention and Control" (1971). For a history of the war on drugs, see, for example, Carpenter 2003; Loveman 2006; Gootenberg 2009. For rates of trafficking through Central America, see United Nations Office on Drugs and Crime 2012. There is an expansive historical literature on the war on drugs, but here it should be sufficient to recognize that drug prohibition as US foreign policy has failed to stem both the production and distribution of drugs while also disrupting countless lives across the hemisphere.

10. For an ethnographic look at parallel drug markets, see Bourgois 1996. For the rise of crack cocaine in Guatemala, see Feilding and Giacomello 2013. For details on Guatemala's homicide rate being more than twenty times the US average, see Jorge A. Restrepo and Alonso Tobón García, eds., *Guatemala en la Encrucijada: Panorama de una Violencia Transformada* (2011), which documents that in 2010 the rate of homicides per 100,000 of population in Guatemala City was 116. By comparison, the United States has a rate of about 5. Of importance here is the recognition that the practice of prohibition has been taken up by Protestant communities. This includes the founding and management of rehabilitation centers that essentially serve as sites of incarceration amid incredibly uncertain times.

11. For the percentage of Guatemala's health care budget dedicated to matters of mental health, see the World Health Organization's "Mental Health Atlas" (2011). For the percentage of Guatemalans that self-identify as Pentecostal or Charismatic Christian, see Pew Forum on Religion and Public Life 2006 and Garrard-Burnett 2015. Note that the aim here is to make some general claims about Pentecostalism in Guatemala and so the book will not engage the important distinctions that exist throughout the region between pentecostal, *evangelico*, *cristiano*, and *católico*. For studies that take greater pains to establish these divisions, see Canton Delgado 1998; Garrard-Burnett 1998; and O'Neill 2009.

12. Guatemala's maximum security prison population is roughly 1,500 prisoners; see International Centre for Prison Studies 2013. My own fieldwork suggests that there are as many as two hundred Pentecostal rehabilitation centers in Guatemala City. This book's

research is based on fifty centers, with a deeper ethnographic focus on one such center. Some centers hold as many as one hundred and fifty people, others as few as ten. A very conservative average would be thirty people per center, putting the total number of people inside Pentecostal rehabilitation centers at well over six thousand.

13. The image of the good shepherd appears in Foucault 2007, 165; the image of the bad shepherd appears in Foucault 2001, 298. For humanitarian intervention, see Redfield 2013. For zones of social abandonment, see Biehl 2005 and Rose 2006, 57. For the progressive animalization of man, see Agamben 1998, 30, who borrows the formulation from Foucault, who states in the third volume of *Dits et Écrits* that biopolitics produces "une animalization progressive de l'homme" (1994, 719).

14. The most common cause of death inside these centers is health complications related to the sudden withdrawal from alcohol and drugs. Predictably, this is more of a threat for elderly and chronically ill captives but can also afflict the young and those heavily dependent on such substances as alcohol and cocaine. However, these centers can also become sites of accident and injury, with the combination of open fire and locked doors creating the conditions for tragedy.

15. The normative assessments of these centers conducted by human rights and public health officials tend to establish a narrowly defined evaluation of coercive and compulsory care. My own research and reports have certainly contributed to this discourse. See Kevin Lewis O'Neill, "Guatemala's Compulsory Rehabilitation Centers," submission to the UN Committee Against Torture (2013). But while Pentecostal drug rehabilitation centers in Guatemala City do not abide by liberal notions of justice, they nonetheless provide the city with an invaluable social resource. This kind of nuance readily appears through the course of fieldwork but remains absent from such definitive reports as UNODC and WHO, "Principles of Drug Dependence Treatment" (2008); UNODC, "From Coercion to Cohesion: Treating Drug Dependence Through Health Care, Not Punishment" (2010); Human Rights Watch, "'They Treat Us Like Animals': Mistreatment of Drug Users and 'Undesirables' in Cambodia's Drug Detention Centers" (2013); C. Zamudio, P. Chávez, and E. Zafra, "Abusos en centros de tratamiento con internamiento para usuarios de drogas en México" (2015); and Open Society Foundations, "Detention and Punishment in the Name of Drug Treatment" (2016).

16. Malinowski 1922, 4, 9.

17. Hunting has an important place in the history of anthropological thought. The hunting hypothesis was one of anthropology's first adaptive explanations of human origins, with the development of predatory skills supposedly distinguishing humans from animals. The South African anthropologist Raymond A. Dart (1953) championed this theory soon after World War II, arguing that the skeletal remains of *Australopithecus* demonstrated that hominoids had learned to hunt. While the discovery of additional fossils ultimately allowed physical anthropologists to argue otherwise (Brain 1970), this midcentury interest in hunting colored the work of social anthropologists, with studies of hunting featuring prominently in classic twentieth-century ethnographies. Focusing on the role of animals in systems of taboo, anthropologists explored principles of social solidarity and selfhood as constituted through these encounters between

humans and animals. Yet the particularities of the hunt, namely the complex relationship between predator and prey, surfaced only briefly with Renato Rosaldo's study of headhunting (1980).

18. Lauren Berlant writes that "the case represents a problem-event that has animated some kind of judgement" and that "what matters is the idiom of the judgment" (2007, 663). Here, the idiom is ethnography, which is both a method and a genre that offers important examples of monographs organized around the life of single person—if only because "the case is always pedagogical, itself an agent" (665). Such monographs include Bourgois's *In Search of Respect* (1996); Ruth Behar's *Translated Woman: Crossing the Border with Esperanza's Story* (2003); João Biehl's *Vita: Life in a Zone of Social Abandonment* (2005); Karen McCarthy Brown's *Mama Lola: A Vodou Priestess in Brooklyn* (2001); and Vincent Crapanzano's *Tuhami: Portrait of a Moroccan* (1980).

19. A decade after the signing of the 1996 Peace Accords, which ended Central America's longest and bloodiest civil war, Guatemala City emerged as Central America's "crime capital" and one of the most violent cities in the world as ranked by rates of homicide per 100,000 inhabitants. This was the result of neoliberal economic reforms, mass deportations from the United States, the rise of transnational street gangs, and the growing power of drug cartels in Central America. A decade after those developments, even with explicit efforts at intervention and justice reform, these assessments did not change in any significant way. See Wilson 2009; Restrepo and García 2011; and Dudley 2016.

20. A sample of this work includes a 2013 report that I submitted to the United Nations Committee Against Torture titled "Compulsory Rehabilitation Centers in Guatemala." I also curated a 2014 photography exhibit in Guatemala City titled "Dios y Vos: Los centros de la rehabilitación" and a 2016 photography exhibit in Guatemala City titled "El Arte del Cautiverio." Both exhibits showcased the visual work of anthropologist and photographer Benjamin Fogarty-Valenzuela, with the latter foregrounding the artwork produced by captives inside these centers. Both exhibits also included round-table discussions between stakeholders and opportunities for public debate. In 2014, I worked with journalist Linda Presley to produce a twenty-eight-minute audio documentary for the BBC World Service titled "Guatemala's Addicts behind Bars."

21. In response to a note written by a pair of Guinean boys who died as stowaways on a flight to Brussels, James Ferguson (2002, 560) makes the following observation about the letter as genre: "Let us read these two young men as they meant to be read: unknown authors of a message in a bottle . . . Let us read this letter, in short, *not* as an ethnographic text but precisely *as a letter*—a letter that demands not a sociological analysis of its author but a response." Other anthropologists have also turned toward the letter as a style of argumentation. Consider Charles Briggs's letter to Sigmund Freud (2014) as a provocation to consider the epistle not simply as a form of address but also a style of thought. In this sense, I take Alejandro's letter both as a letter—in that it deserved a response—as well as a style of thought, even argumentation, about his own claims to such human rights as the freedom of movement.

22. Captivity is a genre of American literature. A foundational example features Mrs. Mary Rowlandson (1682), the wife of a Puritan minister. Narragansett Indians took Mary

hostage for some eleven weeks. She walked with the Narragansett almost 150 miles north until her husband paid for her freedom. From the beginning, Christians converted the political conditions of her captivity into a journey of Puritan spiritual tribulation, subsuming the politics of white-Indian conflict into a religious narrative (Lepselter 2016). Her story's three-part structure (removal, conversion, and return) defined a genre that ultimately justified westward expansion and the origins of American racism (Strong 1998). Yet captivity is more than a narrative genre. It is also a practice and maybe even an affect. That is, captivity is about being literally tied up, but it is also about feeling tethered to a less tangible someone or a something. At its most conceptual, in fact, this book is an extended meditation on being held captive—not necessarily by someone or something but rather by an aspiration. Sobriety, piety, even ethics itself, they all bind the subject to a set of imperatives that are impossible to achieve let alone escape. This makes freedom inside these centers not just an eschatology but also a trap.

THE HUNT

1. For coverage of the fire in March 2014, see "Guatemala City Fire Destroys La Terminal Market" (BBC News 2014).
2. It is as easy as it is dangerous to slip into caricatures when writing about the use of crack cocaine. Driving much of these stereotypes is the hearsay that the drug is instantaneously addictive. The work of psychologist Carl Hart (2013) is instructive, demonstrating that the use of crack cocaine has more to do with social context than with the biochemical power of the drug itself. These caricatures are largely the effect of what Joelle M. Abi-Rached and Nikolas Rose (2010) would call the neuromolecular gaze. By this they mean "a common vision of life itself" (13), "a gaze that immersed itself in the nascent molecular approaches used in biology, chemistry and biophysics and was applied to the realm of neurobiology" (17). The slip is when the biochemical proprieties of a substance tumble into the moral terrain of dependency.
3. Guatemala City sprouted a skyline in little less than a decade. Low level for centuries, kept at one or two stories by earthquakes, a surge in foreign investment prompted the construction of more than one hundred new office towers and condominium complexes over the span of about ten years. All of them are over ten stories with some over twenty stories. For the spatial politics of this rapid urban expansion, especially the vertical forms of segregation, see O'Neill and Fogarty-Valenzuela 2013.
4. Grégoire Chamayou (2012) offers the clearest philosophical voice when it comes to hunting's reflexivity. He writes, "The experience of hunting establishes for the prey a relationship to the world that is structured by a radical anxiety. Each perception, including that of its own body, becomes a foreboding danger. Being constantly on the watch is what characterizes the animal, and it is in this sense that being hunted animalizes humans" (59). For Chamayou, as for this book, "Hunting presupposes a form

of empathy with the prey: to track effectively, one has to put oneself in its place. But this mental operation implied a denial of the absolute social distance between masters and their slaves that the hunting relationship sought precisely to reinstate" (65). This is a matter of strategic empathy that demands a tremendous degree of anthropological anticipation, in the biographical sense (how will the other person react when hunted?) and maybe even in the affective sense (how does the human, as opposed to the animal, react when hunted?).

5. Social scientists have long understood crowds as unpredictable, perhaps most famously Gustave Le Bon (2002 [1895]), who describes them as "always irritable and impulsive" (13). In *Crowds and Power* (1962), Elias Canetti characterizes the crowd as a great equalizer, where "ideally, all men are equal there; no distinctions count" (15), giving the subject a sense of relief and freedom amid the multitude. Meanwhile Michel Foucault's *Discipline and Punish* (1977) details the political challenge that the mercurial crowd poses to sovereign power during public executions. He writes that "the great spectacle of punishment ran the risk of being rejected by the very people to whom it was being addressed . . . [as the part] played by feelings of humanity for the condemned [raised] a political fear of the effects of these ambiguous rituals" (63, 65).

6. The turn of phrase "bound hand and foot" comes from Augustine's *Confessions* and how the saint sees sin as a form of captivity. "The enemy held my will," Augustine writes, "and of it he made a chain and bound me. Because my will was perverse it changed to lust, and lust yielded to become habit, and habit not resisted became necessity. These were like links hanging one on another—which is which is why I have called it a chain—and their hard bondage held me bound hand and foot" (1992, 135). Alongside the material captivity that Pentecostal rehabilitation centers provide, I want to emphasize the moral captivity—the webs of predation—that Christian theology makes possible.

7. Tattoos are a source of concern and regret in Guatemala. Given that tattoos have long been the marker of gang affiliation, it is dangerous to have a tattoo, no matter its significance. A tattoo puts a person at risk of becoming a social outcast and even of being the target of social cleansing. Individuals have been murdered—supposedly for the greater good—because of their tattoos, and so entire industries have emerged throughout Central America to provide the service of tattoo removal, which is a painful and time-consuming process.

8. The hunt's visceral effect on experience can call to mind Louis Althusser's doctrine of interpellation (1971). His theory of subject formation famously posits a primal scene in which a police officer hails a civilian by calling out, "Hey, you there!" A subject emerges, he argues, when the civilian turns around, when he recognizes himself in the police officer's call. The turning subject for Althusser is a guilty subject. Althusser's theory has been rightly critiqued for its theological impulses. The voice of the police officer all too easily echoes the voice of a biblical God (Althusser even references the Hebrew God) and the subject initiated by the call comes equipped with a Christian interiority, one willing to turn toward itself as well as to turn on itself. In fact, Judith Butler (1997, 113) critiques his theory as not simply imbued with a tautological framing but also heavily organized around Christian assumptions. Though debatably

rendering Althusser's theory of subject formation inappropriate for normative liberal politics, its theology fits rather well in Guatemala City. See also Daniel Boyarin's *Border Lines* (2004, 9–11) for a discussion of interpellation and religion by way of Althusser and Butler.

9. The figure of the petty sovereign for Judith Butler is an actor endowed with sovereign power who needs to deem an individual or group to be dangerous to justify a violent intervention. She writes, "These are petty sovereigns unknowing, to a degree, about what work they do, but performing their acts unilaterally and with enormous consequence. Their acts are clearly *conditioned*, but their acts are judgements that are nevertheless *unconditional* in the sense that they are final, not subject to review, and not subject to appeal" (Butler 2004, 65). This is the scale of power that Pedro had over his captives.

10. Pedro is not the only critic of human rights. There is a critical, scholarly tradition of understanding human rights not as liberal, transparent, and accountable, as a key indicator of governmental legitimacy, but rather as a technique of rule that imposes a normative set of assumptions onto a diverse series of contexts. See Englund 2006; Clarke 2009; Babül 2017.

11. Details about Jorge's life come from extensive interviews with family and former captives but also from Manuelo Corleto's *Malasuerte murio en Pavón* (1992). María Elena, an evangelical Christian and benefactor of Jorge's center, commissioned the biography. As source material, it bends far closer to hagiography than historical analysis. Qualifying my use of this biography as evidence is Stephen Davies's *Empiricism and History* (2003), which carefully traces what historians mean by empiricism while also examining the origins of empirical methods in historical analysis. Also instructive is Barbara Caine's *Biography and History* (2010), which looks at the discipline of history and the writing of lives.

12. Matthew Engelke writes about nineteenth-century British evangelicals, namely the British and Foreign Bible Society (BFBS), and how they used numbers and statistics to imagine Christianity as global. In 1867, he notes, the British and Foreign Bible Society distributed 2,400,076 Bibles, "bringing the sum total over sixty-four years to 55,069,865 Bibles. Why not round the numbers out? Why do those seventy-six texts *more* than 2.4 million matter in the report for 1868? In part because the precision contributes to an image of corporate discipline, but just as significantly because as BFBS supporters were encouraged to think, each copy stood for something more important: a person, an owner-reader, a saved soul" (2010, 818). Pedro and these centers pursue a parallel logic, with the number of captives that they keep contributing to their vision of Christianity.

13. The thrill of the hunt cited here is not a cliché or trope but an ethnographic fact. Chamayou writes that "The joys of manhunting occupy a particular place in the history of the dominators' affects—an experience that mixes in a complex way cruelty, pleasure, and the feeling of power" (2012, 69). This pleasure compounds when connected to the thrill of salvation, to the idea that pulling a sinner from the street literally saves them from the depths of hell. It is this affect that makes hunting, in the words of Omri Elisha (2011), morally ambitious.

14. Guatemala presents a neoliberal backdrop familiar to anthropologists. This is a context in which the liberal democratic state recedes from its duties to provide basic social services, insisting instead that civil social organizations begin to the do the work of the state. The literature on neoliberalism is expansive though some of this work resonates better here than others, mainly for its insistence on the emotional and affective labor that citizens must also direct toward themselves. See, for example, Rose 1990; Cruikshank 1996; and Paley 2001.

15. Michel Foucault uses the term "carceral archipelago" (1977, 297) to describe how the logic of the prison has extended to other parts of society. This is a potentially helpful metaphor because there is no single Pentecostal rehabilitation center but rather hundreds of Pentecostal rehabilitation centers in Guatemala City. A quick mapping of some of these structures does calls to mind Michel Foucault's notion of the carceral archipelago. Yet Foucault's metaphor is static. These centers are not islands. They close. They relocate. They reopen. Users also graduate, so to speak, and start their own outfits. Others escape but then return. Recidivism is also common. This assemblage is in constant motion.

16. Historians of the United States have extensively documented the Christian connections between many nineteenth-century reform movements, including antislavery and temperance. See, for example, Robert Abzug's *Cosmos Crumbling* (1994).

17. In the introduction to their oft-quoted edited collection *Law and Disorder in the Postcolony*, Jean and John Comaroff write that "government, as it disperses itself, becomes less and less an ensemble of bureaucratic institutions, more and more a licensing-and-franchising authority. This, in turn, provides fresh opportunities, at all levels, for capitalizing both on the assets of the state and on its imprimatur" (2006, 16–17). In the work of rehabilitation by pastors, part of this franchising necessarily involves intake forms to standardize deviance, fitting neatly with Ian Hacking's notion of "making up people" (1999). Ann Laura Stoler (2010), too, traces the intimacies between commitments to paper and the grids of intelligibility they produce in her examination of colonial regimes of governance. Also see Susan Leigh Star and Geoffrey Bowker's (2000) analysis of classificatory schema and their consequences on the people they categorize.

18. Critical here is how often these centers model themselves after the state and how this modeling often takes the form of paper, for which the work of Matthew Hull (2012) and Ramah McKay (2012) become immediately useful—with the circulation of business cards, fliers, and forms allowing these centers, in the words of Steven Pierce, "to look like a state" (2006). But at a broader register, the process of pastors formalizing rehabs also calls to mind Daniella Gandolfo's ethnographic work on informal markets in Lima, Peru, where she asks: "at what point does simplifying the law, in its aim to bring state regulation closer to the realities of informal vendors, produce, rather, the 'informalization' of the state's legal and bureaucratic apparatus?" (2013, 296). Such a question throws into relief the tethered cord between formality and informality.

19. Ethnographic accounts of postwar Guatemala often explore the politics of unknowing. Diane Nelson writes that "claiming to be duped is a way to admit you did something but to avoid full responsibility. It occurred, but it's not your fault" (2009, 12). In many ways, Nelson echoes Michael Taussig's (1984) sense of epistemic murk. While

her approach to being duped is decidedly about the past, also appropriate here is a reference to Anthony Fontes's (2016) future-oriented notion of mortal doubt, which suggests how doubt illuminates the future amid times of great uncertainty. In this sense, Maria is not duped amid epistemic murk so much as mortally hopeful. On this didactic quality of hope, Hirokazu Miyazaki writes, "I approach hope as a methodological problem for knowledge and, ultimately, as a method of knowledge deployed across a wide spectrum of knowledge practices, as well as of political persuasions" (2004, 1–2).

20. With the state in mind, Anand Pandian asks: "What predators haunt the pastoral fold of good government? Must the state itself prey on threats to the welfare of those in its care? How, in other words, does the exercise of sovereign force aid in the cultivation of subject populations?" (2001, 80). I am interested in a parallel set of questions, but within a context in which the state plays a minimal role. Echoing E. P. Thompson (1975), the work of Peter Evans makes such a set of questions thinkable: "How should we characterize variations in state structure and state-society relations? My strategy was to start by constructing two historically grounded ideal types: predatory and developmental states. . . . predatory states extract at the expense of society, undercutting development even in the narrow sense of capital accumulation" (1995, 12). My intention, however, is to push against the notion that predation and development are mutually exclusive.

21. Chamayou posits a division between sovereign power and pastoral power clearly when he writes, "Christianity continues this opposition between pastoral power and cynegetic power, which it uses chiefly to distinguish between the spiritual and the temporal modalities of governing humans . . . Christianity does not hunt; it fishes" (2012, 17). Chamayou largely builds from Michel Foucault's work on pastoralism in *Security, Territory, Population* (2007) in an attempt at proposing an alternative genealogy to biopolitics. And while I celebrate this effort, the problem with Chamayou's formulation lies with this false dichotomy between predation and care. The dichotomy overlooks longstanding examples of the sovereign's preoccupation with care that extends well beyond the case of Pentecostal drug rehabilitation centers in Guatemala. For more on the intimate relationship between salvation and government, see Agamben 2011.

22. I take my cue here from the anthropological literature on care and its politics. Consider Clara Han's *Life in Debt* (2012), Annemarie Mol's *The Logic of Care* (2008), and Miriam Ticktin's *Causalities of Care* (2011), in the last of which Ticktin astutely asks, "When did it become true that humanitarianism was the best way to do politics? What kind of politics? . . . I turn to think about how humanitarianism and other 'regimes of care' have come to play a greater role in the governance of immigrants. This is despite the fact that such regimes of care do not purport to be about politics, but about emergencies and about protection, care and compassion" (61). The point here is to illuminate the predatory terrain upon which care operates. These are moments when the intent to do good necessarily requires calculated levels of force and coercion.

23. Webb Keane's work on sincerity is important here. He references a convergence of Puritan morality and scientific objectivity that aspires to "language so transparent that it would do no more than refer to those things intended by its speaker, thus serving as a proper vehicle for objectivity" (2002, 66). Keane's analysis evokes, even if unknowingly,

an Augustinian semiotics that pines for a transparency of both speech and soul. This is exactly what Pedro as pastor seeks: outward signs of complete sincerity. For further work on this matter, see Cary's *Outward Signs* (2008).

24. Chamayou writes that "hunting presupposes a form of empathy with the prey: to track effectively, one has to put oneself in its place. But this mental operation implied a denial of the absolute social distance between masters and their slaves that the hunting relationship sought precisely to reinstate. Thus, blacks were used against other blacks, on the racist assumption that the latter understood their 'kind' better, but also in order to avoid having to tangle with them. It was a hunt, not a fight among equals. A third term had to be brought into mediate" (2012, 41).

25. Three things are salient to note here. The first is that hunting as custodial labor aims to cultivate a level of sincerity as well as a sense of purpose among rehabilitated patients, similar to the kinds of volunteerism Juno Salazar Parreñas examines in her work on Malaysian orangutan rehabilitation centers. She writes, "affective encounters between bodies fill a demand for more meaningful purpose among professional workers (usually from the global north) who engage in commercial volunteerism or other efforts that at first glance appear to be altruistic" (2012, 674). The second is that hunting is meant, as Andrea Muehlebach aptly states, "to mak[e] compassion productive." Such affective labor exists as a "curious double . . . [a] complex composite of exploitation and salvation, exclusion and utopia, alienation and [engenders] new forms of sociality" (2011, 76). The last point is that this labor constitutes a form of ethical citizenship for chronically unemployable men. Also see João Biehl's quick reference to caring for "abandoned" subjects as pedagogical (2005, 65).

26. For more on the history of Pavón, see Ordoñez 2007 and Centro de Investigaciones Económicas Nacionales (CIEN) 2011.

27. These four huntsmen striding through the streets, for me, call to mind the work of Erving Goffman in *The Presentation of the Self in Everyday Life* (1961). Yet while Goffman tends to focus more closely on subjectivity and social interaction in the dramaturgy of everyday life, one can very easily extend his analysis to the making of sovereign power. Here hunters "act like a state" (Wedeen 2003) with their material performances invoking what scholars have called the dramaturgy of power (Cohen 1981). Such symbolic action calls to mind Clifford Geertz (1981), who analyzes the theatrical qualities of the state in his work on nineteenth-century Balinese Negara. For other work on performativity and the state, see Judith Butler and Gayatri Chakravorty Spivak's *Who Sings the Nation-State?* (2007).

28. According to research by the National Economic Research Center (CIEN), 75 percent of the economically active population in Guatemala is employed in the informal sector. This makes Guatemala the country with the largest percentage of informality in Central America, a fact reported by CIEN in 2006 and 2016.

29. This strained conversation evokes what Viviana A. Zelizer notes in her work on the purchase of intimacy, that "to label a payment as a gift (tip, bribe, charity, expression of esteem) rather than an entitlement (pension, allowance, rightful share of gains) or compensation (wages, salary, bonus, commission) is to make claims about the relationship between payer and payee . . . Negotiation, then, runs in both directions: from

definition of social ties to selection of appropriate payments, from forms of payment
to accepted definitions of ties" (2000, 826). The insistence that families do not pay pastors but rather provide offerings also intuits what Marcel Mauss (2000 [1954]) noted
about the gift—that gifts contribute to the construction of hierarchy and dominance
while simultaneously building group solidarity. The language of offering also insidi-
ously obscures the labor of circulating business cards, creating advertisements, and the
physical hunt itself—all central practices in the effort to capture users.

30. Gary Anderson writes, "in much of the New Testament, as well as in all of rabbinic
literature and Aramaic-speaking Christianity, the primary metaphor for sin is that of
debt.... For during the era in which sin begins to be thought of as debt, human virtue
assumes the role of a merit or credit" (2009, ix). Marcella Maria Althaus-Reid writes
that "the doctrine of redemption may have been the earliest attempt by Christianity to
sacralise a patriarchal economic order based on *debt*. Here we can detect the origins
of what we can call a 'judicial theology' or a lawyer's account of the rights and wrongs
of commercial spiritual transactions. But more than that, an ontological substratum
where debt is part of the cultural, economic and religious horizon of expectations"
(2007, 293). Her theological reflection reveals the overlapping metaphors that drive
both economy and salvation. She then thoughtfully, if not optimistically, adds, "the
economic system is one of these areas in which the revelation of God is particularly
visible, because economy is by nature a way of relationships, of loving exchanges and
the production and distribution of life" (295).

31. There is great precedence to the Protestant ideal that one cannot pay for salvation.
Salvation comes through faith, not works. Max Weber famously observes the role that
this belief plays in what he calls "the spirit of capitalism," where the faithful try to
discern whom among them God has chosen. "Good works," he writes, "are absolutely
unsuitable to serve as means for the acquisition of this certainty [of salvation]: because
even the saved are still mere humans determined by human wants and desires, all that
even they do falls infinitely short of God's demands. Nevertheless, good works are
indispensable as signs of election. They are technical means, but not ones that can be
used to purchase salvation. Rather, good works serve to banish the anxiety surround-
ing the question of one's salvation" (1905, 68).

32. Jan Van Baal defines an offering as "any act of presenting something to a supernatural
being, a sacrifice and offering accompanied by the ritual killing of the object of the offering" (1976, 161), adding that "a major problem of the gift is that of the inconsistences
of its reciprocity" (164). He rightfully observes that an exchange always traffics in some
level of risk and creates vulnerability: "it is not only that reciprocity is sometimes un-
balanced as in gift-exchange between partners of unequal status, but reciprocity can
also be muddled, unclear, a principle held in latency as a weapon in reserve against
persons who fail to comply with reasonable expectations" (165).

33. Archana Sridhar writes, "The government of Guatemala imposes a range of other,
smaller taxes on its citizens. Many of these also include exceptions for charities. For
example, Article 12 of Decree Number 15–98, the property tax law, grants limited ex-
emptions to certain categories of nonprofit associations, such as universities and other
educational centers. The statute's exemption for religious organizations probably stems

in part from Article 37 of the Constitution, which grants all churches an exemption from property taxes, provided that the property is used for social services, education, or religious purposes" (2007, 214–15).

34. To clarify, the house Pedro used as a center was never intended to be anything other than a family home. This invites a reflection on infrastructure as a social and material construct that provides a concrete means to examine the workings of power in society (Mann 1984; Star 1999). The materiality of abandoned buildings, for example, shapes social relations (Larkin 2013). A warehouse without closets results in men being tied up instead of locked up, and former apartment buildings often provide a world of corners in which captives conspire or simply find much needed moments of privacy. In this way, infrastructure renders ethnographically visible how social problems and possibilities get allocated unequally across communities and neighborhoods, with economic blight providing the spatial conditions for extrajudicial incarceration (Rodgers and O'Neill 2012).

35. As Clare Seelke and her colleagues (2011) note, United States assistance to Central America averaged $1.4 billion a year during the 1980s, but this money largely went to supporting anticommunist military forces. Concern for the region declined in the 1990s, but then surged in 2008 after the introduction of the Mérida Initiative, a multibillion-dollar security plan created to counter drug trafficking and the rise of transnational street gangs (Isacson and Kinosian 2015). Additional US funds were funnelled to Central America for the purposes of supporting counterdrug programs, like the ones that take place in Guatemala City for rehabilitation center directors. These have been funded by the International Narcotics Control and Law Enforcement (INL) and annual counternarcotic defense appropriations ("US Counternarcotics Programs in Latin America" n.d.).

36. The culprit here is a group called Daytop International. Daniel Wolfe and Roxanne Saucier spot the problem when they write, "Abuses are not limited to African, Asian, or post-Soviet countries. Indeed, the break-them-down, build-them-up model used as treatment in Asia finds its origins in a therapeutic community approach supported by Daytop, Inc., a US drug treatment provider that the US State Department has engaged to offer training in Cambodia, Vietnam, and other countries. While stressing the therapeutic value of support provided by drug-free peers, Daytop's philosophy regards active users as 'alone as in death.' This invocation of death in association with drug use, and the refusal to recognize existing social networks as in any way meaningful, echoes what some analysts of slavery and abuses in health care settings have termed 'social death'" (2010, 146). But of note here is how organizations like Daytop demonstrate a deeply familiar humanitarian logic that exports care from the Global North to the South, shipping a particular brand of prevention to places like Guatemala.

37. Chamayou writes, "But cynegetic violence does not occur only at the time of acquisition but also later on, as a means of governing. The hunt continues after the capture" (2012, 8).

38. Anthropologists tend to approach the topic of alcohol consumption as either an individual pathology or a social problem. Mariana Valverde (1998) has called it "a disease of the will," which focuses not on alcohol as a problem but rather on those social forces

that constitute the substance as a problem. In the Latin American context, fellow trav-
elers to this approach include Stanley Brandes's *Staying Sober in Mexico City* (2002)
and Adrienne Pine's *Working Hard, Drinking Hard* (2008). My contribution to these
perspectives is the reminder that alcohol is a depressant that can slow the users down,
which is significant when considering the practice of manhunting. Such a perspective
on alcohol as an object is influenced by the recent work of archaeologists like Michael
Dietler (2006) who examine how the substance as embodied material culture enacts
specific kinds of practices.

39. There are three interconnected points to make when thinking about speed in terms of
drugs and temporality. The first is that speed provides a short boost to users' vitality. In
Jason Pine's work on methamphetamine use in the rural US, a former addict is quoted
saying that he thought using speed would help him "get more life" (2007, 357). This
need for "more life" through drugs may give insight into a second point: how those
who experience precarity and stagnation seek to endure in such circumstances. For
work on endurance in late capitalism, see Povinelli 2011. The third is that this desire for
immediacy reflected in drug culture may be a symptom of life in late modernity. See
Tomlinson 2007 for an in-depth analysis of immediacy in modernity.

40. Michel Foucault writes, "a secret punishment is a punishment half wasted" (1977, 111).
The work of Diana Taylor (1997) makes eminently clear that there is obvious utility
in public disappearances for the sovereign, which is why they are often made into
public spectacles. The shrinking audience that bears witness to the sovereign's brutality speaks to the power of the state, one that can kill its subjects with impunity. Such
impunity operates during not just a civil war but also in the postwar period, as the
pastoral hunting of men in Guatemala City makes clear. Given that, as Schmitt so
aptly puts it, "sovereign is he who decides on the exception" (2005, 5), this raises an
Agamben-inspired analysis that the city is itself a state of exception.

CAPTIVITY

1. A few notes on these photographs. The first is that Heather Curtis (2012) and David
Morgan (2009) write about the relationship between seeing and feeling and how this
is deeply relevant to the study of religion. Of interest here are the optical tropes that
users deploy to evoke sympathy. The aesthetics of this empathy are intended not simply to generate and refine a feeling but also to establish a counterpoint against which
the sinner's eventual transformation will be judged. The second is that Allan Sekula's
"The Body and the Archive" (1986) retains its analytical influence even into the digital age. His concern for a "new juridical photographic realism" (5) underwrites much
of my analysis here, in much the same way that his work influences Shawn Michelle
Smith (1999) on the American archives of the nineteenth century. "Photography,"
Sekula writes, "came to establish and delimit the terrain of the other, to define both
the generalized look—the typology—and the contingent instance of deviance and

social pathology" (7). While these ideologies emerged in the nineteenth century, their resonances still linger in twenty-first-century Guatemala. The third is that the work of Roland Barthes (1977, 21) is helpful to think with here, namely his focus on how social relationships extend beyond the frame of the photograph. A more sociological perspective might also think about this in terms of "front stage" and "back stage," which are concepts that refer to different modes of behavior. Developed originally by Erving Goffman (1961b), the two terms help present a dramaturgical perspective by way of theatrical metaphors in an attempt to explain social interaction. Pedro here obviously has a great appreciation for the differences between these two stages.

2. In "Caught on Camera" (O'Neill 2017), I explore the imbrication of taking photos and taking men, assessing not only the visual technologies that forge new forms of social surveillance but also the Christian ontology that prompts these pastors to see (and seize) drug users. I found that discernment is absolutely central to this story. But rather than a mode of aesthetic judgement, with philosophical concerns for beauty and taste, discernment as a Pentecostal practice distinguishes the truly repentant soul from all the rest. Rooted in scripture (1 Cor. 12:10) and based on a rather dramatic division between good and evil, discernment describes the ability of Christians not simply to assess the spirits that purportedly drive a person's actions but also to appreciate the relative sincerity of the sinner.

3. The "morgue" in some ways speaks to how the newly abducted are understood as less than full human beings, though one must also consider the dynamics of withdrawal and notions of the undead. Some of this could be glossed by the work of Zygmunt Bauman (1992) and Orlando Patterson (1982) on social death, but the "Zombie Manifesto" by Sarah Juliet Lauro and Karen Embry leads us to examine the social and political processes that render men zombie-like: "we propose that reading the zombie as an ontic/hauntic object reveals much about the crisis of human embodiment, the way power works, and the history of man's subjugation and oppression of its 'Others'" (2008, 87).

4. Prison studies has long presumed a division between society and so-called prison culture, with life inside of the prison often imagined as completely set apart from the wider society. Erving Goffman's notion of the "total institution" (1961a) is one obvious point of reference but so too is Michel Foucault's "carceral archipelago" (1977), which acknowledges that penitentiary techniques extend into the entire social body but that nonetheless understands these techniques as contained within architecturally specific sites of discipline: the factory, school, and reformatory, for example. Yet a new generation of prison studies, largely based on research completed in North America, has begun to detail the intimate relationships that exist between these supposedly separate spheres of social relationships. Often understood as a "carceral continuum," in the words of Loïc Wacquant (2001), studies have detailed the many ways in which nonprisoners not only engage prison life but also how prison life extends into the community. See, for example, the work of Megan Comfort (2008) and Philippe Combessie (2002).

5. Here, the work of Chris Garces (2014) is insightful. Garces provides an analysis of Ecuador's prison administrations' demand for visual, digital, or physical strip searches of all adult citizens who establish contact with incarcerated subjects. Garces argues

that the maintenance of carceral boundaries effectively blurs any formal distinctions between desire and duty—insisting that one must always remain attuned to the sexualization of security. For more on the sexual undercurrents of surveillance, see Amar 2013. This is not to say that the strip search here in the center need be explicitly sexualized, but the homosociality of domination is certainly prevalent, with the public nudity of the captive compounding power dynamics.

6. In a photo essay coauthored with Benjamin Fogarty-Valenzuela (O'Neill and Fogarty-Valenzuela 2015), we detail the plight of Frener. It explores the reality of captivity and the rhetoric of positivity, to consider the politics of what Lauren Berlant (2011) would call "cruel optimism." It is this juxtaposition that helps capture the dire circumstances of those held inside these houses. It also reflects larger insights about the moral economy underlying Central America's war on drugs.

7. Émile Durkheim might have called this kind of communion a church, as he had little to say about the volition of ritual actors, but Pedro never went so far. In his distinction between magic and religion, Durkheim insists that magic "does not result in binding together those who adhere to it, nor in uniting them into a group leading a common life. There is no church of magic" (2008, 44). It is this ability for religion (as opposed to magic) to bind people—signified even in the very etymology of the word religion—that informs my sense of this center.

8. It should be noted that in the early twentieth century the Remington Typewriter Company worked with experts in acoustics to reduce the noise produced by its machines (Thompson 2004, 78), but the pastors of these Pentecostal drug rehabilitations centers seek the opposite. The sound of these typewriters envelops the ritual of intake.

9. Böhme writes that "you can be caught by an atmosphere" (2017, 2). For Böhme an atmosphere is an aesthetic impression, a "space with a certain tone of feeling" (2017, 12), and his most immediate analogue is Walter Benjamin's (2007) aura; but he also stays close to the Greek (atmos means "steam") to insist that atmospheres are affective, emotional resonances are nebulous and vaporous, that they are difficult to grasp. And yet Böhme also insists that they grab us. Atmospheres take hold of us, with the affective frame of this kind of captivity critically important to the analysis. Central here is how Böhme decenters subjective experience when considering aesthetics as the imbrication of emotion and space to render atmosphere "an indeterminate spatially extended quality of feeling" (Böhme 2017, 15; see also Böhme 1992).

10. One could follow an interest in the archive here. Most relevant is the incisive work on archives by Ann Stoler, who explores the techniques of classification practices by colonial administrators, "focus[ing] less on taxonomy than on the unsure and hesitant sorts of documentation and sensibilities gathered around them" (2010, 1). Stoler's attention to such archival practices demonstrates how the proliferation of documents, and the social categories they produced, index the ways colonial administrators scrambled to create order amid growing epistemic anxieties about the subjects they sought to govern. But the office's atmosphere is also important. The key reference here is Gernot Böhme (2017). His aesthetic theory of nature pushes away from the philosophy of aesthetic judgment, whose literature largely addresses the work of Immanuel Kant (1790 [2012]), to conceive of aesthetics not as the subjective judgment of art but

rather as perceptions that bind reality together (Chandler 2011, 556). Atmospheres can also be engineered, or what Böhme calls "staged materiality" (2017, 141–47). "Today," he writes, "there is no area of life, no product, no installation or collection that is not the explicit object of design" (2017, 27).

11. An attention to bureaucracy here opens an ethnographic line of inquiry into the practice of holding users captive. It is not just about ropes and razor wire. Centers such as Jorge's generated elaborate archival processes to ensnare their captives with the appearance of legitimacy. In this sense, Max Weber is generally the common point of reference for the social scientific study of bureaucracy (2002, 95). Weber's interest is in how bureaucracy institutionalizes norms through administrative practices. For Weber, "bureaucratic administration means fundamentally domination through knowledge" (Weber 2002, 225; Hull 2012, 25)—and this knowledge, I would like to advance, helps to knit together webs of predation.

12. It is important to note that bureaucracy extends well beyond methods of recording (Riles 1998). The intake and outtake forms are just two moments of this larger process of documenting users. More fundamental, however, is the point that the production of bureaucratic knowledge, and the negotiation of competing claims, mediates between administrators and the social realities with which they engage (Latour 2007). This produces representations that exert influence not only over the formation and character of the communities that they administer but also of individual subjects themselves. The forms and the photographs grip their subjects, interpolating them into a series of subjectivities that ultimately holds everyone in their rightful place.

13. The invocation of ritual here echoes the work of Catherine Bell, who argues that ritualization creates the conditions for a certain embodiment of power; ritual is a strategy that constitutes relations of power. Bell often returns to the work of Michel Foucault to flesh this last idea out. If ritual theory as discourse sets the conditions for conversations about ritual, then Bell, deploying an early moment in the work of Foucault (1972), suggests that the force of ritual activity is "to structure the possible field of actions of others" (2009, 200; see also Bell 1992).

14. An anthropology of waiting tends to juxtapose stretches of nonaction with so-called events. The central concern here is how waiting comes to be understood as prolonged moments of nonaction, epochs without events. Bruce O'Neill's (2014) work connects directly to these concerns, with his focus on homeless Romanians waiting for jobs to one day arrive to postcommunist Romania. This leads to the practice of what Michael Ralph calls "killing time." I am compelled by the captivity narrative that killing time produces for Ralph. He writes, "If access to transnational trade networks enables some youth to 'escape' this postcolonial predicament, it leaves others, imagined as having the requisite masculine characteristics to do so, disparaged for not capitalizing on the opportunities that are allegedly available to all who seek them. The idle young man who, instead of fleeing the civil sector, seems shackled to it thus becomes the index of a pathologically unproductive subject. In this sense, youth are subject to the state's 'frame up,' or 'criminalizing gaze'" (2008, 15).

15. Michel Foucault writes in *Discipline and Punish* (1977, 228), "Is it surprising that prisons resemble factories, schools, barracks, hospitals, which all resemble prisons?" The

limitation to affiliating this quote with Pentecostal drug rehabilitation centers is that Foucault took as his object of study an architectural structure imbued with a moral order. He then extrapolated from the prison and its panopticon to understand surveillance's extensive reach within similarly constructed structures. The flip here is that these Pentecostal drug rehabilitation centers have all been renovated for the purposes of rehabilitation. None of them, minus the occasional factory, have been structured around the practice of surveillance. Single family homes and former apartment buildings do not have the same kind of panoptic form, which made Jorge's efforts to transplant the prison inside of a mansion a difficult task.

16. Tithing is the biblical practice of congregants offering ten percent of their wages to their church. The practice often gets reduced to the sole reason for church growth, the logic being that church planting could very well be the only growth industry in a country such as Guatemala. But the payments one receives from pastoring need not be monetary (Anderson 2009). There are other forms of capital that preaching provides, with alternative kinds of value (and labor) presumed (Bourdieu 1986). Viviana A. Zelizer asks, when trying to extend the range of exchanges implied by payment to a wider range of intimacy: "what forms of payment correspond to which relations, and why? To what extent are correspondences between forms of payment and types of relation subject to historical variability?" (2000, 823). To preach the word for no monetary gain makes sense here because these pastors not only get the opportunity to be called pastor, compensation in its own right, but also to remind themselves of from where they came.

17. This push toward having a positive attitude patently illustrates how the surface of the self operates as a site of governance. From a certain analytical perspective, this pastoral interest in a positive attitude indicates just how successful Pentecostalism has been in getting believers "to write and tell their personal narratives with an eye to the social good" and how "narratives bring people to see the details of their personal lives and their chances for improving their lives [as] inextricably linked to what is good for all of society" (Cruikshank 1996, 233–34). My continued interest in the work of Barbara Cruikshank lies in her ability to identify the self as the field on which political action takes place. While she writes specifically about self-esteem, the notion of a positive attitude can serve easily as an analogue.

18. There is an art to listening. Foucault refers to a distinction between Plato's interest in cultivating dialogue and the Pythagorean cultivation of silence and listening (1997b, 236). These are two very different activities that need to be cultivated, learned, and even practiced. Foucault's use of the term "art" is telling—listening is not inactivity but rather a certain kind of work that takes times to perfect. This includes a balance between discerning what is said and what is not said. Amira Mittermaier addresses this careful art of listening in her introduction to her *Dreams That Matter*: "It was a constant challenge during my fieldwork—a challenge that I hope to pass on in the form of this book—not just theoretically questioning the positivistic premise that the most visible is the most real, but actually suspending this premise to some extent while listening to my interlocutor's stories. I tried to cultivate a mode of listening that does not presume to know better than my interlocutors what kind of experience the dream really is" (2010, 21).

19. Susan Harding notes that social scientists writing about conversion tend to frame converts as "susceptible, vulnerable, and in need of something" (2000, 35). This ends up making conversion sound rather manipulative. To counter, Harding describes her own experience of coming under what she calls conviction. She describes how she found herself "caught up in the Reverend Campbell's stories—I had 'caught' his language—enough to hear God speak to me when I almost collided with another car that afternoon. Indeed, the near-accident did not seem like an accident at all, for there is no such thing as a coincidence in born-again culture" (59). This is a productive contribution, but it leaves unestablished how to regard moments when potential converts find sermons offensive, when the word of God slaps them across the face. There are so many ethnographies that describe when Christianity works but not nearly enough of when it fails or offends. Jessica Johnson's *Biblical Porn* (2018) is the best ethnography to date to spot this line of research.

20. Michel Foucault's later works engage what he calls "self-writing" (1997a, 209), which involves an improvisational elaboration of the self. In his own writings on self-writing, Foucault explores Christian technologies of the self, explaining that it is an ascetic practice. Writing, as Foucault observes, plays an important role in self-training. Foucault also notes the ancients' use of notebooks as a technology of the self. These notebooks not only guided action but also provided advice. In a related sense, Phillip Cary's *Outward Signs* (2008) argues that Augustine (1992) invented an expressionist semiotics. This is an approach to language where outward signs express inner truths. For Augustine, outward signs direct us to a higher source of divine truth with the inner eye of our own mind. Sin has isolated each and every human being, Augustine argues, and this has left humans struggling to communicate ourselves to each other, for no one can properly convey an inner good to the soul.

21. There is a long tradition of identifying letters written from captivity as a distinct genre. These notes invoke a long history of jailhouse letters—from Antonio Gramsci's *Prison Notebooks* (1992 [1948]) to Martin Luther King Jr.'s "Letter from a Birmingham Jail" (1963). Captivity seems to deliver to not just the author but also the page a sense of purpose and clarity, maybe even an immediacy, that ignites the missive with insight. Mohamedou Ould Slahi writes in his *Guantánamo Diary* (2015, 314): "I was in a worse situation than a slave: at least a slave is not always shackled in chains, has some limited freedom, and doesn't have to listen to some interrogator's bullshit every day. I often compared myself with a slave. Slaves were taken forcibly from Africa, and so was I. Slaves were sold a couple of times on their way to their final destination, and so was I. Slaves suddenly were assigned to somebody they didn't choose, and so was I. And when I looked at the history of slaves, I noticed that slaves sometimes ended up an integral part of the master's house."

22. Elizabeth Povinelli articulates endurance as "the problem of substance: its strength, hardiness, callousness; its continuity through space; its ability to suffer and yet persist. . . . Moreover, endurance encloses itself around the durative—the temporality of continuance, a denotation of continuous action without any reference to its beginning or end and outside the dialectic of presence and absence. Enduring isn't a singularity. . . . [E]ndurance is not a homogenous space. Every scene of endurance, and

certainly the scenes that concern this book, is shot through with multiple and incommensurate configurations of tense, eventfulness, and ethical substance and aggregations of life. The alternative social projects that lie within these stretched and striated spaces must survive eventfulness that is below the threshold of the catastrophic and ethical substance as sacrifice" (2011, 32). See also Garcia 2017.

23. To take Santiago's appreciation of ghosts and haunting is to assess both just how presence is constituted but also how absence becomes understood. One point of reference is Jacques Derrida's *Specters of Marx*, especially his term "hauntology." He writes, "*What is* a ghost? What is the *effectivity* or the *presence* of a specter, that is, of what seems to remain as ineffective, virtual, insubstantial as a simulacrum? Is there *there,* between the thing itself and its simulacrum, an opposition that holds up? Repetition *and* first time, but also repetition *and* last time, since the singularity of any *first time* makes of it also a *last time.* Each time it is the event itself, a first time is a last time. Altogether other. Staging for the end of history. Let us call it a *Hauntology"* (1994, 10). See also the work of Katie Kilroy-Marac (2014).

24. Of note is that the most compelling moments of self-expression inside these centers came in the form of Chicano/a prison art. First appearing in the 1940s in penitentiaries across Texas, California, and New Mexico, this genre of art soon flourished in Guatemala's Pentecostal drug rehabilitation centers, quickly laying claim to how interconnected these centers are with state-run prisons in the United States. One point is that the deported bring to Guatemala different modes of cultural production. We see this in the historical work of Martha Henry (2005), but there is also a more theoretical point to make about these images—that they demonstrate how drawings as a medium operates as what Birgit Meyer calls a "sensational form," one that "encompasses the levels of perception . . . feeling . . . and signification" (2015, 22). Of interest is that the immediacy both produced and promised by these drawings evidences the centrality of sensuous media in the experience of captivity. Work by William Mazzarella (2013) and Jill Stevenson (2013) also explores how images have the power to arrest their viewers at the level of the body, across the viewing public's social skin.

25. The question of legibility, namely the Christian rendering himself legible, is a distinctly Pentecostal concern. Amos Yong (2000, 2004) would call this a hermeneutics of life. He defines the phrase, in relationship to what Pentecostals understand as the life of the Holy Spirit, as a "hermeneutics of life that is both a divine gift and a human activity aimed at reading correctly the inner processes of all things." This means that discernment as a "spiritual gift" is "for the specific purposes of providing insight and guidance, and for edifying the people of God" (2004, 84, 98). The artwork, from the perspective of faith, is a confessional moment to externalize the moral dramas that reside within a person.

26. Liberation or salvation, I write elsewhere, is about space, not time. This is distinctly meant to run against a telos of progress: "Today, as a Pentecostal practice, Christian liberation and its formation of the will are not about time (or progress or even the future). It is about space. It is about getting the fuck out of here. From temporality to spatiality, from progress to egress, a 'will to escape,' as I call it, now organizes the practice of Christian liberation. Locked up, tied up, and told to shape up, users come to confess, at times plead, that they want out and they want it now. Pentecostal rehabilita-

tion centers, in response, assure them that captivity is itself liberation" (K. O'Neill 2014, 12). For more on the temporalities of neoliberalism, see also the work of Elysée Nouvet (2014) and Clara Han (2011).

27. The term warehousing is dependent upon the infrastructure at play here. Centers are often staged inside of gaping structures with minimalist floorplans. These are makeshift spaces, cobbled together with secondhand materials that produce cavernous enclosures completely walled off from the outside. The anthropology of infrastructure details the way that the built form regulates the politics of belonging to the city (Anand 2015), to the state (Collier 2011), and to the global economy (Appel 2012). Of interest to the literature is how infrastructure projects often build towards a desired future (Harvey and Knox 2012) but here, through the repurposing of the built form, the ruins of the past get retrofitted to underlie a stalled present.

28. Waiting is a fecund Christian category. The most optimistic approach is found in the work of theologian Jürgen Moltmann, namely in *The Coming of God* (2004). Moltmann stands Christian eschatology on its head: rather than an apocalyptic end, he focuses on what a liberationist perspective might understand as the final solution. "Christian eschatology," he writes, "is the remembered hope of the raising of the crucified Christ, so it talks about beginning afresh in the deadly end" (xi). Sadly, his "horizon of expectation" for transformation in God does not order these centers, with the work of waiting there ultimately taking the form of a frustrated practice.

29. See J. L. Austin, *How to Do Things with Words* (1975). Austin maintains that sincerity is a condition for felicity. For more on sincerity and illocutionary acts, see Hent de Vries, "Must We (Not) Mean What We Say?" (2009).

30. See Erving Goffman, *Relations in Public* (1971), 113. And see Paul de Man, *Allegories of Reading* (1982), for a distinction between the structure of a confession and the structure of an excuse.

ESCAPE

1. Pedro often proved that pastoralism as a technique of governance is alive and well in the very Christian fields from which Michel Foucault drew the concept. It is worthwhile to quote Foucault at length. He writes: "To say that power took possession of life in the nineteenth century, or to say that power at least takes life under its care in the nineteenth century, is to say that it has, thanks to the play of technologies of discipline on the one hand and technologies of regulation on the other, succeeded in covering the whole surface that lies between the organic and the biological, between body and population. We are, then, in a power that has taken control of both the body and life or that has, if you like, taken control of life in general—with the body as one pole and the population as the other" (2003, 252–53; see Rabinow and Rose 2006).

2. The idea that human rights is common knowledge in Guatemala says far less about human rights as a set of universal values and more about the history of the country's

wartime era. If human rights emerged as a technique of governance following World War II, amid the Cold War, then Guatemala became a beachfront amid this battle for human dignity with the publication of *I, Rigoberta Menchú* (2011), which not only garnered the author the 1992 Nobel Peace Prize but also set the discursive conditions for Guatemala to become a site of intervention. This included the rise of international human rights organizations in Guatemala as well as the eventual writing of two truth commission reports that deploy the language of human rights to characterize the country's civil war as genocidal (REMHI 1998; CEH 1999). This movement came with institutional shifts, including the influence of international watchdogs and a new logic through which to pursue diplomacy, but it also included efforts at general education, with the distribution of posters, pamphlets, and fliers that sought to teach all Guatemalans about their inalienable rights (Cardenas 2010). Pedro formed his hunting parties not only amid this sea of concern but also in direct tension with it.

3. There is something ironic about Pedro's Christian refusal of human rights, given that the history of human rights has such a clear Christian history. The work of Samuel Moyn is probably the strongest point of reference. In *Christian Human Rights* (2015), Moyn argues that religious thought within Christian churches just prior to World War II set the conditions for the rise of human rights. Much of this has had to do with the Roman Catholic Church's articulation of human dignity, which is a decidedly different genealogy of human rights than those that focus on the legacy of the French Revolution. Talal Asad has somewhat parallel interests (though motivated by a rather different argument) when he writes about human rights and what they do (2000): "[B]ecause champions of human rights have strong emotions invested in their point of view, I must begin by clearly warning the reader that what may appear to be a criticism of the very idea of universal values is not so at all but simply an attempt to describe something of what it means to apply universal values in the world today, and to inquire briefly into some of their specifically Christian roots."

4. It is productive to situate Alejandro's labor within a much longer history of prison labor. The vast majority of histories of prison labor come from research completed in and from the United States, with the dynamics driven by state efforts to extract as much value from the prison population as possible. Of interest is how Pedro manipulates the intention of this conscripted labor as a form of therapy to assign a redemptive value to the efforts of Alejandro and his fellow captives. These strategies appear repeatedly in prison studies as everything from the chain gang to prison lawyering, becoming imbued with the power of rehabilitation—as opportunities for prisoners to perform not simply their contrition but also their newfound entrepreneurialism. For studies of this process, see Lichtenstein 1996; Lafer 2003; LeFlouria 2015.

5. Labor within the center can be understood as conscripted, with Alejandro working for Pedro in all kinds of ways that allowed the pastor to maintain a large and complicated business without any paid staff. Yet it should also be said that Pedro often pressed Alejandro into the service of immaterial labor—that is, the work of of self-regulation (Parreñas 2012). One must not overlook the fact that the arduous effort of corralling and emplotting all of the center's intensity into sincerity is itself a kind of work. Following Michael Hardt, one can argue that immaterial labor "has assumed a dominant

position with respect to the other forms of labor in the globalist capitalist economy" (1999, 90). Alejandro's emotional labor is not incidental to the pastor's enterprise, and their relationship, however fraught, is not somehow the effect of material labor. It is the work of hunting itself.

6. The work of Winnifred Fallers Sullivan makes clear that the separation of church and state in the United States is not a viable distinction. Her study of faith-based prisons (2009) suggests to her that religious authority "has shifted from institutions to individuals," which makes it difficult to constitutionally disentangle religion from the state. The curiosity that Pedro's center raises is how these two social forces—religion and sovereignty—could ever be understood as distinct in the first place. It is the work of Mark Lewis Taylor (2014), also in the context of the United States, which seems to suggest that Christianity and the language of prison reform have always been entangled. Alejandro's deployment of biblical verses to stitch together theological arguments ultimately makes great ethnographic sense, for the Bible exists as one of the only (if not the sole) moral languages available to him while inside the center.

7. In March 2016, a parallel institution to these Pentecostal drug rehabilitation centers held more than 700 women within high walls and barbed wire. The center caught on fire, resulting in the death of forty people. The investigative reports that followed stitch together a dramatic scene of captives held against their will, with some lighting mattresses on fire as part of elaborate escape plans (Goldman 2017).

8. The history of such an affect clearly stretches back to ethnography's colonial roots, in which ethnographers would engage the so-called savage other to better understand the human condition. Ethnography's exotifying tendencies also mixed with the excitement of intervention, with the righteous subtext of most human rights discourses that know beyond cultural specificities the proper way to respect thy neighbor. Anthropology presented a strong critique of this history in the 1980s and has continued to this day. These artful critiques will surely be applied to this ethnography, which routinely finds itself not simply mediating but also (if involuntarily) adjudicating the intricacies of compulsory drug rehabilitation. For critiques of ethnography as colonial, see the following note.

9. Feminist and postcolonial scholars have positioned ethnographers today to be wary of implementing a well-worn motif, one that Gayatri Spivak (1988) noted decades ago: "The white men are saving the brown women from the brown men." Seminal studies drive home some version of this point, as in the work of Talal Asad (1973), Ruth Behar (1996), Johannes Fabian (1983), and Clifford Geertz (1988). More recently, Victor Rios has commented on "the jungle-book trope" and Laurence Ralph on "Tarzan ethnography," wherein which researchers descend into a dark world and live to tell about it.

10. In *Discipline and Punish*, Michel Foucault writes, "The panoptic mechanism arranges spatial unities that make it possible to see constantly and to recognize immediately. In short, it reverses the principle of the dungeon . . . to enclose, to deprive of light and to hide—it preserves the first and eliminates the other two. Full lighting and the eye of a supervisor capture better than darkness . . . Visibility is a trap" (1977, 200). I want to advance, as so many scholars of Foucault have, the idea not only that visibility is a trap but also that freedom is a trap. By this I draw on the work of Patrick Joyce (2003) to

consider the production of certain kinds of citizens and patterns of social life—all in the name of freedom. Joyce lingers on the material form of the city (its layout, architecture, infrastructure), but I want to think about the Christian promise of freedom from sin and the kind of submissive subjectivity that such liberation demands. This longstanding tension between freedom from sin and slavery to Christ (as well as its inverse: freedom from Christ and slavery to sin) permeates these centers. See also Dale Martin's *Slavery as Salvation* (1990).

11. Michel Foucault writes, "Is it surprising that the cellular prison, with its regular chronologies, forced labour, its authorities of surveillance and registration, its experts in normality, who continue and multiply the functions of the judge, should have become the modern instrument of penality? Is it surprising that prisons resemble factories, schools, barracks, hospitals, which all resemble prisons?" (1977, 227–228).

12. For an analysis of salvation as a constant cycle of redemption and then backsliding, see Austin 1981.

13. During a 1975 interview with the Paris newspaper *Le Monde*, which was later translated and published by the *New York Times Review of Books*, Michel Foucault discusses the prison's invention of the prisoner. I quote him at length: "The social role of internment is to be discovered in terms of a person who begins to emerge in the 19th century: the delinquent. This establishment of the criminal world is absolutely correlated with the existence of prisons. Within the masses, a small core of people became, so to speak, the privileged and exclusive licensees of criminal activity. In the classic age, on the contrary, violence, petty thievery and embezzlement were extremely common and, in the long run, were tolerated by everyone. The malefactor, it seems, was able to melt very easily into society. If he happened to get caught, penal procedures were swift and definitive: death, life in the galleys, banishment. The criminal world was not so closed in on itself, something that developed essentially out of the existence of prisons, out of the 'marinade' of prison society that forms a microsociety in which men find real solidarity that will provide them, on their release, with mutual support. Prison is a recruitment center for the army of crime. That is what it achieves. For 200 years everybody has been saying, 'Prisons are failing; all they do is produce new criminals.' I would say on the other hand, 'They are a success, since that is what has been asked of them'" (Droit 1975).

14. This brief reference to human trafficking is intentional. The United Nations provides a clear definition of human trafficking in Article 3, paragraph (a) of the "Protocol to Prevent, Suppress and Punish Trafficking in Persons." It defines trafficking in persons as "the recruitment, transportation, transfer, harboring or receipt of persons, by means of the threat or use of force or other forms of coercion, of abduction, of fraud, of deception, of the abuse of power or of a position of vulnerability or of the giving or receiving of payments or benefits to achieve the consent of a person having control over another person, for the purpose of exploitation. Exploitation shall include, at a minimum, the exploitation of the prostitution of others or other forms of sexual exploitation, forced labor or services, slavery or practices similar to slavery, servitude or the removal of organs." Accompanying literature then presents elements of human trafficking, with the idea that trafficking in persons has three constituent elements. There is the act of

trafficking: "Recruitment, transportation, transfer, harboring or receipt of persons." There is then the means: "Threat or use of force, coercion, abduction, fraud, deception, abuse of power or vulnerability, or giving payments or benefits to a person in control of the victim." And then there is the purpose: "For the purpose of exploitation, which includes exploiting the prostitution of others, sexual exploitation, forced labor, slavery or similar practices and the removal of organs. To ascertain whether a particular circumstance constitutes trafficking in persons, consider the definition of trafficking in the Trafficking in Persons Protocol and the constituent elements of the offense, as defined by relevant domestic legislation" (UNODC 2017).

15. My hesitation was often colored by disciplinary concerns, with the fear that I might reproduce Gayatri Spivak's longstanding critique that "the white men are saving the brown women from the brown men." For this extended ethnographic engagement took place against the backdrop of an already established anthropology of violence. This includes the work of Ruth Behar (2003), Nancy Scheper-Hughes (1993), and Philippe Bourgois (1996) as well as a more recent generation of ethnographers whose research engages directly with debates over the representation of violence in Latin America (Zilberg 2011; De Leon 2015). The work of Ellen Moodie in postwar El Salvador proves instructive, with her commitment to modulating the talk of crime to avoid tropes of male delinquency. As Moodie reminds the anthropologist, and by extension scholars of Latin America, "the social obsession about crime and criminals . . . is not just about crime and criminals" (2010, 171). I have always wanted to sidestep an unreflexive interest in violence. As a model for this approach, I have looked toward the work of Angela Garcia, whose 2016 essay on an individual prisoner in New Mexico provides a particularly rich understanding of the emotional complexities of incarceration through a single informant.

16. In a passage cited earlier, Chamayou writes: "The problem, in fact, is that hunting presupposes a form of empathy with the prey: to track effectively, one has to put oneself in its place. But this mental operation implied a denial of the absolute social distance between masters and their slaves that the hunting relationship sought precisely to reinstate. Thus, blacks were used against other blacks, in the racist relationship that the latter understood their 'kind' better, but also in order to avoid having to tangle with them. It was a hunt, not a fight among equals. A third term had to be brought in to mediate" (2012, 65).

17. Anticipation is a tactic. A strategy, in contrast, is a blueprint. In *The Practice of Everyday Life*, Michel de Certeau defines strategies as a "calculus of force relationships when a subject of will and power (a proprietor, an enterprise, a city, a scientific institution) can be isolated from an environment" (2011, 5). Strategies tend to draw boundaries around places. Prison plans, for example, comprise a strategy. However, tactics, as understood by Certeau, react directly to strategies. They amount to "clever tricks, knowing how to get away with things, the hunter's cunning, maneuvers, polymorphic simulations, joyful discoveries poetic as well as warlike they go back to the immemorial" (7). Pedro touring his center from the perspective of the captive is an example of tactical anticipation, of the hunter's cunning.

18. James Scott tracks techniques of evasion and resistance among peasants. He writes: "Everyday forms of resistance make no headlines. Just as millions of anthozoan polyps

create, willy-nilly, a coral reef, so do thousands upon thousands of individual acts of insubordination and evasion create a political or economic barrier reef of their own. There is rarely any dramatic confrontation, any moment that is particularly newsworthy. And whenever, to pursue the simile, the ship of state runs aground on such a reef, attention is typically directed to the shipwreck itself and not to the vast aggregation of petty acts that made it possible. It is only rarely that the perpetrators of these petty acts seek to call attention to themselves. . . . The nature of the acts themselves and the self-interested muteness of the antagonists thus conspire to create a kind of complicitous silence that all but expunges everyday forms of resistance from the historical record" (1987, 18–19).

19. Work on recidivism makes clear that a constellation of factors need to combine to make permanent, lasting change possible for those dependent upon drugs and alcohol. Part of the problem can be said to be biochemical, but social scientists also stress the cultural and historical contexts in which people use drugs and alcohol. The work of Philippe Bourgois, for example, is a clarion call to consider the structural conditions of drug dependency, whether it be crack cocaine in New York City or heroin in San Francisco. See also Farmer 2009; Bourgois and Schonberg 2009; Garcia 2010; Contreras 2012.

20. In this sense, the center holds the user captive as much in a moral as in a material sense. The barred windows and locked doors clearly keep the user from leaving the house, but the social dynamics of substance abuse also tether the user to the center, pulling him back to the house with a frightening level of consistency. If the power of the hunt is its potential for reversal, for prey to become predator, then the practical limitations of this power seem to be the social context in which this hunting happens. The broader context of Guatemala City, with its near complete lack of social services and astounding levels of urban violence, tends to make complete reversals relatively unrealistic. Hence these momentary flashes of upheaval, no matter how tricky they appear to be, routinely deliver the user back to the center either by force or through his own will. Captives have tied up their captors, they have stabbed their pastors, and they have flung open center doors with their own force, but to what end? They then stand in broad daylight, a few meters into freedom, but at a complete loss for where to go or to whom to turn.

21. It should not be overlooked that a Christian anthropology, at its most fundamental, presumes at least two things. The first is that everyone is a sinner and the second is that all sinners must change. Variations across denominations quickly emerge about the intricacies of sin and the process by which sinners can change, but these two theological statements structure so much of center life in Guatemala City, allowing pastors not only to presume sin but also to implore individual transformation.

22. The comment that theological therapy is an improvisational practice is not to dismiss it as unformulated or void of content. It is, first, to establish that the practice of theological therapy stretches across a wide spectrum of practices that shuttle between distantly biomedical commitments to illness and symptoms and the Pentecostal pole of possession and spiritual warfare. The one constant is that all of these centers insist that they practice theological therapy, if only to shoehorn themselves into a public

health model of care. This recalls the work of Julie Livingston (2012), whose work in Botswana explores a cancer ward amid an epidemic. Key are the contingencies in spaces where there is an extreme lack of resources, including medicine, machines, and even hospital space itself.

23. It is important to note that Pentecostal drug rehabilitation centers butt up against normative, liberal formations of care. Anthropologists have long explored alternative and indigenous modalities of care in a variety of contexts. See Kleinman 1978; Geissler and Wenzel 1998; Good 2010.

24. Redemption in the Pentecostal tradition is the fulfillment of history, and it begins with eschatological expectation, often with world history signaling the imminent end of this world and the beginning of the next. One problem within Pentecostal communities has been a frustration with an immanent end that never seems to arrive, and so scholars have observed that a growing proportion of Pentecostals have shifted expectations from the redemption of humankind to the redemption of individual people. See the work of Cristiana Giordano (2016), whose ethnography of Catholic nuns involved in state-funded rehabilitation programs for former foreign prostitutes illustrates a Roman Catholic instantiation of biopolitics.

25. Alvarado 2001.

26. The centrality of personal responsibility to Christian subjectivity has been well documented, alongside how this Christian subjectivity folds neatly into neoliberal notions of the self, which celebrates the will as an autonomous faculty. For neoliberalism generally, see Sawyer 2004; Sunder Rajan 2006; Rofel 2007. For the neoliberal Christian generally, see Meyer 2010; Marshall 2010; Smith 2010; O'Neill 2012.

27. It is appropriate to quote Max Weber on domination here, if only because it is clear that Pedro dominates Alejandro within the center but also that Alejandro makes decisions in relationship to his domination. "Every genuine form of domination," Weber writes, "implies a minimum of voluntary compliance, that is, an interest . . . in obedience. [C]ustoms, personal advantage, purely effectual or ideal motives of solidarity do not form a sufficiently reliable basis for a given domination. In addition there is . . . a further element, the belief in legitimacy. . . . Every system attempts to establish . . . the belief in its legitimacy" (1978, 212–13). Alejandro presented a consistent case in which his domination always met a general belief in its legitimacy, such that Alejandro did not become complicit in his own domination so much as he asserted himself as a political actor through the very contours of his domination.

28. The roof of the center was a porous place. It was also elevated, which injected the captive with a newfound perspective on the city as well as on life. Spending time atop the center, inside the kitchen, always called to mind (in obviously far more modest scales) Michel de Certeau's seminal essay titled "Walking in the City," which begins with his experience of viewing New York City atop the World Trade Center. He notes that "to be lifted to the summit of the World Trade Center is to be lifted out of the city's grasp" (2011, 92). I am compelled by the power of verticality that Certeau spots as well as his recognition that cities hold people, that they constrain them. It would be overextended to say that the city, much like Pedro's center, tries to grasp the citizen, but there is something revelatory about standing above it all with the wind on your face.

29. One would not want to stretch this metaphor beyond its limits, but there did emerge inside the center a tacit sense as to when captives overextended Pedro's trust or when they earned more trust from this man. So much of this center functioned through reciprocal economies of material goods but also immaterial, affective charges of sympathy, trust, sincerity, and respect. To misread or misuse this system carried severe consequences, including freedom itself. For keen ethnographies of debit and credit, even if largely in the idiom of political economy, see Chu 2010; Han 2011; Stout 2016.

30. Jacques Derrida begins *The Politics of Friendship* with a quote attributed to Aristotle: "O my friends, there is no friend." Derrida uses this quote to create an analogy between friendship and politics, with survival key to the construction. He writes: "Hence surviving is at once the essence, the origin and the possibility, the condition of possibility of friendship; it is the grieved act of loving. This time of survival thus gives the times if friendship" (2006, 14). He later writes, "Friendship always begins with surviving" (291). In an interview about his work on friendship, Derrida would explain that in Aristotle "we find friendship, knowledge, and death, but also survival in one and the same configuration" (cited in Cheah and Guerlac 2009, 10). It is Derrida's insistence on understanding survival alongside friendship that resonates with this ethnographic effort to highlight the fragile bonds of intimacy, not in some crass functionalist sense that friendship makes survival possible but rather in the philosophical sense that friendship is a political conception of democracy, of belonging.

31. Loneliness and being alone, philosophically speaking, are not the same conditions. Lars Svendsen (2017) defines loneliness as "social withdrawal, a feeling of discomfort or pain that informs us that our need for attachment to others is not satisfied." Being alone has historically been celebrated by such philosophers as Friedrich Nietzsche (1997, 139) for both political and intellectual purposes: "Where there have been powerful societies, governments, religions, public opinions, in short wherever there has been tyranny, there the solitary philosopher has been hated; for philosophy offers an asylum to a man into which no tyranny can force its way, the inward cave, the labyrinth of the heart: and that annoys the tyrants."

32. Throughout the fieldwork there emerged radically divergent senses of risk, with mine always gravitating toward liberal conceptions of public health and these captives always concerned with alternative formations of risk—the risk of being caught and then the risk of being released into the streets, for example. My repeated concerns about fire codes, locked doors, and how sanitized these centers were proved to be a nagging reminder of my own presuppositions about risk, which often fit neatly into what ethnographers have come to understand as techniques to assess future events—such as accidents, attacks, or outbreaks (Defert 1991; O'Malley 1996; Collier and Lakoff 2008).

33. Clothes have long been signs of redemption and sincerity. Formalizing one's appearance has always been central to a new Christian lifestyle. As Jean and John Comaroff note, for the South African rather than the Central American context, "standards of Christian decency applied to dress, and converts had to ensure that their distinction from their fellows was shown in their attire." A refined appearance delivered "a newly embodied sense of self-worth, taste and personhood" (Comaroff and Comaroff 1986; see also Meyer 1999).

RETURN

1. Plato's "Allegory of the Cave" (2017) signals the start of a broader motif that courses through Western thought—that is, a release from the bondage of either ignorance or innocence. The allegory is not necessarily about material captivity, although that is certainly part of the problem, but rather about the intellectual captivity suffered by the slaves. This is what resonates so well with my own moment of leaving the center. Far more than the shackles, the imperative of this allegory is to escape the shadows. It is an imperative familiar to Hegel's master/slave narrative (1979) or Freud's theory of neurosis (1989), even Adorno and Horkheimer's critique of culture (1997). Each wants to see the light.

2. As I have written elsewhere (Benson and O'Neill 2007), conversations about the ethics of fieldwork tend to theorize the product rather than the process of fieldwork. See, for example, the attention to writing culture in the discipline of anthropology, with its insightful attention to ethnographic representation (Crapanzano 1980; Marcus and Cushman 1982; Rabinow 2007; Clifford 1988; Clifford and Marcus 1986). But there is also a need to consider the ethics and politics of the face-to-face encounter between ethnographer and informant as primary to textual representations. Liberal conversation regarding ethics tends to dominate much of contemporary thought and political debate. Against a model of ethics premised upon rights and equality, the anthropologist can also be pushed to consider the self as responsible for the informant and maybe even embedded within an unequal and hierarchical encounter. This emphasis on inequality and responsibility in the work of Emmanuel Levinas (1969) has always challenged me during conversations about the ethics of fieldwork.

3. The clearest articulation of ethnography as a moral economy comes from Philippe Bourgois and Jeff Schonberg's reflections on their fieldwork with heroin users (2009). Two points translate well in Guatemala. The first is that "gifts of money, blankets, and food were the primary means—aside from sharing drugs—they used to define and express friendships, organize interpersonal hierarchies, and exclude undesirable outsiders . . . We had to become sufficiently immersed in the logics of hustling to be able to recognize through an acquired common sense, when to give, when to help, when to say no, and when to be angry" (6). My presence within the center, especially its general population, established the conditions for a moral economy between me and these men, with my access to the outside world and its resources proving to be one of the mediums through which we negotiated our relationships to each other. The second is that "dogmatic rules for researchers with respect to giving money or doing favors for research subjects are out of touch with the practical realities on the street" (6). It is wildly impractical to think that extended research could be completed without some kind of moral economy emerging, just as it would be unthinkable for a friendship to form without an exchange of gifts and favors.

4. There is an important point to make about the efficiency of Pentecostal drug rehabilitation centers. The price placed on Alejandro's freedom is offensive in one perspective, but it also notes an incredibly streamlined process compared to those within

the country's prison system. Underfunded and overcrowded, prisons in Guatemala routinely erupt into riots, and as much as five percent of its prison population remains behind bars well past their court mandated release dates purely because of bureaucratic failures (CIEN 2011). Files regularly go missing while a limited number of government attorneys have proven incapable of keeping up with an ever-mounting stack of paperwork. The convicted enter Guatemala's prisons, but it is increasingly difficult to get them out; the families of drug users know this. This is why so many of them seek out an alternative to prison, and why a growing number of judges offer defendants the opportunity to enter a center rather than a prison.

5. There is a growing anthropological tradition that announces quite predictably that "there is no Archimedean point from which either one's self-interest or means-ends calculations can be objectively perceived and evaluated" (Keane 2010, 82; see also Lambek 2010; Throop 2008). But there are actually few examples of anthropologists directly engaging in conversations over the experience of ethics in an analytically sophisticated way. I am attracted to anthropologists that wrestle with the density of moral experience, such as with the work of Angela Garcia (2014) and Anand Pandian (2010). Pandian writes well (67): "The simple image of a fold, its interior depths formed by the turning of a surface against itself, may provide the clearest means of grasping the openness of this process. What one finds in Nietzsche's account of interiority, Foucault has argued, is a 'glittering exteriority that was covered up and buried': genealogy reveals that personal 'depth was only a game and a surface fold,' an interior volume fashioned through the involution and creasing over of an exterior horizon (Foucault 1998, 273). Building upon such observations, Gilles Deleuze (1988) has suggested that ethics in Foucault's sense are best understood by means of this language of 'folding,' arguing that the ethical practices that Foucault examined in the classical Western world—such as bodily exercises and pedagogic relations to others—should be understood as ways of transforming relations with an 'outside' into relations with oneself."

6. Categorical imperatives, argues Immanuel Kant (1996), form the foundation of our moral duties as humans. They are *imperatives* because they are commands ("Thou shalt not kill") delivered to those who could follow them but not need to follow them. The rational will must ascend to these imperatives because they are nonnegotiable. Abolitionism largely functions along a series of categorical imperatives ("slavery is always wrong"). Crucial to Kant's formulation is the imperative to seek an end that is equal to all people.

7. Utilitarianism often contrasts with Kant's categorical imperative. Utilitarianism (Mill 1879) is a situational ethics in which the guiding principle is not an end equal to all people (as with Kant's categorical imperative) but rather an end that yields the greatest amount of happiness for the greatest number of people. This principle of conduct could also underlie abolitionism but on different grounds, namely that the suffering of slaves far outweighs the pleasure of slave owners. Key here, as with the categorical imperative, is a rational will.

8. How does one conceive of ritual as a strategy? And possibly more interestingly, how might we understand abstaining from ritual or withholding a ritual as a kind of

strategy? There are plenty of examples in the study of religion of religious actors mind-lessly engaging in ceremonies, devotees kneeling without any real consideration as to why, and the faithful supplicating to divine authority without a second thought. While this kind of rote activity can appear in any religious life, the work of Catherine Bell (1992), for example, questions whether this is a sustainable way to consider the struc-ture and function of religion itself. Take the act of kneeling as but one example. There is a temporality to submission and supplication, with the religious subject willing to kneel. However, one may decide to kneel more slowly than or as generally accepted—all to communicate critique. Or the religious subject may not kneel at all, deciding to stand instead. Yet these strategic possibilities remained largely unthinkable within the study of religion until Bell insisted on thinking through the temporality of practice. See also Bourdieu's *Outline of a Theory of Practice* (1977).

9. Durkheim writes often in *The Elementary Forms of the Religious Life* about how the totemic principle binds people together. Again, I am interested in these processes of binding individuals into something akin to society, and, possibly more importantly, I am interested in taking this action of binding quite literally. Durkheim writes: "All the beings partaking of the same totemic consider that owing to this very fact, they are morally bound to one another; they have definite duties of assistance, vendetta, etc." (2008, 190). Of interest for me has always been Durkheim's insistence that semiotics and affect can bind individuals into societies, that more than ropes and shackles it is the words and the sensations they provoke that tether people together.

10. Émile Durkheim always maintained the individual's duality: "It does not owe this to any vague mysterious virtue but simply to the fact that according to the well-known formula, man is double. There are two beings in him: an individual being which has its foundation in the organism and the circle of whose activities is therefore strictly limited, and a social being which represents the highest reality in the intellectual and moral order that we can know by observation—I mean society" (2008, 16). Much of Durkheim's concern, however nostalgic it may have been, centered on how processes of modernization dissociated these two selves such that the individual became distinct from society and, thus, experienced isolation—or, in his own words, anomie (1951).

11. There are a number of ways to interpret Alejandro's concern for the community that he left behind while yet avoiding the psychological pitfalls of reducing his emotions to Stockholm syndrome—that is, when hostages befriend their captors for the sake of survival. That is a trope that stretches back to the very beginning of captivity as a genre, when early colonial Americans were kidnapped and then converted by Native Ameri-cans. Instead, a more productive approach would highlight the historical specificity of such compassion (Berlant 2004) and how Alejandro's affective labor (Hardt 1999) made his time inside the center a matter of managing his heart as well as the hearts of others (Hochschild 2012). By leaving the center, Alejandro could not connect with the very attachments that his conscripted labor made possible, and this detachment proved painful.

12. World Health Organization 2010.

13. Compulsory rehabilitation and extrajudicial incarceration often shock liberal sensi-bilities, yet there is no real answer to the fact that addiction, as it is understood within

a biomedical sense, has no immediate solution. The physical restraint of users is an improvisational effort to keep individuals from harming themselves and others. Maria's
insistence that Santiago must be locked up is a nod to the impossibilities of addiction
as well as Guatemala's extreme lack of social services. Parallel studies appear throughout the social sciences and the humanities, ones that tell stories of societies that make
difficult decisions for the sake of both the one and the many.

14. Genealogies of psychological thought often run through Christian terrain. Matthew
Hedstrom's *The Rise of Liberal Religion: Book Culture and American Spirituality in the
Twentieth Century* (2013) is one point of reference; it provides a history of how psychological forms of spirituality became a part of the American middle class. One need
only combine this history of psychological Protestantism with histories of missionaries in Latin America and with a more critical approach to psychological formations
of the governable person (e.g. Rose 1998) to understand how Protestant Christianity
can become a technique of control.

15. A subset of demonology, spiritual warfare is an age-old biblical metaphor for Christian life. At its most basic, the metaphor provides Christians with a combat-centered
vocabulary through which they can articulate their own prayerful efforts at good-
ness. Images of battle and the language of warfare exist at the heart of the Christian
imagination. Erasmus's *Handbook for the Christian Soldier* appeared in 1503 to solidify
the popularity of spiritual warfare (Harrington and Keenan 2002, 1–8) while Sabine
Baring-Gould's nineteenth-century English hymn "Onward, Christian Soldiers" testi-
fies to the importance of warring for Jesus Christ, of "suffering like a good soldier of
Christ Jesus" (2 Timothy 2:3). As a metaphor rooted in biblical stories, spiritual warfare
has proven a flexible image that communities have molded for their own purposes.
Among early Christians, for example, monastic authors used the metaphor of combat
to "make the monk"—to forge a sense of masculine devoutness and defiance in spite of
Satan (Brakke 2006).

16. The scene called to my mind the work of Javier Auyero, namely *Patients of the State*
(2012), which details the waiting that poor people endure while seeking state social
services in Buenos Aires. Key to his analysis is not simply the mundane interactions
but also people's confusion about the administrative process. Auyero's interest is largely
in the state's manifestation through everyday bureaucratic processes, such as waiting,
but here I am interested in the very practice of waiting in lines. James Holston observes: "Standing in lines for services is a privileged site for studying performances of
citizenship, because it entails encounters between anonymous others in public spaces
that require the negotiations of powers, rights, and vulnerabilities" (2009, 15). See also
Secor 2007.

17. Smell is an important dimension of middle-class respectability. The most immediate
point of reference comes with the work of Lalaie Ameeriar. In *Downwardly Global*,
Ameeriar examines the transnational labor migration of Pakistani women to Toronto.
Rather than addressing this downward mobility as the result of bureaucratic failures, she focuses most acutely on racialized bodily difference, including smell: "The
imagined smelly, sweating, unhygienic immigrant body is central here" (2017, 3). She
writes: "But rather than just smelling or seeing, this book is also concerned with the

experience of being seen and smelled in a particular way . . . How the same sensorial phenomena (smells, tastes, forms of dress, and embodiment) can be a means of both exclusion and including, signifying both racialized Otherness and belonging" (4). See also Hirschkind 2011.

18. Of interest here are the political sensibilities that signal "cultivated, articulate, well-mannered middle-class aspirations," as Tania Ahmad writes (2014, 416). The question here, in this scene, is how to comport oneself properly—in line and for a middle-class audience. This is a performance, to be sure, and one that constitutes cartographies of belonging and exclusion even when in a small, relatively anonymous government office. The imperative to perform respectability within these settings is constant and, thus, easy to overstep or overlook when unsure how to maintain the proper distinctions. See also Freeman 2014 and Bourdieu 1984.

19. There is a clear genealogy to Alejandro's state-issued photographs. In the mid-nineteenth century, first in France and then in the United States, the invention of photography coincided with the rise of criminology. The two practices intersected in the mug shot (Tagg 1993). Inspired by the empiricism of botany and zoology, French police officer Alphonse Bertillon mapped criminal bodies with photographic precision, ultimately standardizing the genre with a split screen. A proper mug shot would consist of a portrait and a profile. The format gained popularity as Bertillon proved prolific, documenting delinquency at a rate that quickly outpaced the possibilities of taxonomy itself. In less than a decade, Bertillon (1896, 12–13) systematized more than one hundred thousand photographs across a vast network of file drawers and identification cards, archiving as many as two hundred images a day. While his immediate intention might have been to create a system that could calculate rates of recidivism, the ultimate consequence of his pursuit proved to be nothing short of a semiotics of the soul (Finn 2009, 23; Sekula 1986, 18).

20. I am hesitant to associate Alejandro with Giorgio Agamben's notion of bare life, which he takes to mean how "*Homo sacer* has been excluded from the religious community and from all political life: he cannot participate in the rites of his *gens*, nor [. . .] can he perform any juridically valid act. What is more, his entire existence is reduced to a bare life stripped of every right by virtue of the fact that anyone can kill him without committing homicide; he can save himself only in perpetual flight or a foreign land" (1998, 183). Not only has Alejandro not been abandoned by the state, his pastor, or even the anthropologist—nor has he been rendered an outlaw—there is also something important about the specificity of his physical state. It is worth noting how life on the streets and inside the center stole his vitality pound by pound until he aged well past his own age.

21. This exchange calls to my mind Robert Orsi's notion of "theology in the streets" from *Madonna of 115th Street* (1982). The phrase captures the optimism of "lived religion," which builds from David Hall's confession that only a few decades ago the field of American religion knew "a great deal about the history of theology and (say) church and state" but "next-to-nothing about religion as practiced and precious little about everyday thinking and doing of lay men and women" (1997, vii). A generation of scholars soon stepped forward. They followed "a wider reorientation rooted in a rethinking

of what constitutes religion" (Hall 1997, viii). From denominational histories and theological anthropologies, the study of American religion shifted its focus from what authorities have said to what practitioners have done. But Orsi's take on theology in the streets always seemed overly complimentary of religious dialogue. He seemed to stop just short of presenting an actual debate, let alone an argument. I appreciate the everyday or ordinary texture of what the term presents but find that Christians speaking to Christians in the streets often looks a lot more contentious than what scholars of so-called lived religion tend to present.

22. Scholarship on Latin American prisons focuses on expanding rates of incarceration, the implementation of structural adjustment policies, the militarization and securitization of Latin American states, and the expansion of a United States–style industrial prison complex. See Wacquant 2008; Ross 2013; Garces, Martin, and Darke 2013. Rather than drug offenders filling the prisons, the key concern has been the recurring observation that states throughout Latin America routinely fail to isolate prisoners effectively. Particularly in Central America and Brazil, where powerful prison-based criminal organizations present open challenges to the rule of law, prisons have become understood as the "hole at the center of the state." Organized prisoners routinely take advantage of aged infrastructure and systemic corruption not only to create self-governing organizations inside of prison but also to project their influence into urban communities. See Denyer Willis 2009; Cruz 2010; Darke 2014; Lessing 2017.

23. Kyle Roberts writes (2006, 234): "Tracts like *The Dairyman's Daughter* have long been acknowledged as a staple of nineteenth-century evangelicalism. Published and distributed by denominational, nondenominational, and enterprising commercial publishers throughout the century, a ready supply of free or low-cost pious literature found its way into British and American cities and across the countryside. Despite the space this literature takes up today on the shelves of libraries, churches, and used bookstores, historians (with a few notable exceptions) have been slow to explore the vital function such texts played in evangelical culture. The testimonial above, however, suggests just how important they were. Evangelicals believed a tract could effect the conversion of its reader, or in this case, its listener. It could transform a person reading a tract aloud into a minister exhorting the unconverted, and in the process, turn the confines of a private home into a sacred space."

24. It is productive to consider the tract as an extension of the captivity narrative, not necessarily a retelling of captivity but rather as itself a technique of captivity—as an active participant in the chase. To conceptualize the tract as such it is important to understand the materiality of the tract as a mediating force. See de Vries and Weber 2001.

25. There is a slippage in these moments with the language of slavery and sin, such that Alejandro begins to take on the figure of the escaped slave—not necessarily because he is no longer slave to Pedro but because he now finds himself on the run from his sins. Grégoire Chamayou writes, "This 'choice' between freedom in death and life in servitude was part of the apparatus of domination—it was the sole kind of choice, an impossible choice—that slave power intended to leave its prey" (2012, 59). This could then be paired with Pennington 1849.

26. It should be noted that *The Forgiven* deviates from the orthodoxy of evangelical visual culture, provoking the insight of Heather Hendershot that "Christian media have not become more secular but more ambiguous" (2004, 7). Hendershot's sense of ambiguity pivots atop a divide between the secular and the Christian, but the point could be extended to note how evangelical images are open to an increasing number of interpretations. Some of the ambiguity here has to do with *The Forgiven* hailing from the United States and taking on a new social life in Guatemala. For more on the context in which evangelical media emerges, see the work of David Morgan (1998) and Heather Curtis (2012).

HUNTED, A CONCLUSION

1. See Foucault 1986.
2. For detailed accounts of Guatemala's civil war, see the country's two truth commissions: Proyecto Interdiocesano de Recuperación de la Memoria Histórica (REMHI) 1998; and Comisión para el Esclarecimiento Histórico (CEH) 1999.
3. A full report of one such disappearance appears in CEH 1999, 6:145–54: "Caso ilustartivo No. 48 Deparciciones forzadas de Edgar Fernando García, Sergio Saúl Linares Morales y Rubén Amilcar Farfán. Fundación del Grupo de Apoyo Mutuo (GAM)."

BIBLIOGRAPHY

Abi-Rached, Joelle, and Nikolas Rose. 2010. "The Birth of the Neuromolecular Gaze." *History of the Human Sciences* 23, no. 1: 11–36.

Abzug, Robert H. 1994. *Cosmos Crumbling: American Reform and the Religious Imagination*. Oxford: Oxford University Press.

Adorno, Theodor W., and Max Horkheimer. 1997. *Dialectic of Enlightenment*. Translated by John Cumming. London: Verso.

Agamben, Giorgio. 1998. *Homo Sacer: Sovereignty and Bare Life*. Translated by Daniel Heller-Roazen. Stanford: Stanford University Press.

———. 2005. *State of Exception*. Translated by Kevin Attell. Chicago: University of Chicago Press.

———. 2011. *The Kingdom and the Glory: For a Theological Genealogy of Economy and Government*. Translated by Lorenzo Chiesa and Matteo Mandarini. Stanford: Stanford University Press.

Ahmad, Tania. 2014. "Socialities of Indignation: Denouncing Party Politics in Karachi." *Cultural Anthropology* 29, no. 2: 411–32.

Al-Mohammad, Hayder. 2012. "A Kidnapping in Basra: The Struggles and Precariousness of Life in Postinvasion Iraq." *Cultural Anthropology* 27, no. 4 (November): 597–614.

Althaus-Reid, Marcella Maria. 2007. "Queering the Cross: The Politics of Redemption and the External Debt." *Feminist Theology* 15, no. 3: 289–301.

Althusser, Louis. 1971. "Ideology and Ideological State Apparatuses." In *Lenin and Philosophy and Other Essays*, 127–88. Translated by Ben Brewster. New York: Monthly Review Press.

Alvarado, Héctor. 2001. *Escapa Por Tu Vida*. Guatemala City: Casa Editorial Héctor Alvarado.

Amar, Paul. 2013. *The Security Archipelago: Human-Security States, Sexuality Politics, and the End of Neoliberalism*. Durham: Duke University Press.

Ameeriar, Lalaie. 2017. *Downwardly Global: Women, Work, and Citizenship in the Pakistani Diaspora*. Durham: Duke University Press.

Anand, Nikhil. 2015. "Leaky States: Water Audits, Ignorance, and the Politics of Infrastructure." *Public Culture* 27, no. 2: 305–30.

Anderson, Gary A. 2009. *Sin: A History*. New Haven: Yale University Press.

Appel, Hannah C. 2012. "Walls and White Elephants: Oil Extraction, Responsibility, and Infrastructural Violence in Equatorial Guinea." *Ethnography* 13, no. 4: 439–65.

Asad, Talal, ed. 1973. *Anthropology and the Colonial Encounter*. London: Ithaca Press.

———. 2000. "What Do Human Rights Do? An Anthropological Enquiry." *Theory and Event* 4, no. 4.

Austin, Diane J. 1981. "Born Again . . . and Again and Again: Communitas and Social Change among Jamaican Pentecostalists." *Journal of Anthropological Research* 37, no. 3: 226–46.

Austin, J. L. 1975. *How to Do Things with Words*. Cambridge: Harvard University Press.

Auyero, Javier. 2012. *Patients of the State: The Politics of Waiting in Argentina*. Durham: Duke University Press.

Baal, Jan Van. 1976. "Offering, Sacrifice, Gift." *Numen*, no. 23: 3.

Babül, Elif M. 2017. *Bureaucratic Intimacies: Translating Human Rights in Turkey*. Stanford: Stanford University Press.

Bales, Kevin. 1999. *Disposable People: New Slavery in the Global Economy*. Berkeley: University of California Press.

Barthes, Roland. 1977. *Image-Music-Text*. Translated by Stephen Heath. New York: Hill and Wang.

Bauman, Zygmunt. 1992. *Mortality, Immortality, and Other Life Strategies*. Stanford: Stanford University Press.

BBC News. 2014. "Guatemala City Fire Destroys La Terminal Market." March 25. http://www.bbc.com/news/world-latin-america-26739763.

Behar, Ruth. 1996. *The Vulnerable Observer: Anthropology That Breaks Your Heart*. Boston: Beacon Press.

———. 2003. *Translated Woman: Crossing the Border with Esperanza's Story*. Tenth anniv. ed. Boston: Beacon Press.

Bell, Catherine. 1992. *Ritual Theory, Ritual Practice*. New York: Oxford University Press.

———. 2009. "Belief: A Classificatory Lacuna and Disciplinary 'Problem.'" In *Introducing Religion: Essays in Honor of Jonathan Z. Smith*, edited by Willi Braun and Russell T. McCutcheon, 85–99. New York: Equinox.

Benjamin, Walter. 2007. "The Work of Art in the Age of Mechanical Reproduction." In *Illuminations: Essays and Reflections*, 217–252. Translated by Harry Zohn. Edited by Hannah Arendt. New York: Schocken Books.

Benson, Peter, and Kevin Lewis O'Neill. 2007. "Facing Risk: Levinas, Ethnography, and Ethics." *Anthropology of Consciousness* 18, no. 2: 29–55.

Berlant, Lauren, ed. 2004. *Compassion: The Culture and Politics of an Emotion*. New York: Routledge.

———. 2007. "On the Case." *Critical Inquiry* 33 (Summer): 663–72.

———. 2011. *Cruel Optimism*. Durham: Duke University Press.

Bertillon, Alphonse. 1896. *Signaletic Instructions, Including the Theory and Practice of Anthropometrical Identification*. Edited by Robert Wilson McClaughry. Chicago: Werner.

Biehl, João. 2005. *Vita: Life in a Zone of Social Abandonment*. Berkeley: University of California Press.

Böhme, Gernot. 1992. "An Aesthetic Theory of Nature: An Interim Report." Translated by John Farrell. *Thesis Eleven* 32, no. 1 (May): 90–102.

———. 2017. *The Aesthetics of Atmospheres*. Translated by J. P. Thibaud. Oxford: Routledge.

Bourdieu, Pierre. 1977. *Outline of a Theory of Practice*. Translated by Richard Nice. Cambridge: Cambridge University Press.

———. 1984. *Distinction: A Social Critique of the Judgement of Taste*. Translated by Richard Nice. Cambridge: Harvard University Press.

———. 1986. *The Forms of Capital: Handbook of Theory and Research for the Sociology of Education*. New York: Greenwood.

Bourgois, Philippe. 1996. *In Search of Respect: Selling Crack in El Barrio*. New York: Cambridge University Press.

Bourgois, Philippe, and Jeffrey Schonberg. 2009. *Righteous Dopefiend*. Berkeley: University of California Press.

Boyarin, Daniel. 2004. *Border Lines: The Partition of Judaeo-Christianity*. Philadelphia: University of Pennsylvania Press.

Brain, C. K. 1970. "New Finds at the Swartkrans Australopithecine Site." *Nature* 225:1112–19.

Brakke, David. 2006. *Demons and the Making of the Monk: Spiritual Combat in Early Christianity*. Cambridge: Harvard University Press.

Brandes, Stanley. 2002. *Staying Sober in Mexico City*. Austin: University of Texas Press.

Briggs, Charles. 2014. "Dear Dr. Freud." *Cultural Anthropology* 29, no. 2 (May): 312–43.

Brown, Karen McCarthy. 2001. *Mama Lola: A Vodou Priestess in Brooklyn*. Revised ed. Berkeley: University of California Press.

Butler, Judith. 1997. *The Psychic Life of Power: Theories in Subjection*. Stanford: Stanford University Press.

———. 2004. *Precarious Life: The Powers of Mourning and Violence*. New York: Verso.

Butler, Judith, and Gayatri Chakravorty Spivak. 2007. *Who Sings the Nation-State?* London: Seagull Books.

Caine, Barbara. 2010. *Biography and History*. New York: Palgrave MacMillan.

Canetti, Elias. 1962. *Crowds and Power*. Translated by Carol Stewart. New York: Continuum Books.

Canton Delgado, Manuela. 1998. "Bautizados En Fuego: Protestantes, Discursos de Conversion y Política En Guatemala (1989–1993)." South Woodstock: Plumsock Mesoamerican Studies.

Cardenas, Sonia. 2010. *Human Rights in Latin America: A Politics of Terror and Hope*. Philadelphia: University of Pennsylvania Press.

Carpenter, Ted Galen. 2003. *Bad Neighbor Policy: Washington's Futile War on Drugs in Latin America*. New York: Palgrave MacMillan.

Cary, Philip. 2008. *Outward Signs: The Powerlessness of External Things in Augustine's Thought*. New York: Oxford University Press.

CEH (La Comisión para el Esclarecimiento Histórico). 1999. "Memoria Del Silencio. Guatemala: Comisión Para El Esclarecimiento Histórico." Guatemala.

Certeau, Michel de. 2011. *The Practice of Everyday Life*. Translated by Steven Rendall. Berkeley: University of California Press.

Chamayou, Grégoire. 2012. *Manhunts: A Philosophical History*. Translated by Steven Rendall. Princeton: Princeton University Press.

———. 2013. *Théorie du drone*. Paris: La fabrique.

Chandler, Timothy. 2011. "Reading Atmospheres: The Ecocritical Potential of Gernot Böhme's Aesthetic Theory of Nature." *Interdisciplinary Studies in Literature and Environment* 18, no. 3: 553–68.

Cheah, Pheng, and Suzanne Guerlac, eds. 2009. *Derrida and the Time of the Political.* Durham: Duke University Press.

Chu, Julie Y. 2010. *Cosmologies of Credit: Transnational Mobility and the Politics of Destination in China.* Durham: Duke University Press.

CIEN (Centro de Investgaciones Economicas Nacionales). 2006. *Economia Informal: Superando las barreras de un estado excluyente.* Guatemala City: Centro de Investgaciones Economicas Nacionales. http://www.cien.org.gt/index.php/tag/economia-informal/.

———. 2011. "El Sistema Penitenciario Guatemalteco—Un Diagnostico." Guatemala: Centro de Investigaciones Económicas Nacionales.

Clarke, Kamari. 2009. *Fictions of Justice: The International Criminal Court and the Challenge of Legal Pluralism in Sub-Saharan Africa.* New York: Cambridge University Press.

Clifford, James. 1988. *The Predicament of Culture: Twentieth-Century Ethnography, Literature, and Art.* Cambridge: Harvard University Press.

Clifford, James, and George E. Marcus, eds. 1986. *Writing Culture: The Poetics and Politics of Ethnography.* Berkeley: University of California Press.

Cohen, Abner. 1981. *The Politics of Elite Culture: Explorations in the Dramaturgy of Power in a Modern African Society.* Berkeley: University of California Press.

Collier, Stephen J. 2011. *Post-Soviet Social: Neoliberalism, Social Modernity, Biopolitics.* Princeton: Princeton University Press.

Collier, Stephen J., and Andrew Lakoff. 2008. "Distributed Preparedness: The Spatial Logic of Domestic Security in the United States." *Environment and Planning D* 26, no. 1: 7–28.

Comaroff, John, and Jean Comaroff. 1986. "Christianity and Colonialism in South Africa." *American Ethnologist* 13, no. 1: 1–22.

———. 2006. "Law and Disorder in the Postcolony: An Introduction." In *Law and Disorder in the Postcolony*, 1–56. Chicago: University of Chicago Press.

Combessie, Philippe. 2002. "Marking the Carceral Boundary: Penal Stigma in the Long Shadow of the Prison." *Ethnography* 3, no. 4: 535–55.

Comfort, Megan. 2008. *Doing Time Together: Love and Family in the Shadow of the Prison.* Chicago: University of Chicago Press.

Contreras, Randol. 2012. *The Stickup Kids: Race, Drugs, Violence, and the American Dream.* Berkeley: University of California Press.

Corleto, Manuelo. 1992. *Malasuerte murio en Pavón: Vida, Pasión, Muerte de Un Drogadicto y Delincuente.* Guatemala: Artemis Edinter.

Crapanzano, Vincent. 1980. *Tuhami: Portrait of a Moroccan.* Chicago: University of Chicago Press.

Cruikshank, Barbara. 1996. "Revolution Within: Self-Government and Self-Esteem." In *Foucault and Political Reason: Liberalism, Neo-Liberalism, and Rationalities of Government*, edited by Andrew Barry, Thomas Osborne, and Nikolas Rose, 231–53. Chicago: University of Chicago Press.

Cruz, José Miguel. 2010. "Central American Maras: From Youth Street Gangs to Transnational Protection Rackets." *Global Crime* 11, no. 4: 379–98.

Curtis, Heather. 2012. "Depicting Distant Suffering: Evangelicals and the Politics of Pictorial Humanitarianism in the Age of American Empire." *Material Religion: The Journal of Objects, Art, and Belief* 8, no. 2: 154–83.

Darke, Sacha. 2014. "Managing without Guards in a Brazilian Police Lockup." *Focaal* 68:55–67.

Dart, Raymond. 1953. "The Predatory Transition from Ape to Man." *International Anthropological and Linguistic Review* 1, no. 4: 201–17.

Davies, Stephen. 2003. *Empiricism and History*. New York: Palgrave MacMillan.

Defert, Daniel. 1991. " 'Popular Life' and Insurance Technology." In *The Foucault Effect: Studies in Governmentality*, edited by Graham Burchell, Colin Gordon, and Peter Miller, 211–34. Chicago: University of Chicago Press.

De León, Jason. 2015. *The Land of Open Graves: Living and Dying on the Migrant Trail*. Berkeley: University of California Press.

Deleuze, Gilles. 1988. *Foucault*. Translated by Seán Hand. Minneapolis: University of Minnesota Press.

de Man, Paul. 1982. *Allegories of Reading: Figural Language in Rousseau, Nietzsche, Rilke, and Proust*. New Haven: Yale University Press.

Denyer Willis, Graham. 2009. "Deadly Symbiosis? The PCC, the State, and the Institutionalization of Violence in São Paulo." In *Youth Violence in Latin America: Gangs and Juvenile Justice in Perspective*, edited by Gareth A. Jones and Dennis Rodgers, 167–82. New York: Palgrave MacMillan.

Derrida, Jacques. 1994. *Specters of Marx: The State of Debt, the Work of Mourning, and the New International*. Translated by Peggy Kamuf. New York: Routledge.

———. 2006. *The Politics of Friendship*. Translated by George Collins. New York: Verso.

Desmond, Matthew. 2016. *Evicted: Poverty and Profit in the American City*. New York: Crown Publishers.

de Vries, Hent. 2009. "Must We (Not) Mean What We Say?" In *The Rhetoric of Sincerity*, edited by E. van Alphen, M. Bal, and C. E. Smith. Stanford: Stanford University Press.

de Vries, Hent, and Sam Weber, eds. 2001. *Religion and Media*. Stanford: Stanford University Press.

Dietler, Michael. 2006. "Alcohol: Anthropological/Archaeological Perspectives." *Annual Review of Anthropology* 35:229–49.

Droit, Roger-Pol. 1975. "Michel Foucault, On the Role of Prisons." Translated by Leonard Mayhew. *New York Times*, August 5. http://www.nytimes.com/books/00/12/17/specials/foucault-prisons.html.

Dua, Jatin. 2019. *Captured at Sea: Piracy and Protection in the Western Indian Ocean*. Oakland: University of California Press.

Dudley, Steven. 2016. "Homicides in Guatemala: The Challenge and Lessons of Disaggregating Gang-Related and Drug Trafficking-Related Murders." Bethesda, MD: InSight Crime.

Durkheim, Émile. 1951. *Suicide: A Study in Sociology*. Translated by J. Spaulding and G. Simpson. New York: Free Press.

———. 2008. *The Elementary Forms of the Religious Life*. Translated by Joseph Ward Swain. Mineola, NY: Dover Publications Inc.

Elisha, Omri. 2011. *Moral Ambition: Mobilization and Social Outreach in Evangelical Mega-churches*. Berkeley: University of California Press.

Engelke, Matthew. 2010. "Number and the Imagination of Global Christianity; or, Mediation and Immediacy in the Work of Alain Badiou." *South Atlantic Quarterly* 109, no. 4: 811–29.

Englund, Harri. 2006. *Prisoners of Freedom: Human Rights and the African Poor*. Berkeley: University of California Press.

Evans, Peter B. 1995. *Embedded Autonomy: States and Industrial Transformation*. Princeton: Princeton University Press.

Fabian, Johannes. 1983. *Time and the Other: How Anthropology Makes Its Object*. New York: Columbia University Press.

Farmer, Paul. 2009. "On Suffering and Structural Violence." *Race/Ethnicity: Multidisciplinary Global Contexts* 3, no. 1: 11–28.

Feilding, Amanda, and Corina Giacomello. 2013. "Illicit Drugs Markets and Dimensions of Violence in Guatemala." Oxford: Beckley Foundation.

Ferguson, James. 2002. "Of Mimicry and Membership: Africans and the 'New World Society.'" *Cultural Anthropology* 17, no. 4: 551–69.

Finn, Jonathan Mathew. 2009. *Capturing the Criminal Image: From Mug Shot to Surveillance Society*. Minneapolis: University of Minnesota Press.

Fontes, Anthony W. 2016. "Extorted Life: Protection Rackets in Guatemala City." *Public Culture* 28, no. 3: 593–616.

———. 2018. *Mortal Doubt: Transnational Gangs and Social Order in Guatemala City*. Oakland: University of California Press.

Foucault, Michel. 1972. *The Archaeology of Knowledge and the Discourse on Language*. Translated by A. M. Sheridan Smith. New York: Pantheon.

———. 1977. *Discipline and Punish: The Birth of the Prison*. Translated by Alan Sheridan. New York: Vintage Books.

———. 1978. *History of Sexuality, Volume 1: An Introduction*. New York: Vintage.

———. 1982. "The Subject and Power." *Critical Inquiry* 8, no. 4 (Summer): 777–95.

———. 1986. "Of Other Spaces." *Diacritics* 16:22–27.

———. 1994. *Dits et Écrits, Vols. 3–4*. Paris: Gallimard.

———. 1997a. *Ethics: Subjectivity and Truth*. Edited by Paul Rabinow. New York: New Press.

———. 1997b. "Technologies of the Self." In *Ethics: Subjectivity and Truth: Essential Works of Foucault, 1954–1984, Volume I*, edited by Paul Rabinow, 223–53. New York: New Press.

———. 1998. "Nietzsche, Freud, Marx." In *Aesthetics, Method, and Epistemology*, edited by James Faubion, 269–78. New York: New Press.

———. 2001. "'Omnes et Singulatim': Toward a Critique of Political Reason." In *Power: Essential Works of Foucault, 1954–1984, Volume 3*, edited by James D. Faubion, 298–325. New York: New Press.

———. 2003. *"Society Must Be Defended": Lectures at the Collège de France, 1975–1976*. Edited by David Macey. New York: Picador.

———. 2007. *Security, Territory, Population: Lectures at the Collège de France, 1977–78*. Edited by Michael Senellart. Translated by Graham Burchell. New York: Palgrave MacMillan.

Freeman, Carla. 2014. *Entrepreneurial Selves: Neoliberal Respectability and the Making of a Caribbean Middle Class*. Durham: Duke University Press.

Freud, Sigmund. 1989. *The Future of an Illusion*. New York: W. W. Norton.

Gandolfo, Daniella. 2013. "Formless: A Day at Lima's Office of Formalization." *Cultural Anthropology* 28, no. 2: 1–35.

Garces, Chris. 2014. "Denuding Surveillance at the Carceral Boundary." *South Atlantic Quarterly* 113, no. 3: 447–73.

Garces, Chris, Tomas Martin, and Sacha Darke. 2013. "Informal Prison Dynamics in Africa and Latin America." *Criminal Justice Matters* 91, no. 1: 26–27.

Garcia, Angela. 2010. *The Pastoral Clinic: Addiction and Dispossession along the Rio Grande*. Berkeley: University of California Press.

———. 2014. "The Promise: On the Morality of the Marginal and the Illicit." *Ethos* 42, no. 1: 51–64.

———. 2015. "Serenity: Violence, Inequality, and Recovery on the Edge of Mexico City." *Medical Anthropology Quarterly* 29, no. 4: 455–72.

———. 2016. "The Blue Years: An Ethnography of a Prison Archive." *Cultural Anthropology* 31, no. 4: 571–94.

———. 2017. "The Rainy Season: Toward a Cinematic Ethnography of Crisis and Endurance in Mexico City." *Social Text* 35, no. 1: 101–21.

Garrard-Burnett, Virginia. 1998. *Protestantism in Guatemala: Living in the New Jerusalem*. Austin: University of Texas Press.

———. 2015. "A Discussion with Virginia Garrard-Burnett, Professor, University of Texas." Berkley Center for Religion, Peace & World Affairs. 2015. http://berkleycenter.george town.edu/interviews/a-discussion-with-virginia-garrard-burnett-professor-university -of-texas.

Geertz, Clifford. 1981. *Negara: The Theatre State in Nineteenth-Century Bali*. Princeton: Princeton University Press.

———. 1988. *Works and Lives: The Anthropologist as Author*. Stanford: Stanford University Press.

Geissler, Peter, and P. Wenzel. 1998. "Worms Are Our Life, Part 1: Understandings of Worms and the Body among the Luo of Western Kenya." *Anthropology and Medicine* 5, no. 1: 63–79.

Giordano, Cristiana. 2016. "Secular Redemptions: Biopolitics by Example." *Medical Anthropology* 35, no. 3: 278–90.

Goffman, Erving. 1961a. *Asylums: Essays on the Social Situation of Mental Patients and Other Inmates*. New York: Doubleday.

———. 1961b. *The Presentation of the Self in Everyday Life*. New York: Doubleday Anchor Books.

———. 1971. *Relations in Public*. New York: Basic Books.

Goldman, Francisco. 2017. "The Story Behind the Fire That Killed Forty Teen-Age Girls in a Guatemalan Children's Home." *New Yorker*, March 19.

Good, Byron. 2010. "Medical Anthropology and the Problem of Belief." In *A Reader in Medical Anthropology*, edited by Byron Good, M. J. Fischer, S. Willen, and M. J. DelVecchio-Good, 64–75. New York: Wiley-Blackwell.

Gootenberg, Paul. 2009. *Andean Cocaine: The Making of a Global Drug*. Chapel Hill: University of North Carolina Press.

Gramsci, Antonio. 1992. *Prison Notebooks*. Translated by Joseph A. Buttigieg and Antonio Callari. Vol. 1. New York: Columbia University Press.

Hacking, Ian. 1999. "Making Up People." In *The Science Studies Reader*, edited by Mario Biagoli. New York: Routledge.

Hall, David D. 1997. "Introduction." In *Lived Religion in America: Toward a History of Practice*, edited by David D. Hall, vii–xiii. Princeton: Princeton University Press.

Han, Clara. 2011. "Symptoms of Another Life: Time, Possibility, and Domestic Relations in Chile's Credit Economy." *Cultural Anthropology* 26, no. 1: 7–32.

———. 2012. *Life in Debt: Care and Violence in Neoliberal Chile*. Berkeley: University of California Press.

Hansen, Helena. 2012. "The 'New Masculinity': Addition Treatment as a Reconstruction of Gender in Puerto Rican Evangelist Street Ministries." *Social Science Medicine* 74, no. 11: 1721–28.

Harding, Susan. 2000. *The Book of Jerry Falwell: Fundamentalist Language and Politics*. Princeton: Princeton University Press.

Hardt, Michael. 1999. "Affective Labor." *Boundary 2* 26, no. 2: 89–100.

Harrington, Daniel, and James Keenan. 2002. *Jesus and Virtue Ethics: Building Bridges between New Testament Studies and Moral Theology*. Lanham, MD: Rowman and Littlefield.

Hart, Carl. 2013. *High Price: A Neuroscientist's Journey of Self-Discovery That Challenges Everything You Know About Drugs and Society*. New York: Harper Collins Publishers.

Harvey, David. 2004. "The 'New' Imperialism: Accumulation by Dispossession." *Socialist Register* 40:63–87.

Harvey, Penny, and Hannah Knox. 2012. "The Enchantments of Infrastructure." *Mobilities* 7:521–36.

Hedstrom, Matthew S. 2013. *The Rise of Liberal Religion: Book Culture and American Spirituality in the Twentieth Century*. Oxford: Oxford University Press.

Hegel, G. W. F. 1979. *Phenomenology of Spirit*. Translated by A. V. Miller. New York: Oxford University Press.

Hendershot, Heather. 2004. *Shaking the World for Jesus: Media and Conservative Evangelical Culture*. Chicago: University of Chicago Press.

Henry, Martha. 2005. *Art from the Inside: Paño Drawings by Chicano Prisoners*. Brooklyn, CT: New England Center for Contemporary Art.

Hirschkind, Charles. 2011. "Is There a Secular Body?" *Cultural Anthropology* 24, no. 6: 33–47.

Hochschild, Arlie Russell. 2012. *The Managed Heart: Commercialization of Human Feeling*. Berkeley: University of California Press.

Holston, James. 2009. *Insurgent Citizenship: Disjunctions of Democracy and Modernity in Brazil*. Princeton: Princeton University Press.

Hull, Matthew. 2012. *Government of Paper: The Materiality of Bureaucracy in Urban Pakistan*. Berkeley: University of California Press.

Human Rights Watch. 2013. "'They Treat Us Like Animals': Mistreatment of Drug Users and 'Undesirables' in Cambodia's Drug Detention Centers." https://www.hrw.org

/report/2013/12/08/they-treat-us-animals/mistreatment-drug-users-and-undesirables
-cambodias-drug.

International Centre for Prison Studies. 2013. "World Prison Brief." http://www.prison
studies.org/info/worldbrief/.

Isacson, Adam, and Sarah Kinosian. 2015. "Obama's Billion Dollar Aid Request to Central
America: How Has It Changed?" WOLA: Advocacy for Human Rights in the Ameri-
cas. November 17. https://www.wola.org/analysis/obamas-billion-dollar-aid-request-to
-central-america-how-has-it-changed/.

Johnson, Jessica. 2018. *Biblical Porn: Affect, Labor, and Pastor Mark Driscoll's Evangelical
Empire.* Durham: Duke University Press.

Joyce, Patrick. 2003. *Rule of Freedom: Liberalism and the Modern City.* London: Verso.

Kant, Immanuel. 1996. *The Metaphysics of Morals.* Translated by Mary Gregor. Cambridge:
Cambridge University Press.

———. 2012. *Critique of Judgment.* Translated by J. H. Bernard. Mineola, NY: Dover Publications Inc.

Keane, Webb. 2002. "Sincerity, 'Modernity,' and the Protestants." *Cultural Anthropology* 17,
no. 1: 65–92.

———. 2010. "Minds, Surfaces, and Reasons in the Anthropology of Ethics." In *Ordinary
Ethics: Anthropology, Language, and Action,* edited by Michael Lambek, 64–83. New
York: Fordham University Press.

Kilroy-Marac, Katie. 2014. "Speaking with Revenants: Haunting and the Ethnographic Enterprise." *Ethnography* 15, no. 2: 255–76.

King, Jr., Martin Luther. 1963. "Letter from a Birmingham Jail." In *Why We Can't Wait,* 77–
100. Boston: Beacon Press.

Kleinman, Arthur. 1978. "Concepts and a Model for the Comparison of Medical Systems
as Cultural Systems." *Social Science Medicine* 12:85–93.

Lafer, Gordon. 2003. "The Politics of Prison Labor: A Union Perspective." In *Prison Nation:
The Warehousing of America's Poor,* edited by Tara Herivel and Paul Wright, 120–28.
New York: Routledge.

Lambek, Michael. 2010. "Toward an Ethics of the Act." In *Ordinary Ethics: Anthropology,
Language, and Action,* edited by Michael Lambek, 39–63. New York: Fordham University Press.

Larkin, Brian. 2013. "The Politics and Poetics of Infrastructure." *Annual Review of Anthropology* 42:327–43.

Latour, Brono. 2007. *Reassembling the Social: An Introduction to Actor-Network-Theory.*
Clarendon Lectures in Management Studies. Oxford: Oxford University Press.

Lauro, Sarah Juliet, and Karen Embry. 2008. "A Zombie Manifesto: The Nonhuman Condition in the Era of Advanced Capitalism." *Boundary 2* 35, no. 1: 85–108.

Le Bon, Gustave. 2002. *The Crowd: A Study of the Popular Mind.* Mineola, NY: Dover Publications Inc.

LeFlouria, Talitha. 2015. *Chained in Silence: Black Women and Convict Labor in the New
South.* Chapel Hill: University of North Carolina Press.

Lepselter, Susan. 2016. *The Resonance of Unseen Things: Poetics, Power, Captivity, and UFOs
in the American Uncanny.* Ann Arbor: University of Michigan Press.

Lessing, Benjamin. 2017. "Inside Out: The Challenge of Prison-Based Criminal Organizations." Washington, DC: Brookings Institution.

Levinas, Emmanuel. 1969. *Totality and Infinity: An Essay on Exteriority*. Translated by Alphonso Lingis. Pittsburgh: Duquesne University Press.

Li, Tania. 2010. "To Make Live or Let Die? Rural Dispossession and the Protection of Surplus Populations." *Antipode: A Radical Journal of Geography* 41, no. S1: 66–93.

Lichtenstein, Alex. 1996. *Twice the Work of Free Labor: The Political Economy of Convict Labor in the New South*. New York: Verso.

Livingston, Julie. 2012. *Improvising Medicine: An African Oncology Ward in an Emerging Cancer Epidemic*. Durham: Duke University Press.

Loveman, Brian, ed. 2006. *Addicted to Failure: US Security Policy in Latin America and the Andean Region*. New York: Rowman & Littlefield.

Malinowski, Bronislaw. 1922. *Argonauts of the Western Pacific: An Account of Native Enterprise and Adventure in the Archipelagoes of Melanesian New Guinea*. London: George Routledge and Sons, Ltd.

Mann, Michael. 1984. "The Autonomous Power of the State: Its Origins, Mechanisms and Results." *European Journal of Sociology* 25, no. 2: 185–213.

Marcus, George E., and Dick Cushman. 1982. "Ethnographies as Texts." *Annual Review of Anthropology* 11:25–69.

Marshall, Ruth. 2010. "The Sovereignty of Miracles: Pentecostal Political Theology in Nigeria." *Constellations* 17, no. 2: 197–223.

Martin, Dale B. 1990. *Slavery as Salvation: The Metaphor of Slavery in Pauline Christianity*. New Haven: Yale University Press.

Mauss, Marcel. 1954. *The Gift: The Form and Reason for Exchange in Archaic Societies*. Translated by W. D Halls. New York: W. W. Norton.

Mazzarella, William. 2013. *Censorium: Cinema and the Open Edge of Mass Publicity*. Durham: Duke University Press.

McKay, Ramah. 2012. "Documentary Disorders: Managing Medical Multiplicity in Maputo, Mozambique." *American Ethnologist* 39, no. 3: 545–61.

Menchú, Rigoberta. 2011. *I, Rigoberta Menchú*. Edited by Greg Grandin. New York: Verso.

Meyer, Birgit. 1999. "Commodities and the Power of Prayer: Pentecostalist Attitudes Towards Consumption in Contemporary Ghana." In *Globalization and Identity: Dialectics of Flow and Closure*, edited by Birgit Meyer and Peter Geschiere, 151–76. Oxford: Wiley-Blackwell.

———. 2010. "Aesthetics of Persuasion: Global Christianity and Pentecostalism's Sensational Forms." *South Atlantic Quarterly* 109, no. 4: 741–63.

———. 2015. *Sensational Movies: Video, Vision, and Christianity in Ghana*. Berkeley: University of California Press.

Mill, John Stuart. 1879. *Utilitarianism*. London: Longmans, Green & Co.

Mittermaier, Amira. 2010. *Dreams That Matter: Egyptian Landscapes of the Imagination*. Berkeley: University of California Press.

Miyazaki, Hirokazu. 2004. *The Method of Hope: Anthropology, Philosophy, and Fijian Knowledge*. Stanford: Stanford University Press.

Mol, Annemarie. 2008. *The Logic of Care: Health and the Problem of Patient Choice*. London: Routledge.

Moltmann, Jürgen. 2004. *The Coming of God: Christian Eschatology.* Minneapolis: Fortress Press.

Moodie, Ellen. 2010. *El Salvador in the Aftermath of Peace: Crime, Uncertainty, and the Transition to Democracy.* Philadelphia: University of Pennsylvania Press.

Morgan, David. 1998. *Visual Piety: A History and Theory of Popular Religious Images.* Berkeley: University of California Press.

———. 2009. "The Look of Sympathy: Religion, Visual Culture, and the Social Life of Feeling." *Material Religion: The Journal of Objects, Art, and Belief* 5, no. 2: 132–54.

Moyn, Samuel. 2015. *Christian Human Rights.* Philadelphia: University of Pennsylvania Press.

Muehlebach, Andrea. 2011. "On Affective Labour in Post-Fordist Italy." *Cultural Anthropology* 26, no. 1: 59–82.

Nelson, Diane. 2009. *Reckoning: The Ends of War in Guatemala.* Durham: Duke University Press.

Nietzsche, Friedrich. 1997 [1874]. *Untimely Meditations.* Translated by R. J. Hollingdale. Cambridge: Cambridge University Press.

Nixon, Richard. 1971. "Remarks About an Intensified Program for Drug Abuse Prevention and Control, June 17." The American Presidency Project. http://www.presidency.ucsb .edu/ws/index.php?pid=3047#axzz1PCJydjl5.

Nouvet, Elysée. 2014. "Some Carry On, Some Stay in Bed: (In)Convenient Affects and Agency in Neoliberal Nicaragua." *Cultural Anthropology* 29, no. 1: 80–102.

O'Malley, Pat. 1996. "Risk and Responsibility." In *Foucault and Political Reason: Liberalism, Neo-liberalism, and Rationalities of Government,* edited by Andrew Barry, Thomas Osborne, and Nikolas Rose, 189–208. London: Routledge.

O'Neill, Bruce. 2014. "Cast Aside: Boredom, Downward Mobility, and Homelessness in Post-Communist Bucharest." *Cultural Anthropology* 29, no. 1: 8–31.

O'Neill, Kevin Lewis. 2009. *City of God: Christian Citizenship in Postwar Guatemala.* Berkeley: University of California Press.

———. 2012. "The Soul of Security: Corporatism, Christianity, and Control in Postwar Guatemala." *Social Text* 32, no. 2: 21–42.

———. 2013. "Guatemala's Compulsory Rehabilitation Centers." Submission to the United Nations Committee Against Torture.

———. 2014. "On Liberation: Crack, Christianity, and Captivity in Postwar Guatemala City." *Social Text* 32, no. 3: 11–28.

———. 2017. "Caught on Camera." *Public Culture* 29, no. 3: 493–514.

O'Neill, Kevin Lewis, and Benjamin Fogarty-Valenzuela. 2013. "Verticality." *Journal of the Royal Anthropological Institute* 19, no. 2: 378–89.

———. 2015. "On the Importance of Having a Positive Attitude." In *Violence at the Margins,* edited by Javier Auyero, Nancy Scheper-Hughes, and Philippe Bourgois, 73–92. New York: Oxford University Press.

Open Society Foundations. 2016. "Detention and Punishment in the Name of Drug Treatment." New York.

Orsi, Robert A. 1982. *The Madonna of 115th Street: Faith and Community in Italian Harlem, 1880–1950.* New Haven: Yale University Press.

Paley, Julia. 2001. *Marketing Democracy: Power and Social Movements in Post-Dictatorship Chile*. Berkeley: University of California Press.

Pandian, Anand. 2001. "Predatory Care: The Imperial Hunt in Mughal and British India." *Journal of Historical Sociology* 14, no. 1: 79–107.

———. 2010. "Interior Horizons: An Ethical Space of Selfhood in South Asia." *Journal of the Royal Anthropological Institute* 16, no. 1: 16–43.

Parreñas, Rheana "Juno" Salazar. 2012. "Producing Affect: Transnational Volunteerism in a Malaysian Orangutan Rehabilitation Centre." *American Ethnologist* 39, no. 4: 673–87.

Patterson, Orlando. 1982. *Slavery and Social Death: A Comparative Study*. Cambridge: Harvard University Press.

Pennington, James W. C. 1849. *The Fugitive Blacksmith; or, Events in the History of James W. C. Pennington*. London: Charles Gilpin.

Petryna, Adrianna. 2002. *Life Exposed: Biological Citizens After Chernobyl*. Princeton: Princeton University Press.

Pew Forum on Religion and Public Life. 2006. "Spirit and Power: A 10-Nation Survey of Pentecostals." Washington, DC.

Pierce, Steven. 2006. "Looking Like a State: Colonialism and the Discourse of Corruption in Nigeria." *Comparative Studies in Society and History* 48, no. 4: 887–914.

Pine, Adrienne. 2008. *Working Hard, Drinking Hard: On Violence and Survival in Honduras*. Berkeley: University of California Press.

Pine, Jason. 2007. "Economy of Speed: The New Narco-Capitalism." *Public Culture* 19, no. 2: 357–66.

Plato. 2017. *The Republic*. Translated by Benjamin Jowett. [Los Angeles]: [Enhanced Media Publishing].

Plumwood, Val. 1995. "Human Vulnerability and the Experience of Being Prey." *Quadrant* 39, no. 3: 29–34.

Povinelli, Elizabeth. 2011. *Economies of Abandonment: Social Belonging and Endurance in Late Liberalism*. Durham: Duke University Press.

Rabinow, Paul. 2007. *Reflections on Fieldwork in Morocco*. Thirtieth anniversary ed. Berkeley: University of California Press.

Rabinow, Paul, and Nikolas Rose. 2006. "Biopower Today." *Biosciences* 1, no. 2: 195–217.

Ralph, Laurence. 2015. "The Limitations of a 'Dirty' World." *Du Bois Review: Social Science Research on Race* 12, no. 2: 441–51.

Ralph, Michael. 2008. "Killing Time." *Social Text* 26:1–29.

Redfield, Peter. 2013. *Life in Crisis: The Ethical Journey of Doctors without Borders*. Berkeley: University of California Press.

REMHI (Recuperación de la Memoria Histórica). 1998. *Guatemala, Nunca Más; Proyecto Interdiocesano de Recuperación de la Memoria Histórica*. 4 vols. Guatemala City.

Restrepo, Jorge A., and Alonso Tobón García, eds. 2011. *Guatemala En La Encrucijada: Panorama de Una Violencia Transformada*. Bogotá: Geneva Declaration.

Riles, Annelise. 1998. "Infinity within the Brackets." *American Ethnologist* 25, no. 3: 378–98.

Rios, Victor M. 2011. *Punished: Policing the Lives of Black and Latino Boys*. New York: New York University Press.

Roberts, Kyle. 2006. "Locating Popular Religion in the Evangelical Tract: The Roots and Routes of The Dairyman's Daughter." *Early American Studies: An Interdisciplinary Journal* 4, no. 1: 233–70.

Rodgers, Dennis, and Bruce O'Neill. 2012. "Infrastructural Violence: Introduction to the Special Issue." *Ethnography* 13, no. 4: 401–12.

Rofel, Lisa. 2007. *Desiring China: Experiments in Neoliberalism, Sexuality, and Public Culture*. Durham: Duke University Press.

Rosaldo, Renato. 1980. *Ilongot Headhunting, 1883–1974: A Study in Society and History*. Stanford: Stanford University Press.

Rose, Nikolas. 1990. *Governing the Soul: The Shaping of the Private Self*. London: Routledge.

———. 1998. *Inventing Our Selves: Psychology, Power, and Personhood*. Cambridge: Cambridge University Press.

———. 2006. *The Politics of Life Itself: Biomedicine, Power, and Subjectivity in the Twenty-First Century*. Princeton: Princeton University Press.

Ross, Jeffrey Ian, ed. 2013. *The Globalization of Supermax Prisons*. New Brunswick, NJ: Rutgers University Press.

Rowlandson, Mary. 1682. *A True History of the Captivity and Restoration of Mrs. Mary Rowlandson*. New York: Garland Publishing.

Saint Augustine. 1992. *Confessions*. Translated by F. J. Shield. Indianapolis, IN: Hackett Publishing Company, Inc.

Sassen, Saskia. 2014. *Expulsions: Brutality and Complexity in the Global Economy*. Cambridge: Belknap Press of Harvard University Press.

Sawyer, Suzana. 2004. *Crude Chronicles: Indigenous Politics, Multinational Oil, and Neoliberalism in Ecuador*. Durham: Duke University Press.

Scheper-Hughes, Nancy. 1993. *Death without Weeping: The Violence of Everyday Life in Brazil*. Berkeley: University of California Press.

Schmitt, Carl. 2005. *Political Theology: Four Chapters on the Concept of Sovereignty*. Translated by George Schwab. Chicago: University of Chicago Press.

Scott, James C. 1987. *Weapons of the Weak: Everyday Forms of Peasant Resistance*. New Haven: Yale University Press.

Secor, A. J. 2007. "Between Longing and Despair: State, Space and Subjectivity in Turkey." *Environment and Planning D: Society and Space* 25, no. 1: 33–52.

Seelke, Clare Ribando, Liana Sun Wyler, June S. Beittel, and Mark P. Sullivan. 2011. "Latin America and the Caribbean: Illicit Drug Trafficking and US Counterdrug Programs." Congressional Research Service.

Sekula, Allan. 1986. "The Body and the Archive." *October* 39:3–64.

Shapira, Harel. 2013. *Waiting for José: The Minutemen's Pursuit of America*. Princeton: Princeton University Press.

Slahi, Mohamedou Ould. 2015. *Guantánamo Diary*. Edited by Larry Siems. New York: Little & Brown.

Smith, James K. A. 2010. "'The Spirits of the Prophets Are Subject to the Prophets': Global Pentecostalism and the Re-Enchantment of Critique." *South Atlantic Quarterly* 109, no. 4: 677–93.

Smith, Shawn Michelle. 1999. *American Archives: Gender, Race, and Class in Visual Culture.* Princeton: Princeton University Press.

Spivak, Gayatri. 1988. "Can the Subaltern Speak?" In *Marxism and the Interpretation of Culture*, edited by Cary Nelson and Lawrence Grossberg, 271–313. Urbana: University of Illinois Press.

Sridhar, Archana. 2007. "Tax Reform and Promoting a Culture of Philanthropy: Guatemala's 'Third Sector' in an Era of Peace." *Fordham International Law Journal* 31, no. 1: 186–229.

Standing, Guy. 2011. *The Precariat: The New Dangerous Class.* New York: Bloomsbury Press.

Star, Susan Leigh. 1999. "The Ethnography of Infrastructure." *American Behavioral Scientist* 43, no. 3: 377–91.

Star, Susan Leigh, and Geoffrey Bowker. 2000. *Sorting Things Out: Classification and Its Consequences.* Cambridge: MIT Press.

Stevenson, Jill. 2013. *Sensational Devotion: Evangelical Performance in Twenty-First-Century America.* Ann Arbor: University of Michigan Press.

Stoler, Ann Laura. 2010. *Along the Archival Grain: Epistemic Anxieties and Colonial Common Sense.* Princeton: Princeton University Press.

Strong, Pauline Turner. 1998. *Captive Selves, Captivating Others: The Practice and Representation of Captivity across Colonial Borders in North America.* Boulder, CO: Westview Press.

Stout, Noelle. 2016. "Petitioning a Giant: Debt, Reciprocity, and Mortgage Modification in the Sacramento Valley." *American Ethnologist* 43, no. 1: 158–71.

Sullivan, Winnifred Fallers. 2009. *Prison Religion: Faith-Based Reform and the Constitution.* Princeton: Princeton University Press.

Sunder Rajan, Kaushik. 2006. *Biocapital: The Constitution of Postgenomic Life.* Durham: Duke University Press.

Svendsen, Lars. 2017. *A Philosophy of Loneliness.* Translated by Kerri Pierce. Chicago: University of Chicago Press.

Tagg, John. 1993. *The Burden of Representation: Essays on Photographies and Histories.* Minneapolis: University of Minnesota Press.

Taussig, Michael. 1984. "Culture of Terror, Space of Death: Roger Casement's Putumayo Report and the Explanation of Torture." *Comparative Studies in Society and History* 26, no. 3: 467–97.

Taylor, Diana. 1997. *Disappearing Acts: Spectacles of Gender and Nationalism in Argentina's "Dirty War."* Durham: Duke University Press.

Taylor, Mark Lewis. 2014. "Christianity and US Prison Abolition: Rupturing a Hegemonic Christian Ideology." *Socialism and Democracy* 28, no. 3: 172–88.

Tello Ordoñez, Edyson Roderico. 2007. "Planificación de Una Granja Modelo de Rehabilitación Penal." PhD diss., Universidad de San Carlos de Guatemala, Facultad de Arquitectura.

Thompson, Emily. 2004. *The Soundscape of Modernity: Architectural Acoustics and the Culture of Listening in America, 1900–1933.* Cambridge: MIT Press.

Thompson, E. P. 1975. *Whigs and Hunters: The Origin of the Black Act.* New York: Pantheon.

Throop, Jason. 2008. "On the Problem of Empathy: The Case of Yap, Federated States of Micronesia." *Ethos* 36, no. 4: 402–26.

Ticktin, Miriam. 2011. *Casualties of Care: Immigration and the Politics of Humanitarianism in France*. Berkeley: University of California Press.

Tomlinson, Jason. 2007. *The Culture of Speed: The Coming of Immediacy*. London: SAGE Publications.

United Nations Office on Drugs and Crime. 2010. "From Coercion to Cohesion: Treating Drug Dependence Through Health Care, Not Punishment." Discussion paper.

———. 2012. "Transnational Organized Crime in Central America and the Caribbean: A Threat Assessment." Vienna.

———. 2017. "Human Trafficking." United Nations Office on Drugs and Crime. https://www.unodc.org/unodc/en/human-trafficking/what-is-human-trafficking.html.

United Nations Office on Drugs and Crime, and World Health Organization WHO. 2008. "Principles of Drug Dependence Treatment." Discussion paper.

"US Counternarcotics Programs in Latin America." n.d. Security Assistance Monitor. Accessed October 26, 2016. http://securityassistance.org/fact_sheet/us-counternarcotics-programs-latin-america?language=en.

Valverde, Mariana. 1998. *Diseases of the Will: Alcohol and the Dilemmas of Freedom*. Cambridge: Cambridge University Press.

Wacquant, Loïc. 2001. "Deadly Symbiosis: When Ghetto and Prison Meet and Mesh." *Punishment & Society* 3, no. 1: 95–134.

———. 2008. "The Militarization of Urban Marginality: Lessons from the Brazilian Metropolis." *International Political Sociology* 2:56–64.

Weber, Max. 2002 [1905]. *The Protestant Ethic and the Spirit of Capitalism*. Translated by Stephen Kalberg. Chicago: Fitzroy Dearborn Publishers.

———. 1978. *Economy and Society*. 2 vols. Berkeley: University of California Press.

Wedeen, Lisa. 2003. "Seeing Like a Citizen, Acting Like a State: Exemplary Events in Unified Yemen." *Comparative Studies in Society and History* 45, no. 4: 680–713.

Wilkinson, Annie Katheryn. 2013. *"Sin Sanidad, No Hay Santidad": Las Prácticas Reparativas En Ecuador*. Quito: FLACSO-Sede Ecuador.

Wilson, Maya. 2009. "Guatemala: Central American Crime Capital." Council on Hemispheric Affairs. Washington, DC. http://www.coha.org/guatemala-central-american-crime-capital/.

Wolfe, Daniel, and Roxanne Saucier. 2010. "In Rehabilitation's Name? Ending Institutionalized Cruelty and Degrading Treatment of People Who Use Drugs." *International Journal of Drug Policy* 21, no. 3: 145–48.

World Health Organization. 2010. "ATLAS of Substance Use Disorders." WHO: World Health Organization. http://www.who.int/substance_abuse/publications/atlas_report/profiles/guatemala.pdf?ua=1.

———. 2011. "Mental Health Atlas 2011." Geneva: World Health Organization.

Yong, Amos. 2000. *Discerning the Spirit(s): A Pentecostal-Charismatic Contribution to Christian Theology of Religions*. Sheffield: Sheffield Academic Press.

———. 2004. "Spiritual Discernment: A Biblical-Theological Reconsideration." In *The Spirit and Spirituality: Essays in Honour of Russell P. Spittler*, edited by Wonsuk Ma and Robert P. Menzies. London: T&T Clark International.

Zamudio, C., P. Chávez, and E. Zafra. 2015. "Abusos En Centros de Tratamiento Con Internamiento Para Usuarios de Drogas En México." Mexico City: Colectivo por una Política Integral Hacia las Drogas, AC.

Zelizer, Viviana A. 2000. "The Purchase of Intimacy." *Law & Social Inquiry* 25, no. 3: 817–48.

Zigon, Jarrett. 2007. "Moral Breakdown and the Ethical Demand: A Theoretical Framework for an Anthropology of Moralities." *Anthropological Theory* 7, no. 2: 131–50.

Zilberg, Elana. 2011. *Spaces of Detention: The Making of a Transnational Gang Crisis Between Los Angeles and San Salvador.* Durham: Duke University Press.

INDEX